MAYDAY!
MAYDAY!

MAYDAY! MAYDAY!

Aircraft Crashes in the Great Smoky Mountains National Park 1920–2000

Jeff Wadley
Dwight McCarter

The University of Tennessee Press

KNOXVILLE

Copyright © 2002 by The University of Tennessee Press / Knoxville.
All Rights Reserved. Manufactured in the United States of America.
First Edition.
This book is printed on acid-free paper.

Library of Congress Cataloging-in-Publication Data

Wadley, Jeff, 1964–
        Mayday! mayday!: aircraft crashes in the Great Smoky Mountains
National Park, 1920–2000 / Jeff Wadley, Dwight McCarter.
        p. cm.
Includes bibliographical references and index.
ISBN 1-57233-154-2 (pbk.: alk.paper)
1. Search and rescue operations—Great Smoky Mountains (N.C. and Tenn.)—History.
2. Aircraft accidents—Great Smoky Mountains (N.C. and Tenn.)—History.
I. McCarter, Dwight, 1945– . II. Title.
TL553.8 .W24 2002
363.12'4'810976889—dc21   2001003545

To the men and women of search and rescue who have risked it all that others might live. In memory of the following who died on searches:

Frank Shults, NPS
Lt. Col. Ray Maynard, CAP
Capt. John Dunnavant, US Army
Capt. Terrance Woolever, US Army
Sgt. Floyd Smith, US Army

To the memory of Dr. Robert Lash, MD, who was instrumental in backcountry pre-hospital care for trauma patients and the establishment of the University of Tennessee Hospital's Lifestar

CONTENTS

ILLUSTRATIONS

TABLES

FOREWORD

Letters of Appreciation from Jeff Shrewsbury and Jennifer Shrewsbury Adelman

February 19, 2000

When Jeff Wadley first contacted me and told me he was trying to piece together the events surrounding December 1, 1977, and asked me to write a few words about my family's experience, I was delighted for the chance to express my thanks to the people who helped us through that terrible time. Some of them I can remember as if it were yesterday. Some I never knew.

But the more I thought about it, the more I got scared. As a former journalist, writing has never been a problem for me, but in this case, I struggled. I've struggled with the words because I'm so afraid that no matter how hard I try, I won't be able to capture accurately on paper what those people mean to me and what happened during those hours on the mountain and beyond. No words exist to describe the love and admiration I feel for them. I owe my life and a little bit of who I am to hundreds of people I have never met. It's a debt I can't possibly repay—not that any of them have ever asked for any thanks. They've never asked for anything, they've only given—given their help, their support, their courage, and their love. Not only did the people of East Tennessee and beyond mobilize in a matter of hours to come pull us off the mountain, they also stayed with us through the rescue, the transit, the surgeries, and the painful moments of recovery. They rallied around us and took my family in as their own and helped lift us up. For that I am in awe and filled with gratitude more than any of them will ever know.

From the first moment I heard the thunderous clapping of the helicopters overhead, to the instant I saw Dr. Robert Lash coming through the brush on the side of that mountain, through all the pain and recovery myself and my family have experienced to this very day, I remain humbled by the effort that was made on my behalf. While lying there in the brush that day and night, barely conscious of the fact that I was within hours of dying, I remember only scattered moments. But I remember the faces of some of the people—Dr. Lash standing over me, his strong voice reassuring me that everything was going to be okay; his son David in the helicopter, talking to me soothingly as they lifted me in and keeping my mind off the one-hundred-foot drop in altitude as we landed at UT Hospital; Peggy and Joann, who stood vigil over my sister and me in intensive care and swabbed our mouths with lemon sticks when we were dry; the countless people in the Knoxville area who showered us with good wishes and cards and offered my family a place to stay and food to eat; the doctors who tended my wounds and saved our lives; and the people of the Civil Air Patrol and Air Force and FAA who coordinated the effort and saw it through in time for us to live.

These are memories that I have that will never fade. It inspires me to think about the efforts of all those people. Thinking about them fills me with pride. I'm no different than the thousands of other people who have been pulled from danger by dedicated souls. I'm just trying to live a life, and pay tribute to them by surviving. Not many days go by that the enormity of what those search and rescue folks did for us doesn't hit me again.

So all I can do is say thank you. Thank you to the CAP and the Lifestar people, and the University and the doctors and the citizens of the area. You saved my life and were there for my family, and I am forever grateful.

> Yours most humbly,
> Jeff Shrewsbury
> February 2000
> Fort Mill, South Carolina

Hi Jeff,

Thanks for coming all the way here to talk with me. I actually found our chat very helpful, since I was never aware of many of the details of my accident before.

After you left, I was thinking about all the people from the UT Lifestar, UT Hospital, and the folks of Knoxville who were so very kind to our entire family. It thrills me to be able to connect Dennis's [Sparks] name to the act of prying me out of the plane, for example. I looked back into my autograph book, where I had all the nurses from the hospital sign, and I was amazed at how many of them gave me their home addresses along with well wishes. When we left Knoxville to go home to Michigan, I really felt as though I was leaving good friends behind.

Of course no one wishes to be a victim of an accident like this, but I believe that we are a sum of all our experiences in life, and this experience made me a better person who appreciates what is given to them. The rescuers and the medical staff in Knoxville were largely the reason that I can look back with joy in my heart.

To all the people who helped Jeff and I back then, and to all the people performing search and rescue operations now, I thank you. You are the reason I am alive today!

Sincerely,
Jennifer Shrewsbury Adelman

PREFACE

I n the realm of airplane crashes in the Great Smoky Mountains National Park, history tends to repeat itself. History also makes for a productive tool in planning for search-and-rescue operations.

This book recounts the "known and reported" aircraft incidents in Great Smoky Mountains National Park, including those that occurred within the park's boundaries prior to its establishment in 1934. Most assuredly, there have been other, unknown crashes. After researching, gathering evidence, and interviewing the people involved, we have documented fifty-four incidents between 1920 and May 5, 1999. We compiled this data for three reasons: as a planning tool for future search-and-rescue missions, as historic documentation, and to caution people who fly over the Smokies.

Eighty years of airplane crashes—dots of metal and fabric caught in trees and strew among the boulders—have changed the face of the mountains. Those involved in aviation search and rescue call the Smokies another Bermuda Triangle. We would add that it is not advisable for the reader to use this work as a guide to finding the old aircraft sites. Most no longer remain in the mountains, and a few have taken us several years to locate and document. So enjoy our work and leave the sites for nature to heal.

For the families of the victims, we are heartily sorry for your loss. It is not our wish to deliberately revive bad memories or point fingers. Each time we visit a crash site, we hurt as well. Having been involved, between the two of us, in search and rescue for the past thirty-six years, we want to preserve your loved one's dignity. Every effort has been made to describe the facts of the events accurately by incorporating official documents, interviews, eyewitness reports, newspaper clippings, and informational web sites. We welcome your input and comments.

Jeff Wadley and Dwight McCarter

ACKNOWLEDGMENTS

The authors wish to thank the following people and organizations for assistance in the creation of this project:

The staff of Great Smoky Mountains National Park

Tennessee and North Carolina Civil Air Patrol

Air Force Rescue Coordination Center

Tennessee Emergency Management Agency

All the survivors of aircraft crashes who gave us interviews, photographs, and encouragement to write their stories

All the family members of persons who died in aircraft crashes for their stories, precious interviews, encouragement in telling their side of the story, and willingness to bring up painful memories and frustrations

Col. Dennis Sparks, Tennessee CAP

Col. Ed Curreton, Tennessee CAP

Kent Higgins, NPS (Ret.) (Kent gave us an incredible amount of details regarding several of the incidents he worked.)

David Wadley, for all the hikes and drives to interview people

George Minnigh, NPS

Jack Piepenbring, NPS

Bud Rice, NPS

Bob Wightman, NPS

Mary Ruth Childs, NPS, for her early comprehensive lists

Kenny Slay, NPS

Dr. Joe Howell

Archivist Kitty Manscill, NPS

Librarian Annette Hartigan, NPS

Dennis Faircloth

Jennifer Shrewsbury Aldeman

Jeff Shrewsbury

Jack Pettit

Duane Devotie

Hank Leonard

The staff at the University of Tennessee Press

Bob Swabe, TEMA

Steve Kloster, NPS

Bud Maples, for getting Jeff started in CAP

Lt. Col. Gary Maples, CAP

Last and certainly not least, our families: Rob McCarter, Joy,
    Brandon, Phillip and Erin Wadley for sacrificing time

CHRONOLOGY

	DATE	AIRCRAFT TYPE
1	1920	Curtis Jenny
2	1922, Oct. 31	Curtis Jenny
3	1925	Curtis Jenny, JN-4A
4	1941, Apr. 12	Light plane (Club Coupe?)
5	1944, Jan. 31	UC-78, Bamboo Bomber (army air force)
6	1944, Aug. 12	Beech Model 17, Staggerwing
7	1945, Oct. 5	UC-45, Beech Model B-18-S (army air force)
8	1945, Oct. 17	L-5, Stinson Sentinel (army air force)
9	1945, Dec. 10	AT-11, Beech Model 18 (navy)
10	1946, June 12	Boeing B-29 Superfortress (army air force)
11	1946, Aug. 8	Single-engine light aircraft
12	1948, Dec. 4	Goodyear FG-1D Corsair (navy)
13	1949, May 5	Single-engine light aircraft
14	1951, Apr. 1	P-51D Mustang (air force)
15	1952, Mar. 12	Single-engine light aircraft
16	1955, Nov. 2	Piper J-3 Cub
17	1956, Aug. 24	Aeronca Champ
18	1956, Dec. 9	A-2 Erocoupe
19	1958, June 22	T-33 jet trainer (air force)
20	1959, Jan. 19	T-33 jet trainer (air force)
21	1959, July 1	Convair F-102A (air force)
22	1961, Nov. 24	Piper Tri-Pacer
23	1962, Nov. 10	Cessna 310, U-3B (air force)
24	1964, Mar. 3	C-130 Hercules (air force)
25	1964, Mar. 6	Piper Commanche
26	1964, Mar. 21	Beechcraft Model 18

	DATE	AIRCRAFT TYPE
27	1966, Sept. 5	Cessna 150
28	1968, Aug. 11	Cessna 150
29	1968, Oct. 3	Cessna 180
30	1969, Feb. 12	Cessna 182
31	1969, Aug. 12	Helicopter
32	1972, Aug. 23	Cessna 172
33	1973, Jan. 27	Cessna 182
34	1973, Apr. 3	Piper Aztec
35	1973, Nov. 2	Cessna 150
36	1974, Feb. 16	Cherokee Six
37	1975, Aug. 13	Cessna 172
38	1977, Dec. 1	Cessna 172
39	1978, Jan. 3	Cessna 421, Golden Eagle
40	1978, Jan. 4	UH-1 (army)
41	1979, Feb. 12	Piper Tri-Pacer
42	1980, July 2	Hot air balloon
43	1983, July 26	Bell 206-B Jet Ranger
44	1983, Aug. 6	Sikorsky S-58-D
45	1984, Jan. 4	McDonald Douglas RF-4C (air force)
46	1989, July 11	Cessna 172
47	1991, Jan. 27	Cessna 337-C, Skymaster
48	1992, Jan. 15	F-15 Eagle (air force)
49	1992, Apr. 26	Cessna 310-R
50	1992, May 24	Cessna 172
51	1993, Apr. 16	Bell 204, UH-1F, Huey
52	1995, Feb. 11	Beechcraft BE-60, Duke
53	1997, Dec. 1	Cessna 182
54	1999, May 5	Cessna 172

ONE

The 1920s: The Pre-Park Years

The Curtis "Jenny" was very popular among military and civilian pilots during and after World War I. Simple to fly and inexpensive to operate, it had a single engine and was fabric-covered ("dope" was applied to make the fabric taunt and watertight). Thin wires crisscrossed between the stacked wings brought strength to the flight surfaces. This lightweight biplane was used for observation missions, flight instruction, war training, and transportation sorties.

Imagine an old black-and-white movie: a pilot and passenger sit in an open cockpit, passenger in front, pilot behind, both wearing goggles, a leather flight cap, and a scarf. This is the image of the Jenny. In the Great Smoky Mountains National Park, the first three aircraft that crashed were Jennys.

The First Incident

According to Glenn Branum, who lived in the mountains and later worked for the Park Service, a Jenny crashed in the Porters Creek section of Big Greenbrier around 1920. When he was young, Branum states, people talked about a new airplane that had tried to cross the mountains but failed. The pilot was uninjured and walked out to safety, he recalls, but the plane was destroyed. Residents of the area searched for the aircraft, Branum was told, but it was never located. Constructed of fabric, wood, and some metal, the plane has no doubt decayed and vanished. No actual documentation has been located to provide additional details.

"The Eagle Soars No More"

On October 31, 1920, not far from the first known incident, the mountains claimed another Jenny. According to the *Newport Plain Talk,* the second known crash in the park's history involved a U.S. Army pilot on a cross-country flight from Atlanta to Washington, D.C.[1] Lieutenant Hunter, an army aviator, apparently was flying north over the Smokies near Cosby when he experienced "engine trouble" and crashed near the summit of the mountains. Like an insect flying into a spider web, his plane hit a stand of spruce trees and came to a stop.

Lieutenant Hunter was not injured, and it is not known if he had a passenger with him. His Jenny was badly damaged. He tried to dislodge it from the trees without success. Realizing that he was in "mountains which are among the roughest in eastern America," Hunter left the aircraft and proceeded to walk out for help.[2] Later that evening he arrived at a private residence in upper Cosby; he spent the night there and made his way into Newport the next day. After wiring the War Department and explaining his predicament, Hunter was given instructions to find the aircraft, disassemble it, carry it out to civilization, and repair it.

Word spread among the residents of Cocke County that a young army aviator needed assistance to recover his machine, and several Cosby residents responded. Those who were familiar with the rugged backcountry and wanted to help the aviator joined the search to locate and bring in the damaged aircraft. The problem was Lieutenant Hunter had no idea where to begin his recovery mission.

The initial plan to locate the aircraft included a ground search. If that proved fruitless, Hunter intended to arrange for an aerial search. It was Hunter's plan to take the aircraft apart piece by piece and "lug it out by hand."[3] Pack animals were considered for the task, but since there was no trail system in place, humans would do the work.

Apparently, Hunter's aircraft was never found despite the search efforts. Our research has not produced even a general area of the crash site. The Smokies are not forgiving when it comes to humans and their flying machines. "The eagle soars no more; the aeroplane has disturbed his place as monarch of the skies," declared the *Newport Plain Talk.* "But *if* the unchanging peaks could break their sphinx-like silence they might reflect that no eagle has ever had engine trouble and had to be carried off the mountain by hand."[4]

The Flying Rooster

The third known aircraft incident in the Smokies occurred in what is known today as the Elkmont Campground near Gatlinburg. To merely state the facts of the crash would shortchange a wonderful story. John "Rooster" Williams had no idea that he would become part of aviation incident history in 1925.[5]

Rooster Williams was from the community of "Boogertown" in Sevier County, Tennessee. Born only twenty years after the Civil War, Williams grew up to fight a war of his own: freedom from being strapped to the land. He had a vision to fly. At the turn of the century, the forests of the Smokies were being loaded onto rail cars and shipped out to provide lumber for construction and furniture. Williams sought his fortune in the lumber business, as did thousands of people on both sides of the mountain range. He held many positions in the industry, including train engineer, steam-shovel operator, and log-loader operator. He reportedly had a habit of drinking, and apparently this got him into trouble on more than a few occasions.

It was Frank Andre of Knoxville who first gave Williams flying fever. After completing his flight training in 1922 at the age of sixteen, Andre earned his pilot's license and eventually trained other wishful students. He became one of the pioneer flyers for Eastern Airlines throughout its first twenty-five years of existence and was perhaps the first person to land an airplane successfully in the Great Smoky Mountains. It is said that he landed a Standard Jenny in Elkmont in 1922, and it was there he first met the Rooster.

Instructor Andre spent many hours with Williams teaching him how to fly airplanes. He first taught him from the landing strip near present-day Sutherland Avenue in Knoxville. On weekends Rooster Williams would drive or ride a train from Elkmont through the Little River Gorge to Knoxville. His passion for flight was obvious. Soon the desire for airplane ownership entered his mind. Where in the early 1920s could someone find an ample supply of airplanes for sale?

In 1923 Ben Bower of Knoxville had just what Williams wanted. Surplus army aircraft, some still in their packing crates, were brought to

Tennessee from Americus, Georgia. Government records showed that these aircraft could be bought by mail order for as little as fifty dollars. The new owners would receive several boxes and had to assemble the aircraft themselves. Rooster could not resist, and according to an article in the *Knoxville News Sentinel,* he "insisted" on buying himself a plane.[6] He bought a Curtis JN-4A Jenny with a water-cooled, eight-cylinder, 90-horsepower OX-5 engine. The plane, which had a maximum speed of ninety-three miles per hour, was covered with linen and coated with "dope" to make the fabric taunt and waterproof.

Rooster and Andre assembled the plane and installed the engine. Can you imagine Rooster's excitement as he saw his new pride and joy come to life before his eyes? Although the plane needed more work, Andre flew it to Elkmont. He landed without incident on the strip that he had probably used several times before (according to Vic Weals, this dirt strip was used as a race track).[7]

The plane evidently needed a little more dope, but in August 1925, on a Saturday or Sunday afternoon, Rooster decided that the day had come to stop talking and begin flying. His first and last solo in his home-made airplane was about to take place.

Ben and Maude, Rooster's son and wife, walked to the strip and watched with other employees of the Little River Lumber Company. According to Weals, Maude must have felt apprehensive about the flight. He states she "had no thought of going with him, or of agreeing to let their son go aloft," even if his maiden flight was without problems.[8] More than likely, Williams was not giving it a second thought.

Williams, with the help of fellow loggers, started the engine. They pulled away the scotches and the airplane rolled down the runway. Pulling back on the yoke, the plane became airborne, but not high enough to avoid a large boulder at the end of the strip. A wing tip hit the rock, and the flight of the Rooster came to an abrupt halt. The engine stopped, dust covered the scene, and Rooster Williams emerged from the damaged aircraft unhurt. His pride, however, was crushed.

Embarrassed in front of his co-workers and family, Williams disassembled much of the plane. It was rumored that he placed the engine in an automobile in Sevierville. But perhaps the plane flew again after it was transported by train and reassembled in Townsend.

The first witnessed plane crash in the Smokies was recorded in the memories of those present; some are still telling the story. Through the photography of Frank Wilson and Laura Thornborough, for instance, we

have photographs of Rooster's plane.[9] The story does not end on that fateful summer day in 1925 for Rooster Williams, though. He left Tennessee and worked in New Mexico for a while. He divorced Maude by letter but soon became homesick for the mountains. Williams told the woman he was living with that he was leaving. She did not appreciate the news, so she shot and killed him. He is buried in New Mexico.

Rooster Williams's Curtis Jenny JN-4A. Courtesy of Great Smoky Mountains National Park Library Archive.

TWO

The 1940s

O n January 31, 1944, "W. H. Garvin at Bat Cave, said he heard a plane between 12 and 12:30 o'clock, but could not see it. He said it evidently was twin engine and was flying low, and passed along a valley toward either Little Pisgah or Shumont."[1] This quotation from the *Asheville (N.C.) Times* was typical of the dozens of leads in the search for a UC-78 Bamboo "Bobcat" bomber in the western area of the Smokies. The U.S. Army Air Force (AAF) was in charge of the search, which continued for years. The plane has never been found.

Bamboo Bomber Mystery

The UC-78 is a powerful, medium-sized trainer built by Cessna for bombing. It was a "tail-dragger," with front retractable landing gear under each wing. It had twin blade props, was fabric covered, and had a large cabin area. The two eight-cylinder radial engines (Jacobs R-755-9) produced 245 horsepower each, and the plane could stay aloft 750 miles before refueling—ample time to have made it over the Smokies from Charlotte. It cruised at 175 miles per hour and had a twenty-two-thousand-foot ceiling.

The olive drab–colored UC-78 left Morris Airfield at Charlotte, North Carolina, en route to Nashville on Monday, January 31, 1944. On board were George Michael Maty Jr., Lt. Thomas B. Wheeler,

2d Lt. Irving Bumberg (the pilot), and Carlton D. Haigis, a scientist working on the Oak Ridge Project. The plane apparently went down between
10:00 A.M. and 1:00 P.M. Several people heard and saw what they thought
was a plane in trouble flying toward the mountains. Witnesses reported
hearing a sputtering aircraft engine and seeing a low-flying plane, a circling plane, and a plane that could not have made it over the main
Smokies range. Search headquarters listed sightings from Bat Cave,
Asheville, Horseshoe, Fletcher, Burnsville, Marshall, Fontana Dam, Del
Rio, Waynesville, Franklin, and Bryson City. The weather the day of the
flight included high winds, low clouds, and snow—not ideal mountain
flying weather.

The preliminary search began on the evening of the thirty-first and
grew larger in the following weeks. It was hampered due to high winds,
mist, and snow, but a fleet of aircraft was available to cover the large search
area. Leads continued to pour in from all over the region, and the army
assured the public that each was researched adequately despite criticisms
that not enough work was being done (the pressure was on the searchers
even in 1944). A very promising lead came from a schoolboy near Franklin
who described the airplane exactly to an officer before the details were
broadcast publicly.[2] The search concentrated in the Franklin area, but no
solid clues were found.

Involved in the search was the U.S. Army Air Force, the National
Park Service (NPS) (on their first official search for an aircraft since the
park's dedication), local law enforcement agencies from Tennessee and
North Carolina, the Pisgah and Nantahalia National Forest Service, the
Air Rescue Service, volunteers from area communities, and a new organization called the Civil Air Patrol. Mrs. Thomas B. Wheeler, wife of one
of the crew members, and her sister-in-law searched for the missing
plane during the week of April 24, 1944 by themselves (three months
after the apparent crash).

The Civil Air Patrol, or CAP, as it was called, was a new, congres-
sionally chartered organization that evolved from a group of civilian
pilots who lived along the seacoast prior to World War II. These volunteers took it upon themselves to patrol the coastlines looking for enemy
submarines. The CAP flew both private and military airplanes to search
and destroy the encroaching subs. The U.S. Army Air Force saw their volunteer spirit and gave these civilian pilots more responsibility. Today CAP
handles more than 85 percent of all inland search and rescue involving
missing civilian and military aircraft.

In searching for the missing UC-78, the commanding officer at Morris Airfield, gave much of the responsibility to the North Carolina CAP under the direction of Lt. Oscar Meyes, the local CAP commander. The CAP, on their first search inside the Great Smoky Mountains National Park, used private and AAF planes to perform their duties. On Friday, February 4, CAP scoured the mountains in hopes of turning up evidence. Maj. T. J. Hieatt of the AAF led the ground search.

Two and a half years later (September 10, 1946), two lumber workers, John and Ernest Smathers, found what they thought was the aircraft near Maggie Valley. The search was moved to an area called Rattlesnake Cove. What was found were the remains of a plane that crashed on Campbell Knob in 1943. Not knowing this at the time, it was reported that they had discovered "bits of metal and then the large piece of plane fabric which had Navy gray and olive-drab camouflage paint and a part of a blue insignia."[3] The AAF. returned to the area and searched for three more days from the air and ground. The result of the lead was a "negative find."

This operation marked the first use of a helicopter in a Park search. A Bell Coupe helicopter was borrowed from the Bell Aircraft Corporation of Buffalo, New York, while it was on a demonstration flight in Asheville. Russell Case, assistant manager of the helicopter division, and Harry Mitchell, the pilot, donated their time to the search. On January 28, 1947, three years after the disappearance, the search continued with the Air Rescue Service. Two more military helicopters, several L-5 observation planes, and a C-47 observation plane were assigned to the search.

During the January 1947 search, ground crews found but later disregarded two clues that were carefully checked. One was a parachute harness found by Junior Riggens near Black Camp Gap, and another was a possible sighting through "high powered binoculars" near Polls Gap of an airplane seen "laying under a tree."[4] Once all leads had been investigated, the "official" search was halted.

The UC-78 is still listed as "missing" in U.S. Army and U.S. Air Force files. The whereabouts of the plane and its crew remains an unsolved mystery.

Leonard's Staggerwing

As the Second World War was on the mind of the nation, the Oak Ridge National Laboratories were in their prime. Seven months after the disappearance of the army Bamboo bomber with an Oak Ridge scientist on board, another search began for another Oak Ridge official.

In 1932, just prior to the creation of the Great Smoky Mountains National Park, Walter Beech began to manufacture an airplane that today is referred to as "the Lear Jet of the 1930's."[5] The Beechcraft Company produced the Model 17 Staggerwing, or "Stag," until 1946, making a total of 760. According to a report in the *Maryville-Alcoa Daily Times* in 1974, 125 were still flying and another 100 were being rebuilt.[6] The Stag was, and still is, a popular aircraft among enthusiasts.

The Stag was a very impressive "tail dragger" aircraft with retractable landing gear, an enclosed cabin, a large radial engine that could reach a speed of two hundred miles per hour, and an interesting "negative stagger" wing arrangement: the top set of wings were set behind, not in front of, the bottom set. A. E. "Eddie" Leonard flew one of these wonderful aircraft into the Big Greenbrier section of the park on August 12, 1944, and became involved in the sixth aviation incident in the Smokies.

Leonard was raised in Charlotte, North Carolina, during the Roaring Twenties. According to his son Hank, he had an early love for aviation.[7] In grade school he had a collection of more than one hundred model airplanes put together using wood and metal scraps. Hank Leonard has kept a journal about his quest to return to his father's crash site, thereby providing a terrific record of Smoky Mountain aviation history.[8] The journal begins with the story of Eddie announcing to his parents that he had caught a "passion for flying." At age fifteen he dropped out of school and began his career as an aviator.

The young Eddie Leonard worked his way through flight training and was very successful. He began his aviation pursuits by selling scenic airplane ride tickets in Charlotte, and for each ten he sold, he received one free flying lesson. Quickly he earned his license, and by the time he turned eighteen he was a flight instructor. He was reportedly one of the best acrobatic pilots in North Carolina and traveled throughout the Southeast performing air shows. "I would set quietly and watch as he performed loops, Cuban 8s and spins overhead," Hank recalls. "One of his maneuvers I remember very clearly was an inverted pass about twenty feet over the runway with both arms dangling from the cockpit. This never failed to get the crowd excited. Needless to say, I was very proud."[9]

Acrobatics and flight instruction briefly occupied Eddie's time and interest. His desires changed during the Second World War as pilots were being recruited for battle and he wanted to be a part of the action. At the Cannon Airport near Charlotte, Eddie became the chief instructor for a military flight program, training many of the pilots who flew in the

European theater. His next assignment was in Knoxville, Tennessee, at the McGhee Tyson Airport.

Oak Ridge National Labs was developing nuclear weapons and energy in the 1940s, and Eddie found himself assisting the war effort as a pilot flying for the Stone-Webster Personnel and Engineering Corporation of Oak Ridge. He flew officials throughout the United States on a Model D-17 Staggerwing supplied by the Clinton Engineering Works and based at McGhee Tyson.

On board the aircraft with him on August 12 were Shelby Parham and Reuben Johnson. As an airplane mechanic, Johnson worked at Wood's Flying School in Knoxville. An interesting story about Johnson and his family involves a near-death experience. Apparently he, his wife, and daughter were hit by a lightning bolt before moving to Knoxville. Reuben survived, but his daughter was injured and his wife died.

Between 10:03 and 10:20 A.M. on Saturday, August 12, 1944, the Stag departed McGhee Tyson for Pittsburgh with a stop at Charlotte. They should have arrived in Charlotte for lunch, but the plane did not make it over the Smokies, crashing at approximately 10:30 A.M. A search began soon after the plane was noticed overdue and was closed two and a half years later.

The Tennessee Civil Air Patrol had no idea the work that was before them. The CAP and park rangers could not imagine the disappointment they would feel after flying hundreds of hours and hiking hundreds of miles and not finding the crash site. The search story begins with Lt. C. E. Dunn of Maryville receiving a mission authorization for the Stag disappearance.

The first lead in the search placed the airplane near the community of Hartford. W. L. Striggs Jr. and A. W. Baxter of Hartford reported seeing an airplane in trouble around noon on the day of the crash. The plane flew into the clouds, they said, losing altitude as its engine sputtered. In their thoughts, the plane could not have made it over the mountains.[10] A search began, but no evidence was found to establish for certain that the plane they saw was the Stag. A reward of one thousand dollars was offered by an individual in North Carolina, and leads continued to pour into search headquarters. The search was expanded and soon began to tax the resources of the Park Service and the CAP.

Before the park was officially dedicated and the existing property tracts were acquired, individuals and groups enjoyed the waterfalls, creeks, animals, and trails. In 1924 the Smoky Mountain Hiking Club (SMHC) was formed to organize hikes and hikers in the Smokies wilderness. Today, with hundreds of members from all walks of life—ministers, carpenters, retirees, business executives—the organization is not so much a club as a historical presence in the mountains. Guided hikes into the backcountry were and still are a prominent feature of the SMHC. In 1947 one of the guided hikes turned into a surprise when the group made a discovery . . . an airplane.

It all started with a notice mailed to all club members in January 1947: "Come along and let's take a little jaunt into one of the prettiest and roughest sections of the Park!"[11] The hike was planned for Wooly Tops on the morning of Sunday, January 19. They began their hike in a cold rain. In and out of showers, the group finally made it to their destination deep into the backcountry.

Walking a short distance from the rest of the group, young Ernest M. Dickerman found the first pieces of the puzzle: small strands of olive drab cloth tangled in tree limbs. He summoned the hiking party, and the group, finding themselves in a one-hundred-yard-diameter debris field, combed the mountainside. They had found the missing plane.

Eddie Leonard's Beech Model 17 Staggerwing was lost in the Greenbrier section of the Great Smoky Mountains National Park in August 1944 and was not found until January 1947, when a young hiker briefly wandered from his hiking group and came upon the wreckage. Courtesy of H. A. Leonard.

After looking for human remains and finding none, the group walked off the mountain and reported their findings to the National Park Service. At first the wreckage was thought to be that of a plane that had crashed in 1945, but after additional investigation, park rangers decided that it might be the missing Stag. Military officials and family members were notified and told that this was probably the missing aircraft.

Due to an expected long-term search for the bodies, the Tennessee Highway Patrol (THP) and Oak Ridge officials set up a staging area in Greenbrier. Several investigation teams led by Lt. W. J. Stanton of the U.S. Army and consisting of twelve military personnel, a military police officer, park rangers, highway patrolmen, Dickerman, a newspaper photographer, and Leonard family members, made their way up the snowy mountains during the next week. On January 26, one team—Frank Leonard Sr. (Eddie's brother), Hank Leonard (Eddie's son), Dickerman, and two soldiers—reached the site. The party searched through the debris and found articles they recognized as Eddie's. The serial number on the aircraft matched the missing aircraft's number as well. It was the Stag. After a cold, wet, and emotional hour, the group left and returned to the parking area.

In the following days, state and federal officials searched for clues that might lead them to the men's bodies and to the cause of the crash. No evidence of a cause was found, and the bodies were never recovered. The crash remains a mystery.

Double Trouble

Mount Sequoyah was named in memory of a Cherokee who created a written language and alphabet for his people. Creative and patient, Sequoyah struggled to help the Cherokee nation keep its heritage and not conform entirely to the white man's ways. He stands tall as one of the most famous and respected members of his nation.

On the North Carolina side of the 6,003-foot Mount Sequoyah two airplanes mark three significant events in the aviation history of Smoky Mountains National Park: the first death of a woman in an aviation incident, the crash of the first "working" aircraft, and the first aerial photographs of airplane wreckage.

Two months after Japan surrendered at Tokyo Bay in 1945, a U.S. Army UC-45 became the first authentic "war plane" to make its final flight into a mountainside in the national park. Basically, World War II was over.

The United States lost a quarter of a million soldiers to the fight and many more to noncombat incidents such as this.

The C-45 was a military version of the Beechcraft Model 18. Military, civilian, and commercial pilots commonly used this highly regarded and versatile aircraft. Its popularity stemmed from its reliability and easy modification. The Beech 18 that crashed on Mount Sequoyah was the UC-45 (serial number 43-33351). Its basic shape and interior design was the Beech Model B-18-S, but Beechcraft custom-built dozens of models to meet exact specifications for the military. This UC-45 was built for the U.S. Army Air Force by Beech on October 1, 1943, as a high-speed personnel transport plane. It carried four passengers, a pilot, and copilot. It could haul up to 147 gallons of fuel and 103 pounds of baggage with six persons or more fuel with a smaller crew. It could fly at 234 miles per hour powered by two Pratt and Whitney R-985-23 (or 17) engines rated at 450 horsepower. The aircraft was thirty-five feet long, nine feet high, and forty-nine feet wide. It weighed 8,727 pounds and had 912 hours on the engines. All these details were converted into a debris field on Mount Sequoyah.

Details are unclear regarding the purpose of the flight, but one report from the "Office of Flying Safety" states that the plane was transporting discharged personnel home from the war. The authors have a copy of the censored, illegible report dated October 8, 1945.[12] There was also speculation that there was another C-45 lost on this same flight path at the same time. The AAF had to determine if they actually had one, two, or no searches before this search progressed.

Piloting the UC-45 from Youngstown, Ohio, was 1st Lt. Robert W. Barton, who was assigned to Squadron C of the 3500th Group of the U.S. Army Air Force Base Unit (AAFBU) at the Eastern Technical Training Command (ETTC) on Lambert Field in St. Louis, Missouri. He was a twenty-four-year-old pilot with 717 flight hours, 82 of them in the UC-45. He received his pilot rating two years prior to the crash, was instrument rated, and was flying on instrument flight rules (IFR) as he left St. Louis.

Also on board was Cpl. Winifred R. Haines of Cleveland; SPEC 3/2 Lena E. Allred, a WAVE (Women Appointed for Voluntary Emergency Service, a service branch of the U.S. Navy) of Charlotte, North Carolina; S.Sgt. Hollis E. Brobrick of Waltham, Massachusetts; 1st Lt. Stanley M. Lerner of Greensboro, North Carolina; and the crew chief, S.Sgt. Raymond H. Kerkela of Minneapolis.

Lieutenant Barton received a clearance at 4:50 P.M. Central Time for a direct flight from Lambert Field to Morris Airfield on October 5, 1945.

His requested cruising altitude was 5,000 feet, and at 180 miles per hour for a 550-mile flight, his time en route was two and a half hours. Before he departed, Cincinnati Airway Traffic Control Center changed his clearance to 7,000 feet due to the range of mountains that extend to 6,684 feet. The cloud ceiling was estimated at 6,600 feet, with a 3-mile visibility and intermittent rain. Barton departed at 4:54 P.M., speaking with no one on the radio along the way. The UC-45 crashed into the Smokies. Flight Officer Jack Petitt noted that when he flew over the wreckage a few days later, the aircraft looked as if it had flown straight into the mountain heading toward Tennessee. In that case, it is likely that the plane turned around and was heading back or that the crew became lost in the clouds and turned into the mountain.

At 5:01 A.M. on October 7 the operational chief at Lambert Field declared the plane "missing" and search operations began. The first action was to contact the home bases of the crew and determine if the plane had landed. The second action was to check all military airstrips along the flight path. This did not reveal any leads. An expanded search began promptly with Maj. W. B. Jones of Asheville in charge.

An incredible air search began and eventually extended from St. Louis to Atlanta and from the Atlantic Coast to the Mississippi River. It was estimated that the plane probably made it to the Smokies, and there the intensive search was centered. This was determined from theorizing that maybe the pilot did not comply or did not understand the instructions to fly at seven thousand rather than five thousand feet.

Reports from citizens in the area suggested that a plane might have been in trouble. One report, taken from a man who lived near Roan Mountain, was that a plane was flying very low, dipped, then "failed to reappear."[13] Aircraft saturated the airspace above the mountains during the search. For an unknown reason, the Park Service was not notified to begin its search until five days after the plane was reported overdue. The Tennessee Rescue Service in Nashville alerted the Park Service of the search and asked the rangers to be on the lookout for evidence.

Three local mountain guides from Cosby were called upon to help lead the army search team through the backcountry. Bill Baxter, J. A. Valentine, and John A. Fowler spent a considerable amount of time searching with the army and Park Service. The next day, October 14, nine days after the crash and in the prime autumn color season, wreckage was spotted by a search plane. The Emergency Rescue Control Center in

A U.S. Army Air Force UC-45 in thick rhododendron. Note the steepness of the hillside and the jungle appearance of vegetation. Courtesy of Great Smoky Mountains National Park Library Archive.

Atlanta notified the Park Service of the sighting and asked that they support the mission by sending rangers in to perform a ground search.

On the morning of the fifteenth, a Park Service ground team consisting of Stupka, Morrell, Ownby, Wingier, Ogle, and Smith hiked up the Snake Den Truck Trail at Cosby to the Appalachian Trail in "one of the roughest *areas* in the entire Park—and equally unaccessible to hikers."[14] Later on the fifteenth their team was joined by Maj. W. B. Jones and Capt. Harold Guzzo of the military and led by Park Ranger Wilson. The weather continued to hamper the search. Harold Davis, a *Knoxville News Sentinel* photographer, said, "The *search* plane was above the mists that hid even nearby mountain peaks and blurred the trail 50 yards ahead." The prospect of the crew members' survival was deemed bleak. According to the *Knoxville News Sentinel,* the mountains were so cold that "hikers couldn't pause more than two minutes at a time for fear of frostbite."[15] Additional food, blankets, and a radio were parachuted to the search crews that day.

Another search team, led by Captain Dwyer, departed from the North Carolina side of the park on the sixteenth (day eleven) and met the original team on the Appalachian Trail. That morning Assistant Chief Ranger Light flew above the wreckage with members of the Emergency Rescue Control Center. At 9:50 A.M. the search plane circled over the ground team and led them to the site at 11:02 A.M. "An observation plane radioed back that rescue squads were spotted at the wreckage," Superintendent Blair Ross told the *Sentinel.* "However those at the scene were without portable radio and conditions at the crash site were unknown immediately."[16] The army took control of the scene after confirmation that it was in fact the missing UC-45. All crew members were accounted for, and two days later the bodies were removed from the park with an organized effort by the Park Service, the AAF, and a Civilian Conservation Corps crew from the Kephart Prong Camp. Records indicate that the carryout from the site to the Appalachian Trail was up a sixty-five-degree slope over an undetermined distance. Once at the Appalachian Trail, horses transported the bodies to ambulances at the Bradley Fork Truck Trail. The wreckage was "obliterated" by the AAF and Park Service prior to their departure from the scene.

For their service to the U.S. Army Air Force, the Park Service received a letter of commendation from Brig. Gen. A. Hornsby and a letter of commendation from Brig. Gen. Ivan L. Farman. A "Memorandum for the Director" from the park files records this message: "We sincerely hope that there will never be a month with so much tragedy and disaster as occurred in the Smokies in October, 1945."[17]

The day after the UC-45 was identified by a ground team and recovery work was underway to carry out the victims, the rescue workers were faced with another problem: the crash of an observation plane. On October 17 an L-5, a military version of the popular Stinson Sentinel, crashed near the Appalachian Trail on Mount Sequoyah. Each year hundreds of hikers pass within a few feet of the site, but the plane was dismantled by the AAF soon after the crash.

The L-5 was a fabulous light aircraft built for private pilots and the military. It was powered by a Lycoming 0-435-1 185-horsepower engine. It had a wooden propeller, and its metal tubular airframe was covered with fabric. It had a maximum speed of 130 miles per hour and cruised at 90 miles per hour. The two-person airplane allowed the pilot and passenger to sit one behind the other rather than side-by-side. It was very useful for photography because it had an ample glass-enclosed cabin for viewing above, in front of, and to each side of the plane.

Flight Officer Jack R. Pettit, a twenty-five-year-old pilot from Memphis, and Sgt. Edward Aptt, based at a Greenville, South Carolina, U.S. Army Air base, were the crew members on the slow-moving, light observation plane.[18] Their mission was to photograph the UC-45 incident site. According to Pettit they were flying low and slow, and as the plane crossed the main ridge, it hit a downdraft and quickly fell into the trees.

Pettit said that when he realized they were going to crash, he yelled to Aptt to "put the camera down and brace yourself." Aptt placed the large camera on his lap and held tightly to the steel tubes that made up the airframe. As the plane hit the trees and then the ground, the force of the impact caused Aptt's chin to hit the camera's lens very hard. The lens broke and made a deep cut on his chin. When the plane came to a stop, Petitt looked at Aptt in the back seat and was shocked at the copious amount of blood coming from the laceration. Aptt and Pettit crawled out of the wreckage and promptly decided that there was no time to sit and think.

The men realized they were not seriously injured but knew they had to find their own way out to civilization. Walking in a cold drizzle through "the wildest country" they had ever seen, the two men traveled down the Appalachian Trail toward Gatlinburg.[19] Aptt was not a happy camper. He was a very large man (almost three hundred pounds of solid muscle), and in his discontent with Pettit, walked up to the Appalachian Trail and never looked back. Pettit did not see the photographer again until they met up with each other in Gatlinburg. The last image Pettit had of Sgt. Aptt was of the stout man walking briskly west, bloody camera at his side, mumbling something about pilots.

After hiking for thirteen and a half hours (beginning at 11:00 A.M. and finishing at 12:30 A.M. that night) the two waved down separate cars on the Newfound Gap Road and rode to Gatlinburg. Once in town, Pettit called home and told his father he was "shaken up but otherwise unhurt."[20]

The whereabouts of the UC-45 black-and-white photos are unknown. The film was returned upon Pettit's arrival at the base, but unfortunately the photos have not been located. Commenting on the UC-45 wreckage, Pettit described it this way: "There wasn't much left to see then, let alone now."[21]

Now almost eighty years old, Jack Pettit lives in Chouteau, Oklahoma, and is still sharp as a tack. He recalls details of the crash with great accuracy and was extremely happy to tell his story. He is the earliest Smoky Mountains plane crash survivor still living and is currently building a scale model of his L-5, which will be remote control operated.

A Plane with No Occupants

Seven months. That was the duration of the search for the second Beech Model 18 that crashed in the park. This search receives notoriety because it is the first incident in the park in which parachutes were used to free the crew from harm's way. There are two reasons it took so long to locate the aircraft. First, there was no "search urgency" because the crew landed on the ground in Morristown, and second, the crew did not know in which direction the crewless plane was headed. This training flight became real for the crew of U.S. Navy flight 51174 when they had to put their training into practice in order to save themselves.

The Beech Model 18s were first built in 1937 and were in continuous manufacture until 1969. Not very popular in the United States at first, the aircraft found service elsewhere. Lt. Col. Dwight Eisenhower saw the military possibilities for it and contracted with Beechcraft to manufacture the aircraft according to specifications for diverse mission objectives. The model that crashed in the Cosby area of the park was probably an AT-11 "Kansan," also designated as a T-11-BH. It was basically a Beech 18 with a gun turret in front. The AT-11 was designed to carry ten one-hundred-pound bombs. Powered by two Pratt and Whitney R-985-AN1 engines rated at 450 horsepower, the machine could reach speeds up to 215 miles per hour. The navy version of the T-11BH was the SNB-1. For ease of reading the plane will be referred to as an AT-11.

Four U.S. Navy flyers were on a flight from Chicago to Atlanta on the night of December 9, 1945, when they slowly got into trouble and made aviation history in the Smokies. The flight was going well as they flew over Kentucky heading toward a stop in Nashville before making their way to Atlanta. As they approached Nashville the weather became worse and they were forced to divert to Knoxville. Trying to fly around the storm, they became lost in their attempt to locate the airport and found themselves east of Knoxville. Suddenly, their radio stopped working and they lost communications with the air traffic controller. To make matters worse, their fuel supply was depleted. A decision was made to abandon

the aircraft because they knew the mountains loomed not too far way.

Preparing for the jump, the pilot climbed to forty-five hundred feet and locked the flight controls. The men jumped from the doomed airplane a few moments before midnight on the ninth, and they all landed within three miles of the Morristown Airport. They were unsure of the direction the plane would take to its demise. It apparently crashed just after midnight on December 10. One crew member said it "could have gone up around Greeneville."[22] The search began at 1:45 A.M., when the Hamblen County Sheriff's Department was contacted to locate the four crew members—Lt. Cmdr. J. B. Dewilde, Ens. S. R. Cummings, Lt. O. N. Anderson, and the pilot, Lt. E. E. Johnson—and the presumably destroyed aircraft. Sheriff J. E. Burke was the search manager along with Trooper Carl Gilbert. Within minutes the crew woke residents and made calls to regroup.

The search for the airplane began the morning of the tenth as the search for the crew ended. Two pilots from Morristown, Tom Moore and Bob Jones, began an air search and flew for several hours with no results. Due to the large search area, additional resources were called. The crew

Lost in a storm, their plane low on fuel, four navy flyers parachuted to safety before their AT-11 crashed in the Cosby area of the park in December 1945. Pictured here are the aircraft's engines. Photo by Dwight McCarter.

could not offer much help. "They didn't know where the plane was headed for, because they were lost," the sheriff said.[23]

On July 11, 1946, seven months after the crash, a hiker digging ramps found the crash site in the Cosby section of the park. For years various written records indicated that the plane was a "flying boat," also referred to as a PBY.[24] This is not true and through the years the plane has disintegrated.

B-29 Superfortress

Clingmans Dome is widely known for the white, cement lookout tower that sits atop it, providing visitors with a 360-degree view of the Smokies. The "Dome" is, in fact, the mountain itself. It received its name as a memorial to Thomas Lanier Clingman, an early surveyor in the park. The altitude on the mountain top is 6,643 feet, the highest point in Tennessee and the park. This is what caught a massive B-29 and ended its flight. An airplane could not hit a higher mountain in the area, except for Mount Mitchell in North Carolina (6,684 feet). Hundreds of Appalachian Trail hikers each year walk through this crash site and never realize it. On June 12, 1946, the bomber became a part of Smoky Mountains National Park aviation history as its tenth aircraft incident.

The B-29 "Superfortress" was a bomber built for the U.S. Army by Boeing. It had four massive engines (Wright R-3350-23) with a combined 8,800 horsepower. With an impressive range of more than 5,800 miles, it could fly at 220 miles per hour, it had a ceiling of 31,850 feet, and its maximum weight was an enormous 141,100 pounds. It was held aloft by a 141-foot wingspan and was 99 feet long and 27 feet high.

This particular aircraft was on a routine navigational night-training flight leaving MacDill Field near Tampa, Florida, at 7:00 P.M. on Tuesday, June 11. The flight was to arrive in Chicago and return to MacDill on Wednesday, June 12. The last known radio contact with the crew was made with the Knoxville Airport at 2:16 A.M. as the plane was returning to Tampa. The mountains were cloud-covered during the night, and scattered thundershowers were in the forecast.

At approximately 3:00 A.M. a Sevierville police officer reported what he thought was an abnormally low flying airplane flying south over Sevierville. His attention was drawn to the plane, he said, because Sevierville is not along any regular flight routes.[25] Apparently the officer was correct in his report because the estimated time of impact was between

3:30 and 4:04 A.M. (3:30 A.M. was the time a watch found at the scene had stopped).

U.S. Army Air Force Boeing B-29 Superfortress near Clingmans Dome. The aircraft crashed at night colliding with the Tennessee side and resting in North Carolina. Courtesy of Great Smoky Mountains National Park Library Archive.

Flying at a southeasterly heading, the plane began to hit treetops one-eighth of a mile east of the tower, two hundred to four hundred feet below the crest on the Tennessee side. "Dozens of trees, some more than two feet in diameter, were clipped in a 60 yard wide swath and carried towards the mountain top with the plane," the *Knoxville News Sentinel* reported. "They lie there now, tops pointing backward the way grass is left after the stroke of a sickle."[26] The swath suggested that the pilot began to climb at the last minute, but his attempt was fruitless, as he hit the very top of the summit just a few yards north of the Appalachian Trail.

The fuselage hit the ground, sheared its wings, and continued a quarter of a mile into North Carolina, resting a few feet from the Clingmans Dome Road. The plane's fuel capacity was about six thousand gallons. Most of the fuel had already been spent, but the remainder ignited and the plane and forest were engulfed in flames. The plane was shredded into thousands of pieces, the largest being the engines—one of which landed on the opposite side of the road. The plane burned during the night and smoldered for several days.

From 2:16 until 5:00 A.M. the MacDill Field in Florida was oblivious to the fact that anything had happened. These training flights were common, and no one expected trouble. When the B-29 did not check in or land on time at MacDill, however, the operations officer began to worry. The usual procedure was to continually try to contact the overdue plane by radio on different frequencies. Also, other air bases and airports were usually called to determine if the plane had made an unexpected landing.

After all these methods failed to produce good news, the U.S. Army Air Force tried to track the plane by communicating with its contact points to determine the progress of the flight. They knew the B-29 made it to the Knoxville area because the tower operator said the crew reported in at 2:16 A.M. with an "all's well."[27] The search began in Knoxville and moved south to Tampa. Planes were launched from Greenville, South Carolina, to begin a search. The sky was overcast above the mountains, and clouds held tight to the ridge tops.

On a routine drive to the Clingmans Dome pumping station, two Civilian Public Service employees discovered an unusual sight at 8:15 A.M. Three-quarters of a mile from the Forney Creek Parking Area, on the Clingmans Dome Road, Adam Dixson and L. D. Hancock found a burnt airplane engine. Stopping, they immediately saw a two-acre debris field on the west side of the road. Walking through the wreckage scene, they found several bodies. They left the scene to get help.

During the course of the day on Tuesday, June 11, the Park Service closed Clingmans Dome Road at Newfound Gap and began the gruesome task of recovering the bodies of the crew. The AAF investigation team arrived the next day and began to map the scene and collect clues. During the initial investigation it was determined that all twelve bodies were located inside North Carolina; seven were thrown clear, and five were still in the wreckage. The Third Air Force Headquarters in Greenville confirmed that all the bodies were removed from the scene by noon and were taken to Rawling's Funeral Home in Sevierville on Wednesday, June 12. From there, the identified crew members would receive a military escort to their hometowns.

On Thursday, June 13, under a partly cloudy sky and rain showers, the Clingmans Dome Road was reopened and sightseers were allowed to drive near the site. At the same time a seven-person team of U.S. Army Air Force investigators, led by Lt. Col. Kenneth Holbert, could be seen sifting through the remains of the Superfortress. Instruments and other important pieces of the wreckage were carefully packaged and removed from the site as possible clues to the mysterious crash of the million-dollar aircraft.

Today a person hiking from Clingmans Dome Tower to Collins Gap would never know the B-29 had crossed the ridge top, knocking down trees and moving boulders. The site has been picked clean of wreckage.

This is a story in memory of

Capt. Robert C. Morre, thirty-two, of LaGrange, Illinois
1st Lt. James H. Reid, twenty-nine, of Montgomery, Alabama
1st Lt. Eugene B. Selleck, twenty-six, of Park Ridge, Illinois
1st Lt. Frederick Lee, thirty-one, of Lockport, New York
1st Lt. Carrol L. Wilkinson, twenty-nine, of Wasco, California
2d Lt. John R. McElwee of East Orange, New Jersey
2d Lt. O. C. Cook, twenty-five, of McRae, Georgia
M.Sgt. Taylor Powell, twenty-seven, of Mountain View, California
M.Sgt. Charles E. Bausch, twenty, of Bettendorf, Iowa
M.Sgt. Frank S. Smith, twenty-seven, of Cibolo, Texas
T.Sgt. Alfred G. Parker Jr., twenty-three, of Forest, Louisiana
Sgt. Julius N. Guest, twenty-two, of Tampa Florida.

Rest in peace

A Corsair, a Parachute, and a Model A Ford

The only evidence that a Corsair once sat on a hilltop in the Abrams Creek area is a few cut poplar trees and a good-sized hole. This site was the most visited crash site in the Smokies until the plane was completely removed in the winter of 1992. So many people visited the site that the manway leading to it was wider and more recognizable than the maintained Little Bottoms Trail.

Curiosity was probably spurred in part by the television program *Blacksheep Squadron,* which featured Corsairs (made famous by Col. Gregory "Pappy" Boyington) similar to the one that crashed. The plane was easily accessible, and a trek to it made a fine day hike for children as well as adults. Little by little the plane disappeared, partly due to nature, but mainly due to souvenir hunters and, eventually, a salvage company.

Lt. Dwight C. Follin's Goodyear FG-1D Corsair, which crashed in the Abrams Creek area of the park on December 4, 1948. This site was the most visited crash site in the Smokies until the plane was completely removed in 1992. Photo by Jeff Wadley.

All this interest began on the night of Saturday, December 4, 1948.

Navy reserve pilot Lt. Dwight C. Follin, twenty-six, was a 204-pound senior football player at Kent State University in Ohio majoring in traffic management. He played professional football for the Cleveland Browns and the Toronto Argonauts, but long before he would tell stories of tackles and blocks, he would tell about the cold winter night he spent in the Smokies. Follin's flight was in a U.S. Navy FG-1D Corsair. He was en route from Akron, Ohio, to Jacksonville, Florida, on a ferry flight, but his flight was interrupted near Abrams Creek.[28]

Corsairs had one 2,100-horsepower Pratt and Whitney eighteen-cylinder engine that turned a thirteen-foot, three-blade propeller.[29] It could cruise at 446 miles per hour and had a 3,870-feet-per-minute rate of climb. Goodyear built this particular aircraft, but Chance Vought and Brewster built other models of the same plane. With its "gull" wing pattern and distinctive red, white, and blue "star" logo on each side, the plane was easily recognizable.

Flying at 7,200 feet, Follin found himself running low on fuel and began looking for McGhee Tyson Airport. Flying past the planned refueling stop and over the Smokies, he radioed at 7:05 P.M. that he was in trouble. He climbed to 8,000 feet, leveled off, then cruised at a speed of 90 knots (104 miles per hour). He decided he had two options: jump or ride. He chose to jump. He turned the aircraft away from the lights on the ground in order to avoid populated areas and pulled his rip cord so hard that he bruised his chest. Follin's parachute opened, and he found himself floating above the Smokies so quietly that he could hear the Corsair go through the trees below him. He landed unhurt atop a thirty-foot pine tree near Goldmine Road. After climbing limb to limb down the tree, Follin discovered he would be spending a long, cold, and hungry night alone in the backcountry.

During the night he survived quite well. He inventoried his belongings and found he had two cigarettes and one match but no food. Using pine needles and the cigarette package, he started a fire and kept warm throughout the night, just being satisfied that he survived the crash and was not hurt.

A search had started immediately after the tower lost radio contact with Follin. Law enforcement agencies in Tennessee and North Carolina and the Park Service searched throughout the night and into the late morning for the missing plane. Plans were made to do an aerial search southeast of McGhee Tyson and into the mountains when word reached the searchers that Follin had been found.

At daybreak on Sunday, December 5, Follin decided to leave the parachute and campsite and try to find his way out of the mountains. After walking for four hours and following Abrams Creek, he found a dirt road. While walking along the road he heard a car's engine and spotted a four-door Model A Ford with two teenage boys in the front and "the mother, father and grandfather in the backseat."[30] They were on their way home from a worship service, and Follin flagged them down. The car was not licensed, apparently, but the boys told the navy flyer that they could take him to a place where he could get help. Imagine the story they would tell their friends that afternoon!

The boys let Follin out at a dirt road, where he hitched another ride to a paved road (the second car also was not licensed). At the paved road Follin began to hitchhike, after being told that someone "will come along with plates."[31] Eventually he got a ride to a gas station, told some men his story, and they took him to the Maryville Police Station. He told his story to the police, the search was halted, and the Marine Reserve Center was contacted.

The marines from the center came for him and took him to the airport, where they began a search for the plane's wreckage. What a trip for Follin—a Corsair, a Model A Ford, three other cars, a marine vehicle, and then another airplane!

The marine pilot and Follin began an aerial search, and within minutes they located Follin's parachute hanging in a tree. Shortly thereafter they spotted the actual crash site about two miles from the parachute. The plane was demolished. Follin hiked into the site with the marines on Wednesday, December 8, and retrieved his personal effects and important papers. The blue fabric-and-metal-covered airplane was partially buried in the soil amid poplars and white pine trees slightly off a ridge top. The weapons were removed from the plane, as were other sensitive items, but the rest remained until 1992.

A second operation began for the plane in the late autumn of 1992, this time by a salvage company. Bootstrap Aircraft Restoration of East Haven, Connecticut, removed the vintage war bird from the Smokies on Wednesday, December 11. One of Vertiflite's Bell 206 Jet Ranger helicopters, piloted by Winston Chelf, gave flight to the Corsair. The wings and fuselage were airlifted to a waiting flatbed truck, and all the remaining pieces were bundled together for the trip to Connecticut.

The owner of Bootstrap rebuilds crashed airplanes and claimed the Smokies Corsair would fly again. Another reason for recovering the Corsair, he said, was to remove a "non-conforming, man-made structure" from the site.[32] Although the company removed the object of a good day hike, it is to be credited for helping return the area to its appearance before the crash. Except for a few trees that had to be cleared for the recovery, the site is virtually spotless.

THREE

The 1950s

April Fools' Day Disaster

Hannah Mountain rises as a beautiful ridge near Abrams Creek in the western end of the Great Smoky Mountains National Park. The area contains many historic sites, such as flint pits, pre-park home sites, and some mining sites. When twenty-eight-year-old Robert Hartman crashed onto a slope of Hannah Mountain, he became an unfortunate casualty. The mountains claimed another pilot and his flying machine on Sunday, April 1, 1951.[1]

Hartman's P-51 was powered by a Rolls Royce (Packard) Merlin V-1650 engine. With 1,650 horsepower, the plane could travel 1,000 miles at 250 miles per hour. It had a forty-one-thousand-foot ceiling, stood thirteen feet high and thirty-two feet long, and had a thirty-seven-foot wingspan.

Lieutenant Hartman was flying a P-51D "Mustang" single-engine fighter during a rainstorm. Along with him was another P-51 and a C-47 transport plane. The trio had departed from Warner Robbins Air Force Base near Macon, Georgia, and were en route to Louisville, Kentucky, with a final destination of Wright-Patterson Air Force Base near Dayton, Ohio. They were all assigned to the 164th Fighter Squadron of the Alabama Air National Guard.

At approximately 10:30 P.M. on Sunday night, the lead plane broke through the clouds at 22,500 feet, fifty miles south of

Knoxville, and radioed the other two planes to follow. Lt. Hartman radioed and said he had reached 22,000 feet and was experiencing icing very fast. That was the last word they received from Hartman. The other P-51 and the C-47 continued their flight, thinking Hartman was above the storm and with them. After receiving negative radio transmissions from Hartman, the two planes landed in Bowling Green, Kentucky, and reported the pilot as missing.

The search began with the usual radio calls and airport checks. Hartman was not located either by radio or on the ground, so a larger-scale search was coordinated by the Air Rescue Service. Weather did not cooperate until the fourth day, when Civil Air Patrol search aircraft were able to retrace his route into the park from the south. The Asheville CAP dispatched planes on April 2; however, visibility was only four miles, and

The wreckage of Lt. Robert Hartman's U.S. Air Force P-51 Mustang, ANG 4654, which crashed due to extreme icing on April 1, 1951. The aircraft struck the east slope of Hannah Mountain with such force that from the air only small pieces of the plane were visible and it took searchers four days to locate the debris field. Photo by Dwight McCarter.

the ceiling was not above the mountain tops. The Chattanooga CAP and the Georgia CAP were also involved, following the known route and flying over possible "escape routes" out of the mountains.

Finally, at 7:00 A.M. on Wednesday, April 4, fifty airplanes from the Civil Air Patrol, friends of the missing man, and other military pilots were able to conduct widespread searches from Georgia to Tennessee. In the science and art of searching, incident commanders train their aircrews not to search for the missing airplane, but to search for signs that an airplane might leave in a forest. Most airplanes that hit mountainsides do not look like they did in the hangar at the airport. It is much easier to look for broken treetops, a glimpse of a small piece of metal, or perhaps a ray of the sun reflecting off broken glass. This "lead collection" technique distinguishes expert trackers from nonexperienced sightseers.

Leads continued to flow into the mission base from citizens, and with the fine coordinator, Lt. F. C. Rice of Maxwell Field in Alabama, on top of things, no doubt each lead was well investigated. Two reports of "flares" were noted. A Knoxville resident reported seeing a crashed airplane five miles off Highway 441 between Cherokee and Newfound Gap. Another lead was on Mount LeConte, where a hiker noticed several newly broken trees. Elmer Petty, of the Calderwood area of south Blount County in Tennessee reported seeing a fire around 11:00 P.M. Sunday in the mountains. Records kept of the search log more than thirty people who saw a flash of light or a fire or heard an explosion in the Happy Valley area of Blount County the night of the crash. According to records, citizens' reports led searchers to concentrate the search near Happy Valley. The Park Service, CAP, and other investigators were sent to further question the residents of the valley in order to narrow the search area.

One lead that proved to be very helpful came from Lt. E. J. Keen, the squadron commander of the Oak Ridge CAP. In a search grid near the Tennessee–North Carolina state line, he reported seeing a tree with a broken top. Although Keen did not see wreckage near the tree, his tip eventually paid off because the mission coordinator did not disregard the information just because an actual "plane" was not spotted at the base of the tree. Being a sharp coordinator, Rice, made sure the tree and the area around it was searched by other aircrews later that day.

The Knoxville Municipal Airport was the search base for the operation because the search actually involved areas within three states (Georgia, North Carolina, and Tennessee). This was the first search mission for the newly formed Knoxville Civil Air Patrol. Their commander, Capt. Fred

Human, led much of the effort on the Tennessee side of the mountain. Human, along with Lt. Rice of the Fifth Rescue Squadron, did a wonderful job of organizing resources and assigning search areas. For instance, two resources were the pilot of the other P-51 and a twin-engine amphibian Air Rescue Service plane from Wright-Patterson. Another gesture of cama-raderie came from Cook's Flying Service in Knoxville, which donated the use of all its aircraft to the CAP for the search effort. In North Carolina, C-46s and C-47s were used, and another base was set up for communi-cations at the Andrews, North Carolina, airport by the North and South Carolina CAP.

Search areas were marked off in "grids" so the pilots and observers could conduct a "microscopic" low-altitude search. Each sortie was recorded: the name of pilot, the identity of the search plane, the grid number, departure time, estimated time in the search area, and expected time of return to the base. Each crew was briefed on its mission before it left, and crew members were questioned upon their return. Information such as places that need another search, unusual land and foliage features, and possible sightings were noted. At the end of each day the sectors were reassigned for another search the following day.

After flying 350 search hours and concentrating the search in the Happy Valley and Abrams Creek area, the wreckage was located. Civil Air Patrol members Capt. Robert Tucker of Maryville and Sgt. Jim Squires, a Maryville College student, were flying a search area between Cades Cove and Chilhowee Mountain when Squires became airsick and leaned out the plane's window to vomit.[2] As he did this, he lost his bridgework, but he noticed broken tree branches beneath the plane and saw what appeared to be a debris field on an east slope of Hannah Mountain. This was at 1:00 P.M. on Thursday, April 5, 1951, almost four days after the crash. A ground team of park rangers was ready to hike into the site with hopes of finding the pilot still alive.

In the late afternoon a ground team made it to the crash site. A CAP aircraft piloted by Lt. Hurdle J. Goddard and carrying crew member Sergeant Squires and *Maryville-Alcoa Daily Times* reporter Chuck Parvin flew over the wreckage as the ground team made its way to the area. Once the team was in position to leave the trail and head for the site, the CAP plane led them cross-country through the underbrush to the wreck-age. The six-person team, led by Chief Ranger Murnin, reached the site at 4:35 P.M., with three hours of sunlight remaining in the day.

The team found the aircraft in thousands of pieces within a fifty-yard radius with only a small amount of underbrush disturbed. Apparently, Hartman struck the mountainside straight on and the aircraft burned at impact. From the air, only small pieces of the plane could be seen reflecting in the sun. The team searched for Hartman, hoping that he had parachuted, but to their disappointment they found his body in the debris field.

When the wreckage was confirmed and the body found, the ground team built a signal fire to alert the CAP plane that this was the missing P-51. The search plane returned to the Knoxville airport to tell the good and bad news: the plane had been identified, but Hartman had perished. By 10:30 P.M. on the fifth, the pilot's body had been carried out to a waiting ambulance and transported out of the park.

After the search and carryout, Lieutenant Rice critiqued the operation. He complimented the residents of Blount County for their cooperation, telling them that information they supplied was what enabled CAP to concentrate the search in Happy Valley. "The C.A.P. flyers," Rice continued, "also should be commended for leaving their jobs for four days and giving their time, without pay, in the search." In addition, he expressed his appreciation to the Cook's Aero Service, which provided his staff with a facility from which to coordinate the search.[3] This major search was conducted admirably by the National Park Service, Civil Air Patrol, local sheriffs' departments, and the Air Rescue Service.

Hard to Believe!

It had been almost four years since the last aviation incident in the Smokies. But in 1955 physician Samuel Sullenberger proved unwillingly that he could put a bright yellow airplane into the mountains and still go undetected for several days, even with searchers flying directly over it multiple times.

Sullenberger, forty-two, practiced medicine at the Sullenberger Clinic and made his home in Dandridge, Tennessee. On November 2, at 3:30 P.M., he departed Swan's Airport near Dandridge for a short flight to test a newly purchased aircraft and look for good places to take photographs of the Smokies.[4] He flew to McGhee Tyson Airport and then over the mountains, planning to arrive back home at 5:30. However, he did not bring his new Piper "Cub" back to McGhee Tyson or Dandridge. His wife reported him overdue.

The Piper Corporation built the famous J-3, better known as the Cub. It had a simple 64-horsepower Continental A-65 engine with a range of three hundred miles. Its top speed was eighty-seven miles per hour. This particular aircraft was painted bright yellow. It would seem that a yellow aircraft would be a very easy target to locate from the air, but the search pilots said it was like trying to find a needle in a haystack.

Civil Air Patrol volunteers from Tennessee and North Carolina were called upon by the Air-Sea Rescue Unit from Eglin Air Force Base in Florida to coordinate and operate the search. In the Sullenberger case, the CAP was just over ten years old and had only been involved in a handful of searches in the park. Together with the Park Service, local guides, and the U.S. Air Force, the CAP conducted a well-organized search which ended when the pilot was found—alive.

On Thursday, November 3, fifteen aircraft from the CAP and one air force plane began a search. Sullenberger was a former CAP pilot, and this probably placed additional psychological urgency on the search. Fog hampered the aerial search on the first day, but leads were collected at the search base. CAP commander Maj. Bill Cook was the search mission coordinator (SMC).

On day two, the sky clear over the mountains, twenty-five planes from across the state flew grids. Fourteen sorties were flown very low in hopes of seeing the yellow plane. Leads were investigated, but none turned up valuable information. A report came from Del Rio, near Newport, of a small plane flying low over Morgans Gap. The reporting party thought the plane crashed but did not see a fire. Another person who was hunting in the area at the time saw smoke rising but did not see anything that lead him to believe there was a crash. Witnesses in Haywood County, North Carolina, saw what they thought was the plane near Fines Creek and the Test Farm.

On day three, November 5, Sullenberger was found alive and well. The interesting twist to this story is that he found his own way out of the mountains. His own chronology of events began with engine trouble at 5:00 P.M. on Wednesday, the second. Sullenberger said he experienced a loss of power due to carburetor icing and began to descend. Before he could escape the mountain ridge, he was caught in the force of a downdraft and his plane crashed into a densely wooded area within two miles of the summit of Mount Guyot.[5] He received a small cut to his head and was knocked unconscious for a short period of time. The plane came to rest on the top of a tree, which was bent low enough that Sullenberger could open the plane's door and climb to the ground. The Cub received very minor damage, enduring the downdraft without breaking the propeller or cracking a window.

Sullenberger realized he was in a very remote section of the park and a hike from the crash site to civilization would not be feasible that night. With only a bag of peanuts and a can of sardines to eat, he stayed at the crash site overnight in frigid temperatures. He later spoke to rangers of walking for three days in and out of Big Creek and often seeing search planes fly directly overhead without noticing him signaling below. Despite low-level, slow flights over leafless trees, the CAP pilots could not see him or the plane. They attributed the problem to the density of small trees and heavy underbrush. Sullenberger walked out to Big Creek Ranger Station on Saturday, November 5, with only minor injuries.

Once at Big Creek, Sullenberger called Chief Ranger Granville Liles on a mobile radio and reported that he was "hungry, tired and apparently not injured" from the crash.[6] "I'm in pretty good shape, in good spirits, but have some minor injuries," he said. His injuries were the result of a fight with a bear over his can of sardines. Apparently, Sullenberger wanted the sardines worse than the bear and a fight commenced. According to the pilot, a small bear cub approached him while he was eating sardines and Sullenberger tried to chase it away as the mother bear arrived and tried to chase him away. In the scuffle, Sullenberger received a cut to his stomach by the mother bear's claws. The injury was not debilitating, and after treating the wound Sullenberger decided it was time to walk out and not wait on help to arrive. He walked fifteen miles to the ranger station and was met by Ranger Jess Stamey. Sullenberger was treated by Stamey, ate a big breakfast, and was driven home. The rangers described him as "scratched up" but "in fair shape."[7]

The CAP flew 115 sorties and covered two thousand square miles in the three-day search. The Haywood County CAP located the missing aircraft just after Sullenberger walked into the ranger station. McConnely Ford and Charles Balentine spotted the wreckage from four thousand feet. They descended over the site to look for the doctor, then flew to Jonathan Creek Airstrip to report the "find."

Sullenberger had another problem on his hands: his airplane was stuck in a tree four miles from a road. In appreciation for the time the volunteers gave in trying to locate him, he donated the plane to the Tennessee Civil Air Patrol. The CAP gladly received the generous gift, but when it realized how difficult it would be to remove the wreckage, it suggested Sullenberger grant the Cub to another group. The North Carolina CAP sought the plane, but Sullenberger gave it to an aviation club at the McGhee Tyson Airbase. A crew of thirteen men cleared a swath from the Appalachian Trail down to the plane, disassembled the craft, and hauled it to the trail and down to Walnut Bottom, where it was loaded onto a truck and transported to Knoxville.

Toomey, Tallent, and the Champ

On Friday, August 24, 1956, two young men were involved in a crash of an Aeronca Champ into a steep and thickly vegetated section of the park near Elkmont.[8] Dan Toomey of Alcoa, age twenty-three, piloted the plane, and his nineteen-year-old cousin Quentin Tallent, also of Alcoa, was a passenger. They departed the Sky Ranch Airport (near the intersection of Highway 129 and the present-day John Sevier Highway) for a flight over the mountains. The crash occurred around 5:30 P.M. in a very rugged drainage northwest of Mount Collins and northeast of Clingmans Dome. The two received very minor injuries, stayed the night in the woods, and walked out to civilization the next morning.

Richard M. Cox was the founder of the Cox Sky Ranch, where the Champ was based. He had an interest in aviation and was employed by the Aluminum Company of America (ALCOA) as a millwright. He served in the armed forces during World War II and the Korean War. Cox, who oversaw construction of the Maryville Greenway as an employee of the city of Maryville, formed the Sky Ranch from a piece of leased property between the Tennessee River and Highway 129. He was a crop duster and a flight instructor as well. Cox died on August 30, 2000, at the grand age of eighty.[9]

The Champ, also known as the Traveler, was manufactured between 1948 and 1952 by Aeronca and until 1964 by the Champion Aircraft Company. The "tail-dragger" was a two-place, high-winged aircraft that was highly maneuverable and very popular among private pilots. Modified, it was favored in flight instruction and for use in the military. Small, inexpensive to purchase and operate, and possessing the ability to fly low and slow, the military used the Champ as observation aircraft. The L-16B, with larger windows than its civilian counterpart, was the military version of the plane.

The Champ had an 80-horsepower Continental O-205-1 engine that allowed it to reach a top speed of 110 miles per hour and a cruising speed of 87 miles per hour. Its empty weight was 890 pounds—perhaps the lightest plane that has crashed in the park.

Dan Toomey crashed in a horrible place for hikers even today to reach. He crashed his Champ in a drainage that requires an all-day walk though briars, rhododendron, and thick, immature firs and spruces. The plane, by the way, was eventually removed.

The Alcoa High School graduates (Toomey in 1951 and Tallent in 1955) were students at the University of Tennessee (UT) at Knoxville and were working at ALCOA for the summer to earn money for school. Toomey had served four years in the U.S. Air Force and was at UT studying engineering (perhaps his studies helped him with the mandatory task of removing the damaged wreckage from the park). Tallent and his wife had married the year before at Christmas.[10]

On Friday afternoon (August 24) the pair rented the Champ from Elmer Wood at the Sky Ranch for a couple hours of sightseeing. The plane held about three hours of fuel in the tanks, and the men had plans to return to the airport before dark. After flying over several points of interest in the park, Toomey turned up the valley above Elkmont and headed south at 3,000 feet. Although they were still gaining altitude, they had more than 3,643 feet to go (plus the height of the trees) to clear Clingmans Dome. Toomey stated that although the plane was still climbing, he had to "put the plane into a power stall so the aircraft would pancake into the treetops."[11]

Just as Sullenberger had spent the night in the woods a year prior, the two students spent the night at their crash site wondering what to do next. On their minds during the night were probably words of thanks that they were alive but also worries about how they were going to tell Wood that his airplane was lying in a dense forest in the Smokies. When the two did not return to the Sky Ranch on time, they were reported as overdue and a search began immediately. The Civil Air Patrol began an air search around the water-bounded Sky Ranch and the surrounding area. The mountains were searched, but the plane was not spotted by the first CAP flyers. In fact, one of the missing aviators tried to signal a search plane that flew directly over them to no avail.

During the night, Tallent and Toomey survived by using some of the fabric off the plane's fuselage as bedding and a fire starter. After a long, sleepless night, the men began to walk through the tangled, thick foliage. Finding a road and catching a ride, they were taken to the Wonderland Club in Elkmont. While there, they contacted their relatives and were returned home later that afternoon, August 25, by a friend.

The CAP sent two ground team members into the area to locate the wreckage, estimate the damage, and get an idea of how to recover it. The

CAP personnel returned with word that the propeller and windshield would have to be replaced and that the fabric on the fuselage would need to be repaired. Elmer Wood determined that the plane was worth the effort of recovery and decided that the task would be given to the two who put the plane in the woods in the first place. Toomey was given an ultimatum: "pay for the plane, replace it or repair it."[12] The plan was to disassemble the plane, drag it through the woods to a fire road a mile away, then load it onto a truck for transportation back to the Sky Ranch, where it would be reassembled. Several friends volunteered to help with the task, and the plane was removed.

The Erocoupe at Hazel Creek

Owned by T.Sgt. Dexter Short of Maryville, N3915H was an A-2 Erocoupe based at McGhee Tyson Airport in Knoxville. Short loaned the small, single-engine aircraft to T.Sgt. Pete Suteu of Maryville to fly from McGhee Tyson to Florida. Suteu usually flew a U.S. Air Force helicopter, but on this occasion flew the two-person Erocoupe. He departed McGhee Tyson around 8:00 A.M. and was last heard from at 11:10 A.M., when he radioed that the weather had turned bad and he was returning to Knoxville. The Smokies claimed another flying machine in the Hazel Creek section of the park on Sunday afternoon, December 9, 1956.[13]

While flying south from Knoxville, Suteu flew into some severe winter weather near Madisonville and had to make a decision to abort or continue the flight. Thinking that the safest way out of the weather was to return to Knoxville, he turned the plane and vectored away from the storm toward the east. At six thousand feet and with two hours of fuel remaining, Suteu thought he had it made, but the storm kept pestering him. As he tried to maneuver around the ice and clouds, the visibility dropped to almost zero and he began to look for an emergency landing area.

Suteu's plane suddenly began to lose the ability to stay airborne. Trying to warm the carburetor by applying carburetor heat was unsuccessful in sustaining power. The engine finally quit. Through the clouds and to his right, Suteu saw a mountain peak, so he banked the plane in the opposite direction and escaped a crash. After that close call, Suteu tried to glide as long as possible but saw a hillside in front of his plane. With a split-second reaction, he stalled the plane into the poplars and beeches, which cushioned his crash and probably saved his life.

Once the noise, awkwardness, and violence of the crash had passed, Pete Suteu found himself to be unhurt but very lost. The traumatic stress of undergoing a crash, coupled with being lost without food or shelter, would be debilitating to most people, but Suteu was determined to make it out on his own—and that he did.

Around noon on Sunday the ninth, Suteu decided to leave the wreckage and walk out to find help. After several hours of walking through very thick rhododendron, cold, lost, and shaken, Suteu crossed Hazel Creek and found an old logging road (present-day Hazel Creek Trail). Once he found the road, he opted to continue walking downstream, hoping to come across a ranger or dwelling. The Hazel Creek Trail is a slight downhill walk, and the lost pilot eased his way to Fontana Lake in the late afternoon. He found an unmanned ranger station and a Park Service jeep. Turning on the jeep's radio, he was elated to hear noise and tried to call for help. He tried several times, but no one heard his distress call. Realizing he was lost and would probably not be able to find a way to civilization that day, he began to make plans for the night in order to survive the cold, damp conditions.

Hypothermia is a medical condition in which the human body is unable to maintain its proper inner-core temperature. This deadly condition usually affects hikers and other outdoor enthusiasts who may be well prepared for bad weather but do not recognize they are in trouble. Suteu's situation—hiking, using a lot of energy, becoming sweaty then cold—is a common scenario. Many hypothermia patients become victims when their body loses more heat than it can produce. The patient dies from what many people call "exposure." Suteu was set up for hypothermia. It was a cool night, he was cold and sweaty, and he was not able to eat well or protect himself from the environment. His cool, wet skin was robbing him of heat, and he had to make a decision to bed down for the night. He remembered the ranger station he had passed earlier and returned. That decision also saved his life.

Suteu entered the station and hunted for supplies to make it through the night or until help arrived. He found some blankets, matches, and sugar. He would be fine. With no trouble, the pilot slept throughout the night, awakened only by bears and wild boar on the porch of the cabin. The next morning, Monday, December 10, he awoke to a clear sky and warmer temperatures. While he was making plans for a possible hike out, the search for him began its second day.

When Suteu did not make it back to McGhee Tyson Airport and the tower's efforts to contact him by radio failed, a search began in the early afternoon on the ninth. It was thought that the Erocoupe was on the ground somewhere north of Madisonville and south of Maryville, but without radar tracking, the plane could be almost anywhere between the two points. The Tennessee Civil Air Patrol was contacted and given mission status, and the volunteer aircrews geared up for a search they hoped would produce quick results. However, the same clouds that hampered Suteu's safe return to Knoxville prohibited the CAP planes from doing an effective search on Sunday afternoon and evening. Pilots reported low clouds, poor visibility, and icing, so the air search was postponed. Ground investigation and phone calls dominated the effort on the first day.

On Monday morning (day two), the search intensified as the weather improved. The CAP and park rangers drove to Clingmans Dome and set up a mobile communications post. Ground crews and a boat patrol were organized, and the aircrews were briefed. Once daylight revealed clear skies and smooth flying, the search began. After a couple of hours of searching, a CAP plane spotted the Erocoupe on a flat spot near the top of a ridge. The plane was not greatly damaged, but the aircrew did not see signs of life. Moments later, at 8:30 A.M., the mission coordinator received word from the Park Service dispatcher that Suteu had contacted a ranger via two-way radio that he was all right.

Suteu left the ranger station early on Monday morning, taking with him a 1933 map of the area he found in the cabin. Walking down the road, he soon came to the banks of Fontana Lake. The map did not show the lake but did show the town of Proctor and the Little Tennessee River. After realizing he could not cross the lake, Suteu returned to the jeep at the station and tried again to summon help on the radio. Over the speaker came the welcoming voice of a ranger who heard the lost pilot's call for help. Suteu explained his predicament, said he was in good health, and requested directions out of the mountains. The ranger instructed him to walk back to the lakeshore and wait for a boat that would take him to the Fontana Boat Dock. The pilot returned to the lake and waited.

Immediately, word spread about the wonderful news, and a boat was launched to pick up Suteu at the mouth of Hazel Creek. At 11:00 A.M. (almost twenty-four hours after the crash) Park Ranger Messer and the CAP arrived. Park Service personnel, Civil Air Patrol officers, and a U.S. Air Force crew were overwhelmed at the sight of the pilot "scratched, unshaven, but otherwise unharmed."[14] News spread quickly to the search base, Suteu's family, and the media that the sergeant was safe. At the boat dock, a U.S. Air Force rescue team transported him to the McGhee Tyson Air Base infirmary for a checkup.

After the infirmary declared Suteu to be well, the rescued pilot, along with CAP and Park Service rangers, returned to Hazel Creek to find the crash site. They found the jeep, the cabin, and the place Suteu crossed Hazel Creek from his cross-country hike. From there, the search party crossed the creek and began the long journey off the trail to the airplane. After climbing a hillside on hands and knees, crawling through thick rhododendron, and walking in and out of a small stream, the crew reached the site. Once Suteu's personal belongings and important papers were recovered, the search crew and the pilot left the scene to face another long hike through the rhododendron.

On July 26, 1999, Peter Paul Suteu died in Nokomis, Florida, at the age of seventy-two. He spent thirty years in the U.S. Air Force, retiring as a chief master sergeant. He was buried at Memorial Cemetery in Sarasota, Florida.

T-33

It seems like the Smokies had it in for local military flyers. The past few crashes in the park claimed aircraft and personnel from the military, and on June 22, 1958, two Tennesseans crashed their T-33 jet trainer. Strangely enough, the T-33 crashed within three miles of the Erocoupe crash in the Hazel Creek area. This time the crew was able to exit the plane safely with parachutes rather than riding the plane into trees as Pete Suteu had done.

First Lt. William Oliphant and Capt. John Hayes were assigned to the 151st Fighter-Interceptor Squadron at the Tennessee Air National Guard base at the McGhee Tyson Airport in Knoxville. This squadron was known for its F-104 "Starfighters," which at one time were not thought of highly by the regular air force. After the aircraft proved itself in the Berlin crisis, the planes were reassigned to the regular air force.

The twenty-nine-year-old Oliphant lived in Knoxville and worked as a department manager for Tri-State Roofing Company. Hayes, thirty-four years old, lived in Nashville and was a widely known traveling salesman. They were flying a T-33 fighter trainer over the mountains on a routine training flight to Travis Field in Savannah, Georgia, when the aircraft began to have trouble. They could ride the plane into the mountainside, hoping for a safe emergency landing in the trees, try to return to

Knoxville, or abandon ship. They decided to bail out. At 2:51 in the afternoon, ten minutes after departure, the pilot radioed the tower and said
his plane was flaming out.[15] Ejecting from the airplane, the two air force
reserve officers opened their parachutes and watched their plane hit a
mountainside.

Once they were on the ground near Bone Valley, they realized they
were both hurt. Oliphant had received an injury to his left arm and
minor cuts and bruises. Hayes had suffered
more extensive injuries, including damage to
his back and nose and numerous cuts and
bruises. As lucky as they were, they still had to
summon aid.

Air Force T-33 Jet Trainer in
which two persons survived
near Hazel Creek. Photo by
Dwight McCarter.

When McGhee Tyson Air Base lost contact with the T-33, a search was initiated. A hasty search was launched flying the intended route of the plane, and ground crews were alerted. Stewart Air Force Base near Nashville was contacted, and three rescue helicopters were dispatched to the search area. At the same time, the two men had found their way down the same road as had Suteu a year and a half earlier. The trail down the mountain to the road was steep, wet, and overgrown with rhododendron and underbrush. The men began to walk down stream toward Fontana Lake and hoped the airport would miss them and a search would begin. By the time they had reached the lakeshore, a search had already begun.

While waiting for a search plane or helicopter to fly over them, the two officers caught the attention of some fishermen. What a story the fishermen would have to tell their friends! They helped the soldiers reach the ranger station at Proctor, and there the reservists waited for more help. Within a couple of hours an air force helicopter located the wreckage. The men were located at the mouth of Hazel Creek. The helicopter landed and took the men to the University of Tennessee Medical Center, where they received treatment for their injuries and were given sedatives "so they could sleep."[16]

The next day Park Service and air force ground crews were sent into Hazel Creek to locate the wreckage. An air force helicopter aided in the search, with Ranger Norman Roy as an observer. What they found was a partially burned jet and burned woods. Apparently, when the plane crashed, its fuel bladders were severed, spilling fuel onto the mountainside. The fuel ignited and caused a .74-acre forest fire that self-extinguished.

Extremely Dangerous Artifact

Although not exactly an aircraft crash, an incident on a cold Monday night, January 19, 1959, is still a part of the Smokies' aviation history. A two-man crew in another T-33 almost died—not by the plane hitting the ground, but by hypothermia in midair.

The T-33 was flying at thirty-two thousand feet over the Smokies en route to Wright-Patterson Air Force Base in Ohio. It had departed Donaldson Air Force Base, South Carolina, an hour or so earlier. On board were the pilot, Capt. James Fraser, and the copilot, Maj. W. A. Callis, both stationed at Wright-Patterson.[17]

Near Bryson City, their glass canopy blew off. The air force investigation showed no immediate reason for the jettison. Local governments in Tennessee and North Carolina were warned about the canopy, and the Tennessee and North Carolina Highway Patrols, the National Park Service, and Forestry Service officials searched for it. The problem was the canopy was not just a piece of glass; it could explode.

Most canopies and ejection seats house some kind of explosive charge that separates the canopy from the plane. When a pilot makes a decision to eject, one of the crew members would pull the ejection handle and the canopy's charge would explode, opening the canopy allowing it to clear the cockpit. In the next instant the crew would be projected out of the plane by means of an explosive designed to push them up and to the side of the plane. In the case of this T-33, the canopy did not separate from the plane via the explosive charge but opened slightly and was quickly torn off by the wind.

The canopy went over the plane and fell thirty-two thousand feet to the ground. Somewhere in the vicinity of Bryson City and Cherokee lies a T-33 canopy with a problem: attached to it is a live thirty-seven-millimeter explosive charge. According to the air force, if the charge did not explode upon impact, it may still be armed and "extremely dangerous." Officials said it could discharge if someone simply lifted the canopy off the ground or moved it. Although the canopy probably exploded upon impact, no one knows for sure. It has not been found, or if it has been located, the finders did not call proper authorities for safe removal and disposal.

Although the two crew members, Fraser and Callis, were not injured by the incident, their nerves were on edge because they did not know why the canopy had blown off or if it had damaged their aircraft in the process. The loud engine and the sound of the wind were deafening. Fraser carefully flew the aircraft through the night sky and landed safely. Callis suffered frostbite from the extreme cold before the plane reached the ground back at Donaldson. It was definitely a life-or-death situation, but both men survived.

Peterson's F-102

When native East Tennesseans tell you that hiking off trail in the Smokies is like walking in a jungle in South America or Asia, believe them. The backcountry is a beautiful and diverse sanctuary for animals, fish, and foliage. Foliage in the low and high altitudes can change from simple grasses on the "balds" to rhododendron and dog hobble so thick that a cross-country hiker could walk for several yards without touching earth. In

the Abrams Creek section of the park there is one example of a character-
istic "rhododendron hell." Right in the middle of a rhododendron thicket
are the remains of an F-102 fighter jet. The plane exploded into a fireball
upon impact, scattering wreckage, no piece larger than a trash-can lid, into
the surrounding creeks, drainages, and, of course, rhododendron thickets.[18] Not much remains of the jet except recorded and oral history.

On Independence Day weekend 1959 citizens were preparing to
celebrate the nation's birthday. Communities were preparing for parades
and picnics, families were traveling, and children were waiting until the
Fourth to shoot fireworks and light firecrackers. On July 1, 1959, 1st Lt.
Russell Peterson of Skokie, Illinois, became another part of aviation
incident history in the Smokies as the mountains claimed yet another
flying machine.

The F-102A was the first delta-winged jet developed, produced,
and flown in the U.S. Air Force. Nicknamed the "Delta Dagger," it was
capable of cruising and fighting at altitudes as high as fifty-four thousand
feet and was extremely fast for a fighter jet in the 1950s. Convair began
manufacturing this one-seater aircraft in June 1955. With a cruise speed
of six hundred miles per hour, it was sixty-eight feet long and had a wing
span of thirty-eight feet. The engine was a Pratt and Whitney J57-P-25,
which produced 17,000 pounds of thrust. It could stay aloft for a thousand miles before exhausting its fuel capacity.

The plane and pilot were assigned to the 71st Fighter Interceptor
Squadron of the U.S. Air Force. Lieutenant Peterson was twenty-eight years
old and flying alone in the jet over Murphy, North Carolina, on a 750-mile
flight from Selfridge Air Force Base in Michigan to Tyndall Air Force Base
at Panama City, Florida. At forty-two thousand feet and six minutes from
McGhee Tyson Airport, the plane's single engine "flamed out" and the
pilot was in serious trouble.

At 7:48 P.M. the engine quit producing thrust and Peterson began to
prepare for a "worse case" scenario. After trying to restart the stalled
engine, Peterson contacted the McGhee Tyson Airport by radio and declared
an emergency. His intentions were to glide from 42,000 feet to the airport,
which was at 981 feet above sea level, and make a safe landing. He had
plenty of altitude, and the only obstacle in his way was the Smoky
Mountains. On his way to Knoxville he realized he was losing altitude too
fast and did not think he would be able to make it all the way to the airport. He decided to try a power dive. The idea was to force air through the
engines turbines, add fuel, and "kick start" the engine. It worked, but not

in time for him to regain control of the craft. He began to pull the plane out of the dive when the engine caught fire and tragedy struck.

Perhaps Peterson did not realize how close he was to the mountains, or perhaps he blacked out from the G-force of the power dive, but the plane, under full power, struck a ridge at approximately six hundred miles per hour. First, a high-angle swath was made the through the trees and rhododendron thickets as the jet loudly buzzed the side of the mountain, sending treetops to the ground and snapping large tree trunks like toothpicks. Out of control and doomed to crash, the F-102 violently penetrated the earth, dug itself deep into the soil, and exploded into a large fireball, creating a crater approximately 150 feet in diameter.

The plane exploded into thousands of pieces, some disintegrating upon impact and some burning in the fireball. Other pieces were propelled like missiles into the air, then rained down into the steep drainage, coming to rest in tree trunks, in the ground, in creeks, and in thickets. Although it was foggy and rainy, many residents of Happy Valley heard and felt the explosion. Some even saw the bright initial fireball rising out of the black, cloud-covered mountains. The vegetation, wreckage, and trees burned all night and smoldered for days. Peterson did not eject.

Phones calls were made by southeastern Blount County residents to the local sheriff's office. The airport's phone began ringing also with reports of an explosion and fire in the mountains. The authorities quickly realized what had occurred and began a search. The Air National Guard set up a search base at McGhee Tyson while the Civil Air Patrol and three park rangers started a ground search in the Abrams Creek area. Early on the second day of the search, a plane piloted by Capt. Robert Bennett of the Air National Guard spotted the burnt wreckage near Abrams Creek. Ground crews hiked several hours cross-country to the site, where they found no signs of life—or death.

In the days after the crash, investigators hoped to find a lost and uninjured pilot wandering in the mountains trying to find his way out after parachuting to safety. Hope shrunk for the family, the air force, and the community of searchers when a burned ejection seat was found nearly half a mile away in another drainage. Elgin Kitner, the Blount County coroner, was called to the scene of the debris field. There he found positive proof that the pilot rode the plane into the ground. Peterson's fate was settled, and the search for him was suspended.

In the years that followed, the crash site has been visited by only a handful of people who know exactly where to look for the very small

pieces. The trees have healed. Rain, snow, and the freeze cycle have cam-
ouflaged the crater. Only a few burn scars and several dozen pieces of
wreckage remain. The mountains are reclaiming the land, and only the
trained eye can catch a glimpse of the F-102. Only in the memory of the
family and the searchers do the pilot and plane remain.

In 1995 Jeff Wadley (coauthor of this book) and two friends
returned to the scene. It was a warm, clear day, just perfect for hiking.
The Smokies, however, almost claimed three more lives surrounding the
plane crash. Leaving a maintained trail, the three hikers were prepared to
walk to the wreck scene, take photographs, and return before dark. After
walking almost three hours through rhododendron and in and out of
creeks, the three decided that they must have walked down the wrong
drainage. They looked at their map and decided not to return the same
way they came but to continue walking downhill to Abrams Creek. They
hoped to stay on the creek bank and cross the footbridge near the ranger
station. It was 3:30 P.M.

Quickly the hikers realized they had made an error in judgment
because the rhododendron became thicker and blow-downs from a
recent storm made travel very slow and tiring. By 4:30 the three just "happened up" on the F-102 wreckage and had time to take a few photographs. Realizing how long it had taken to hike to the wreckage, the three
knew they could not get out by dark.

At 5:30 they reached Abrams Creek and immediately knew they
were "up the creek." There was no way to stay on the riverbank. Wadley
knew of an old road on the west side of the creek, so they forded the
frigid water and began to look for the road. At dark they were well on
their way but still had half a mile to go. Blow-downs and rhododendron
made passage much more difficult than expected, and again the three
had to wade the knee-deep stream. Without warning, Wadley, who was in
front, stepped off an underwater ledge and found himself chest deep in
cold water. Before he could turn and stop the others, they too fell in. The
hiking party was in a fatal position.

All three hikers quickly exited the water, shed their wet clothes,
and ate their remaining food. Knowing that they had no tent or sleeping bag, the three decided to keep walking and talking to encourage
each other. Hypothermia was creeping up on them very quickly. Wadley
knew they were close to the footbridge and kept the group moving.
Their spirits began to fade by 6:45 P.M. It was dark; they could barely see
each other.

Wadley soon crawled over a small ridge and saw the most beautiful sight in the world: the footbridge. The last one hundred yards of hiking brought laughter, excitement, and relief to the three men. They popped out of the rhododendron thicket just above the bridge and briskly walked to Wadley's vehicle. They said they had earned respect for the mountains—again. One of the hikers, Brent Thatcher, said he thought they were going to die.

The lesson of the hikers' story is simple. Walking off trail in the Smokies is very dangerous. Not only did this book's coauthor almost become a search statistic himself, but he almost lost his life. The advice of McCarter and Wadley in regard to anyone walking off trail to visit crash sites is *do not do it.*

FOUR

The 1960s

I n the autumn of 1962, John F. Kennedy was president of the United States. The war in Vietnam had already killed thousands of soldiers and civilians, and in the 1960s, the Smokies claimed other lives.

God Have Mercy on Us All

Snow—an estimated six inches—had fallen in the upper reaches of the Great Smoky Mountains National Park, and temperatures were in the twenties. Brig. Gen. John I. Lerom, forty-seven, of Falls Church, Virginia, assigned to the Second Air Force Reserve Regional Head-quarters at Andrews Air Force Base near Washington, D.C., was flying with Capt. Ludwig Gesund, thirty-one, who was assigned to the Office of the Deputy Chief of Staff for Plans and Programs in New York. The two were on board N06067, a twin-engine Cessna 310 aircraft with the military designation U3-B, on a flight to Warner-Robbins Air Force Base in Georgia from Andrews Air Force Base.

On Saturday afternoon, the tenth, the men notified McGhee Tyson Airport that they were flying over Greenville, Tennessee, at seven thousand feet and were experiencing a radio problem. They asked per-mission to descend to six thousand feet. The pilot said he was altering his course to land at Knoxville, but moments later radio contact was lost. When the plane did not land and there was no additional radio contact, a search was initiated by the Eastern Air Rescue Center.

The Tennessee and North Carolina CAPs were notified, as were sheriff departments in eastern Tennessee and western North Carolina. By Sunday, day two, thirty aircraft were scouring a 180-square-mile search grid. Maj. K. B. Maxfield, commander of the CAP in Knoxville, reported that the search would concentrate in the Smokies. Ground crews drove hundreds of miles, knocking on the doors of homes in the search area, hoping to hear a good word from the residents. The CAP requested that hunters keep an eye open in the area. As expected, several leads came into mission headquarters. Blount County authorities received a call reporting a loud noise and what sounded like an explosion near the Christy Hill community. All leads were checked out, with no luck.

One lead in particular was very interesting. In Clinton, Tennessee, a ham radio operator, George Hoskins, heard a distress call at 10:45 A.M., supposedly from General Lerom: "Down in Smokies somewhere east of Knoxville, or in mountain country. Plane in bad shape. Battery almost gone. God have mercy on us all. John."[1]

The Federal Communications Commission was called to verify the message and recipient. They concurred that it was possible that the message could have been from the downed aircraft. The radio traffic gave searchers a boost, thinking that possibly one, if not both, of the men could still be alive. In researching this book, the authors were unable to locate George Hoskins to verify his report.

The emergency message, the pilot's contact with the Knoxville tower, and several other leads led the CAP to believe that the missing aircraft had crashed in the eastern section of the Smokies at or below six thousand feet. Search officials speculated the pilot thought he was near Greenville but may actually have been more southwest. "There's no doubt that the plane is down somewhere in these mountains," predicted Major Maxfield.[2] On Monday (day three) the CAP flew a total of twenty-one aircraft over a corridor seventy-five miles long by twenty miles wide along the Smokies main ridge. By Tuesday (day four) searchers from the air force, CAP, army, and air national guard units had realized that the foliage and steep mountainsides could easily hide the wreckage, but they continued their work, flying dozens of sorties.

On Tuesday afternoon, a search plane was assigned to a section of the Smokies near Inadu Knob with army captain William Volk of Fort Knox, Kentucky, on board. As he was searching, he spotted something that did not fit the landscape and foliage of the mountainside. What he saw was the crashed Cessna 310 on a slope just inside Tennessee. He

made five passes within three hundred feet of the plane and identified it by the red, white, and blue star insignia on the side of the fuselage and the large "U.S.A.F." on the wings. He also noted a large orange wing tip. He said that the plane appeared to have burned.

By 5:00 P.M. the CAP had plotted the information and notified Superintendent Fred Overly of the Park Service that the missing aircraft had been located near Inadu Knob. With Bob White in charge, Bill Worthington and Bud Cantrell left park headquarters forty-five minutes later en route to Cosby. There, Frank Oliver, McKinley Phillips, and Doyle Kline met the NPS ground team. They had driven jeeps to Cosby Knob and begun a ground search under the illumination of the moon, hoping to find survivors.

The NPS had assumed control over the ground search, setting up a base of operations Tuesday evening at Cosby Campground, turning the usually quiet campground into a busy scene. On Wednesday morning at 4:00 A.M., day five, fifteen NPS team members and five CAP team members left the campground in six jeeps to join the searchers already on the mountain.

On November 10, 1962, a twin-engine Cessna 310 aircraft with the military designation U3-B crashed near Inadu Knob on a flight to Warner-Robbins Air Force Base in Georgia. One person was thought to have lived, called for help, and later died. Photo by Dwight McCarter.

After meeting with the other team, the men walked down the Appalachian Trail from Low Gap, watching the search plane circling the debris field. Walking off the trail and following the orbiting search aircraft, the ground team spotted an orange piece of wreckage at 7:53 A.M. Once they arrived on the scene, they found that the two missing airmen had died. The plane was largely intact and had not burned as previously reported. Positive identification of the men and the plane was made. It was thought that the officers were carrying "top secret" documents, so security at the site was tight. After an inventory of the aircraft, the scene was investigated to determine the cause of the crash.

By 8:20 A.M. the carryout began. The bodies were carried to the Appalachian Trail, then down the Snake Den Trail for three and a half miles. At 11:50 A.M. crews arrived at the Cosby Campground, where dozens of onlookers and officials were waiting with cameras and questions. Air force officials took possession of the airmen, delivering the bodies to Greenville, South Carolina, for examination. Two rangers remained at the crash site overnight until investigators arrived.

The Hercules Incident

Throughout the Smokies' aviation history there has never been an aviator death that has not involved a crash. On Tuesday, March 3, 1964, the Smokies claimed the life of an aviator but this time only a small piece of an aircraft.

A C-130 is a very large, powerful, and heavy transport plane used for search and rescue, transporting troops and gear, radar and radio reconnaissance, and various other duties in the armed services. The "Hercules," as it is nicknamed, has four turboprop engines, each wielding a four-bladed propeller. The aircraft is unique in that the vertical stabilizer stands very high above the fuselage and the back of the aircraft has a door that can be raised during flight for dropping personnel and equipment.

U.S. Air Force Hercules 961 was on a fighter-support flight to Myrtle Beach, South Carolina, from Stewart Air Force Base near Nashville when the incident occurred. The aircraft was piloted by Lt. David W. Parsons, an exchange officer from the British Royal Air Force. The plane neared the Smokies at nineteen thousand feet above sea level and almost 350 miles per hour. The cloud-covered Smoky Mountains were fourteen thousand feet below.

At 8:25 A.M., as the plane approached the halfway point in its flight, the crew heard an "explosive-like" sound.[3] The cargo door on the left side of the C-130 opened, and the force of the howling wind tore a large chunk of metal and other materials from the bottom of the plane, along the side, to the top of the fuselage. In a split second, two crew members were in grave danger.

S. Sgt. Jose Gallegos, thirty-one, of San Luis, Colorado, was sucked toward the gaping hole in the side of the airplane. Aircraft parts and personal belongings were blowing inside the plane. Gallegos was able to hold onto a chain attached to the body of the plane and his toolbox, and for dear life he would not let go. Original media broadcasts stated that he was sucked out of the hole and dangled outside the C-130 until other crew members pulled him to safety, but those reports were in error.

Not so fortunate was Airman 2d Class Gary D. Back, twenty-one, of McLean, Texas. Airman Back was sitting near the cargo door when the incident occurred and was immediately sucked from his seat. Gallegos never saw Back leave the aircraft. "He was about four feet from the door. He never made a sound. I'm sure he didn't know what happened," explained Gallegos.[4] Falling from nineteen thousand feet to the national park mountains lasted a moment or so; what was going on in Back's mind during the freefall? Searchers and relatives prayed that he died from injuries sustained exiting the plane and was not conscious during the fall to earth.

Once Gallegos had been rescued and secured, the flight crew assessed the damage. It was obvious to them that an emergency landing was necessary. The closest airport that could handle the size and weight of the Hercules was Knoxville's McGhee Tyson. The C-130 declared an emergency and turned toward Knoxville.

The tower cleared the way for the crippled aircraft to enter the airspace and land at the airport. The C-130 crew realized they had another problem. When the door and part of the side of the aircraft blew off, the metal skin and frame also ruptured electrical, hydraulic flight controls and monitoring devices. The worst problem was that the front landing gear would not move into position. Preparations were made at the airport for emergency equipment to move into position to help rescue the crew if a fire erupted upon landing.

The giant aircraft turned onto its final approach, lined up on the center line of the runway, and, without a front landing gear, hit the hard-surface runway and skidded down the asphalt. With sparks shooting like fireworks and smoke pouring from behind the damaged aircraft, the plane finally stopped with emergency crews in tow. The crew was rescued quickly. Everyone was removed from the plane, and a positive count was made to determine if other crew members were also lost. Gallegos was taken to the Blount Memorial Hospital in Maryville, where he was treated and released. Airman Back was the only person not accounted for.

Damage to the aircraft was extensive. The side door and surrounding metal airframe was missing. An engine, propeller, and tail surfaces were also damaged. Apparently, the wind carried the debris from the side of the aircraft along the wing and tail surfaces causing significant damage. Damage during the emergency landing was minimal due to the expertise of the pilot.

Where was Airman Back? After a debriefing of the crew, a preliminary search area was mapped out, and other agencies were asked to assist in the search for the missing airman and the aircraft's cargo door. More than one hundred persons combed the neighborhoods, roads, and forests near Greenbrier and Dudley Creek. Gatlinburg residents claimed to have seen debris falling from the sky. For instance, Bud Maples, who was painting a house just off Highway 73, noted the C-130 circling over east Gatlinburg and was one of several people who reported seeing pieces of the airplane raining on the community.

Although it was assumed that Airman Back did not survive the fall, searchers still had hopes that a miracle saved his life. The C-130's door was found, and other debris was located. Back's flight jacket was located near a highway outside of Gatlinburg that evening, but his body was not found. A parachute, thought to have belonged to Gallegos, was also located.

By Wednesday evening more than three hundred persons had participated in the search, including law enforcement, rescue crews, and civilians. The search base was set up at the Gatlinburg Fire Department in the city's municipal building. A team from Tennessee Civil Air Patrol, Stewart Air Force Base, and the Robbins Air Force Base Air Rescue Team coordinated the effort with Col. J. G. Dunkleberg acting as the incident commander. The search centered in the Glades community of Gatlinburg, approximately two miles from the main part of town. Additional troops and military helicopters were ordered to the scene as the search continued.

On Thursday, after two days of a concentrated ground and aerial search, the body of the airman was found six hundred yards off Highway 73 near the present-day Gatlinburg Fire and Police Department. Jefferson and Knox County Rescue Squad members located Back's body lodged against a tree and indented a foot into the soft earth. Once identification was made and an investigation was performed, the body was carried out to Highway 73 to a waiting Harrill Funeral Home ambulance. The body was transported to Maryville and on to Stewart Air Force Base.

Although Back's body was not found inside the national park, some aircraft debris was located near Dudley Creek inside the park boundary. In this case, the park had an aircraft "fall to pieces" above its mountains and an aviator lost his life as a result.

Beechcraft Model 18

A week before Easter of 1964, six persons died in a fiery airplane crash near the summit of Parsons Bald in the Great Smoky Mountains National Park. With this fatal crash, the park also lost its first searcher. The story of the Beechcraft B-18 will remain in the hearts and minds of rescuers.

N110WP was the identification number on the large, twin-engine Beechcraft B-18 (D-18-S) owned by the Fabick Company, an implement-distributing business in St. Louis. The red, black, and white "Twin Beech" was very popular among private and commercial pilots because of its large cargo area and great powerhouse motors. The roomy airplane carried six persons the day of the crash on a flight from St. Louis to Miami, Florida. Noble Miles was piloting the airplane and had with him his wife, Josephine, Mr. and Mrs. Alfred S. Fetto, Elizabeth Fabick, and Mary Ellen Fabick. Miles was flying the teenage Fabick sisters to meet their mother for the Easter holiday.

The flight apparently was uneventful into Knoxville, where they had a planned stop for fuel and a break. While having the plane refueled, for some unknown reason someone in the party approached an Avis Rental Car attendant about renting a car for the rest of the trip to Miami. An attendant of Cherokee Aviation told the *Maryville-Alcoa Daily Times* that he did not know why that person had inquired about renting a vehicle.[5] The drive from Knoxville to Miami would have been in excess of eight hundred miles. They had just flown four hundred to Tennessee. Mileage-wise, the trip was not half over.

One solution to the mystery could have been the weather. On the day of the crash, Saturday, March 21, 1964, visibility was fifteen miles below two thousand feet with a solid overcast cloud layer and snow above two thousand feet. Poor visibility, high terrain, and heavy topped-off fuel tanks do not mix well in the Smokies. With full tanks, the plane took off for Miami on air route 267 out of McGhee Tyson at 11:30 A.M.

Just as cars travel on highways and interstates, airplanes travel on regulated air routes. Route 267 is a line on a map. It is not a visible or tangible route such an interstate. Pilots fly these routes by directing the airplane to fly toward a radio transmitter called a VOR, a "very high frequency/ omni/ range radio beacon." VORs broadcast a radio signal monitored by receivers on airplanes. On the instrument panel a dial shows the pilot which direction to fly to get to the VOR. The Beechcraft was flying from the Knoxville VOR to a VOR at the state line near Blairsville, Georgia. Once Miles flew over the Harris VOR in Georgia he would "pick up" another heading and continue his flight to his next refueling stop. The only problem was that Miles was flying at approximately 4,200 feet and flight route 267 goes just to the west of Parsons Bald. Parsons Bald is 4,732 feet high.

According to Lt. Glenn Haun of the Tennessee Highway Patrol, the controllers at McGhee Tyson watched N110WP leave the airport on radar and followed him routinely for twelve miles (which would have been over Look Rock Observation Tower at 2,500 feet).[6] At that point the pilot did a "navigational check" with the tower as he was gaining altitude, and a few minutes later the "blip" that represented the airplane disappeared from the radar screen. The plane made it twenty-one miles from McGhee Tyson. Perhaps if the pilot had been a mile to the west he would have cleared the Smokies. Field elevation at McGhee Tyson is 981 feet, and Look Rock is at 2,500 feet. Apparently, Miles was climbing all the while. The seemingly routine flight suddenly turned into tragedy at approximately 11:45 A.M.

For one hundred feet the plane trimmed treetops in a probable blinding snowstorm before it hit the mountain straight on. A Federal Aviation Administration (FAA) spokesperson, Harold Byerly, said the plane struck the ground and burst into flames. Evidently, clouds and snow shrouded the mountains as the plane made its fatal crash. All aboard were killed.

Park Service personnel reported that snow amounts ranged anywhere from four inches to two feet in the higher elevations. The wind, clouds, and snow slowed search efforts. Phone calls were made, local airports checked, and residents were asked to report anything that would lead the searchers to the missing aircraft. The search began. It was Saturday, day one.

An air search began in the general area the plane went off radar, which was just northwest of Parsons Bald. On the second day of the search, Sunday, the Civil Air Patrol spotted the wreckage and called a Tennessee Highway Patrol helicopter to the scene to get a closer look. Lieutenant Haun of the THP was one of those who spotted the wreckage.

The helicopter tried to land in the area but returned to the airport, where Haun remarked that the plane was "totally burnt with no sign of life."[7]

The Civil Air Patrol plotted the coordinates, evaluated the situation, then notified District Ranger Ward of the National Park Service at 6:30 P.M. Sunday night. They were confident that the missing aircraft had been located near Parsons Bald. Ward organized a ground team with six members. The team left Cades Cove around 10:30 P.M. and drove to Sams Gap on the Parsons Branch Road, where they began the four-mile hike to Sheep Pen Gap and then on to Parsons Bald.

It was at this point in the story that the unexpected happened. For the first time in the park's history a rescuer died while on a search. Frank E. Shults, forty-four, a resident of Townsend and a heavy-machine operator with the maintenance division, died while hiking toward the crash site. Without warning, he began to feel very ill, and within a few minutes an apparent heart attack took his life. The entire search crew suspended their part in the mission and brought their friend's body off the mountain. Hearts sank. For the remainder of the mission, rescue workers and employees were numb. The search crew arrived back at Sams

Six persons died in the fiery crash of this Beechcraft Model 18. Heavy with fuel, the plane was unable to clear the mountains and went down near the summit of Parsons Bald on March 21, 1964. Photo by Jeff Wadley.

Gap at 9:20 A.M., where they delivered Frank to a waiting ambulance. The Shults family received friends on Tuesday, and Frank's funeral was held at the Coker Hill Primitive Baptist Church. Pallbearers were members of the park's maintenance division. The interment was at the church's cemetery.

Despite dampened spirits, there was still a search and rescue to perform. On Monday morning, day three of the search, the THP helicopter was used to transport Robert Lash, a local doctor, to the scene. Lash and an FAA agent hiked over loose rocks and snow and through high wind and thick underbrush to the crash site. Once it was determined that there were no survivors, the men returned to the helicopter and flew back to the mission base at Cades Cove. Another ground crew consisting of park employees, the Civil Air Patrol, Blount County sheriff's deputies, Joe Fabick (a co-owner of the plane), an FAA representative, Sheriff Roger Trotter, and Coroner W. L. Kidd departed Sams Gap Monday morning in an attempt to reach the site. At 12:30 P.M. they arrived on the scene and began the task of removing the bodies from the wreckage and carrying them to Parsons Bald.

The rescuers had to deal with high winds and snow, fatigue and emotional shock, numbness, tough terrain, and the tragic crash site. After the crew completed their investigation, they documented the scene and prepared the bodies for transport off the mountain. Following a steep climb over a boulder field and snow-covered bramble, the searchers arrived at Parsons Bald with the bodies of the crash victims. There they were met by another crew who brought the passengers off the mountain to Sams Gap using a trail tractor and trailer. The recovery operation was completed on day three, Monday night, at 7:45 P.M.

Decoration Day Crash

Cataloochee is a beautiful and out-of-the-way section of the Great Smoky Mountains National Park. It was once home to several hundred residents who farmed, herded, and lumbered in the steep slopes and meadows. The Hannah Mountain Cemetery (approximately fifty graves) that served the mountain families in that area is located in "Little Cataloochee." It is near State Highway 284, south of Mount Sterling Gap, and was the site of an airplane crash that took the lives of two people.

Walter C. Bowsman, age forty-four, and his elderly mother, Margaret W. Bowsman of Elgin, Illinois, were flying home from a visit in Leesburg, Georgia, when their Piper Comanche fell from the sky around noon on

Saturday, June 6, 1964. The pilot's intention was to fly to Knoxville for refueling before heading north for Illinois. The last contact with Bowsman was made at 11:01 A.M. with the Columbia tower, so he probably crashed within the next hour while en route over the mountains.

The authors have been unable to determine the complete history behind this crash, and several questions remain unanswered. For instance, on a direct flight or a VOR flight from Albany, Georgia, to Knoxville, the Bowsman plane was tremendously off course to the east. If Bowsman intercepted the Harris VOR at the Georgia–North Carolina state line and flew to Knoxville, he would have flown over Abrams Creek at the extreme western end of the park instead of the extreme eastern end. Maybe he was flying through South Carolina then to Knoxville because he spoke with the Columbia, South Carolina, tower. Perhaps he was using the Snowbird VOR as his navigational tool if he made a stop in Asheville and was flying to Knoxville. If a line is drawn from Asheville to Knoxville, the crash site is only six miles north of the line. The authors do not know why there is such a discrepancy in this crash history. Documentation through the media, however, states that Bowsman was on a flight from Leesburg, Georgia, to Elgin, Illinois, with a stop in Knoxville.[8]

Apparently the plane was not reported overdue when leads began to come in to the Haywood County Sheriff's Department. Citizens reported hearing what they thought was a plane in trouble over Waterville. One person said he heard what sounded like an explosion. These leads were determined to have been just after noon on Saturday, which coincided with the possible crash time. More specifically, if the plane flew from Asheville to Knoxville, Bowsman would have flown over Waterville before he got into Cataloochee. Several persons began a search on Saturday to try and determine the source of the explosion and to see if there was credence to reports of an airplane in trouble.

Park Ranger Mark Hannah and his family were attending the annual Decoration Day ceremonies at the Hannah Cemetery on Sunday, June 7 (day two). In the late afternoon, his sons-in-law, Claude Trentham and Sam Smith, took a walk up an old road that is now Long Bunk Trail. As they were hiking, the men looked into the woods near an old farm and spotted what they thought was a tent. They walked three hundred feet off the road into the woods and came upon the crash site. Trentham saw that the foliage was freshly broken and that an elderly woman, still strapped to her seat, was dead. The plane was badly crushed and had evidently nose-dived into the ground, finally landing on its top.

The two men ran back to the cemetery and told their father-in-law, Ranger Mark Hannah, who responded to the scene. Hannah radioed park headquarters, and because radio communication in Cataloochee was marginal at best, a friend of Ranger Hannah, Dick Stokes, relayed information from headquarters to Hannah in the backcountry. Soon Rangers Foster, Oliver, and Penny arrived on the scene, and there they remained until the carryout and investigation were completed.

Coroner George Brown arrived and aided the investigation. It appeared, he said, as if the plane had made a "straight fall from the skies."[9] On Monday, Sheriff Jack Arrington and the FAA officials combed the wreckage with the Park Service, searching for clues as to the cause of the crash. Brown told the press that the two passengers in the plane died from multiple injuries received as the plane nosed into the ground. The plane flipped over, pinning the man and woman under the debris. Both occupants died instantly. The bodies were removed from the plane and taken to a funeral home in Newport late Sunday night. The aircraft itself has also been removed.

Thankful to Be Alive Today

Balsam Mountain is an indescribable wonder atop the Smokies. This area of beautiful views, year-round cool temperatures, and steep, rugged slopes is backcountry at its finest. The section is remote and definitely "the road less traveled." Two peaks that make up Balsam Mountain are Big Cataloochee at 6,155 feet and Luftee Knob at 6,234 feet. This long ridge runs south of the main crest of the Smokies that boasts names such as Inadu Knob and Cosby Knob, which are just under 6,000 feet. Flowing very low under the shadow of the two ranges lies the Big Creek drainage. Well-known spots in the drainage is the Walnut Bottom and the actual Big Creek. If an airplane flying from the east flew into the Big Creek drainage too low, it would more than likely not get out because the two ridges form a canyon. The Big Creek drainage is a trap for low-flying aircraft. On Monday, September 5, 1966, the drainage and the two tall ridges trapped an airplane and added it to the Smokies' aviation incident history.

The Cessna Corporation built several small aircraft that the general public, commercial businesses, and the military bought with a fury. The famous Cessna 172 is probably the best-known light aircraft in existence. Another well-known Cessna, the 150, is popular with students taking flight instruction and with private pilots for inexpensive traveling. The Cessna

150 is a two-person, single-engine aircraft that has been and still is highly regarded among aviators. In September 1966, one Cessna 150 became a new fixture near Gunter Fork, as it stalled into a mountainside thick with rhododendron, birch, and cherry trees. The good news is that the two people on board not only lived through the crash but walked approximately fifteen miles to tell about it.

Two air force officers who were stationed at the Fifteenth Student Squadron at Craig Air Force Base, Selma, Alabama, were on a flight from Roanoke, Virginia, to Selma in a rented Cessna 150 when they crashed in the Great Smokies. They had planned a fuel stop at the Sossamon Airstrip in Bryson City, North Carolina, but became lost en route.

The pilot was 2d Lt. Henry Pasquet, twenty-four, of Winchester, Virginia. His passenger was 2d Lt. Salvatore Giardina, age twenty-three, of New Jersey. The two were flying at an altitude of forty-five hundred feet when they entered the eastern section of the Smokies over Big Creek in the red, black, and white Cessna. It was 5:00 P.M.

As they flew into the mountains it was just a matter of moments before the pilot realized that he had flown into a canyon and there was not enough room or time to climb an additional fifteen hundred feet to escape. They were trapped. The aircraft experienced a downdraft as the pilot made a left turn toward Big Cataloochee Mountain, and the plane fell through the lush tree canopy. It rested intact against some trees, enabling the men to literally open the door and step out.

They had been fortunate in that many plane crash victims had not been able to merely open their damaged plane's door and walk away unharmed. Nevertheless, the two officers still had a problem on their hands: they were very lost! The men were dressed in light summer clothing and had only two matches and a small survival kit. The temperatures were dropping into the forties, and they had no idea how to get out. To make matters worse, they had not filed a flight plan that would have alerted authorities when they did not arrive in Selma on time. They had to decide whether to stay with the plane and wait for help or try to find their way out. Opting for the latter, the men began an overnight journey into a wilderness area that few have seen.

Pasquet and Salvatore used their dime-sized survival compass to begin their walk in a northeast direction, the way their plane was facing. They walked until dark, when they realized they were in deep trouble because they had not yet found their way out. It would be the next afternoon before they would make it to safety. Pasquet noted that it was so

This Cessna 150 encountered a downdraft and stalled near Gunter Fork in September 1966. The aircraft came to rest intact against some trees. The two air force officers on board were uninjured and were able to walk fifteen miles to find help. Courtesy of Dr. Joe Howell.

cold he had to stand up just to stay warm. They tried to start a fire, but the wood was wet. Waiting out the night near a creek, the two aviators were unable to sleep. At daybreak they continued their trek through underbrush so thick that at times they had to crawl. At noon on Tuesday they came upon a person camping near Walnut Bottom (site 37) who told them how to find their way out to a ranger station. They continued their hike up the Low Gap Trail to Cosby Ranger Station, arriving there at 2:30 P.M. "We are just thankful to be alive today," said Pasquet.[10]

The officers were taken to the Gatlinburg Medical Clinic by Ranger Frank Oliver and were treated for minor scratches and bruises. Ranger

An aerial photograph of the Cessna 150, N3083J, which crashed intact near Gunter Fork. Courtesy of Dr. Joe Howell

Robert Morris interviewed the men before they were given a ride by a reporter from the *Knoxville Journal* to Knoxville, where they caught a bus to Selma.

The plane was not found for several months as rangers and the Civil Air Patrol waited for the leaves to fall. From the air N3083J looked totally intact, as if it had landed safely. It has been slowly looted through the years, and the mountains have their own way of making planes disappear.

Eagle Creek Cessna 150

Eagle Creek is a popular drainage for historians and trout anglers. One can hike the drainage from the Appalachian Trail to Fontana Lake and discover an abundance of trout, rhododendrons, an old Cherokee footpath and mines. Before the Little Tennessee River was flooded to create Fontana Lake, small towns and logging and mining camps existed. There are still fenced-in copper mines in the area as a reminder of a once-thriving operation. Although the footpath is overgrown with a jungle of rhododendron, the observant hiker can imagine a great hunting and trading route over the Smokies for the Cherokee through Eagle Creek.

On Sunday, August 11, 1968, the Smokies caught another Cessna 150 with two occupants on board. It crashed on a flight from Atlanta, Georgia, to Lexington, Kentucky. The pilot, Don Wheeler, and a passenger crashed their airplane at approximately 6:30 P.M. and spent the night traveling in the mountains. They both walked away from the plane with minor injuries. The airplane crashed approximately half a mile west of Spence Field on Mount Squires after the two men encountered "low storm clouds" near the Smokies. They tried to fly under the clouds at forty-five hundred feet when they contacted the trees. The next day the pilot and passenger managed to walk down the creek several miles to the mouth of Eagle Creek, where they attracted the attention of a fisherman who took them by boat to the Fontana Boat Dock.

In the early afternoon the men reported their misfortune to Ranger Bud Phillips at the dock, who in turn reported the incident to park headquarters. Following information provided by the pilot, a search was launched for the aircraft. Twelve days later, on Friday, August 23, Chan Norris of Knoxville spotted the airplane while hiking on the Appalachian Trail. Norris said the plane could be seen from the trail, "but only if one looked at the right spot."[11] The entire wreckage was carted out to Cades Cove on a trailer and an all-terrain vehicle. Nothing remains today.

An Equestrian Find

In 1968, just as leaves in the Smokies were beginning to change to autumn shades of orange, red, and gold, another aircraft crashed. On a flight from Bainbridge, Georgia, to Toledo, Ohio, Thomas Crawford crashed his single-engine Cessna 180 into a remote section of the Smokies near the Spruce Mountain Lookout Tower. It was Thursday, October 3, 1968.

The search began for Crawford two days after the actual crash, when he was reported overdue by his family. His last known position was near Blairsville, Georgia, when he asked for weather information from the Knoxville tower at 3:37 P.M. It was believed that he flew the route from the Young-Harris VOR to the Snowbird VOR and while on course may not have had enough altitude to clear the Smokies. According to searchers, he could have been flying "on instruments" due to the occasional haze and cloud cover that covers the park a great deal of time. The Civil Air Patrol launched a search along the pilot's intended route and a large portion of the southeastern part of the park. Poor visibility hampered the search efforts from the beginning and periodically throughout the search. As time went on, the search wore on the teams as well as Crawford's family.

On October 13, ten days after the crash, the plane and its lone occupant were located. While on a horseback ride near the old Spruce Mountain Lookout Tower, a three-member group from Waynesville, North Carolina, came upon the aircraft, which was easily seen from the trail. The wreckage was first spotted at 11:30 A.M. by ten-year-old Dave Satterfield III that Sunday morning. After determining that what they had seen was in fact an aircraft, and that one person appeared to have been killed in the tragedy, the riders reported their discovery to a maintenance worker at the Oconaluftee Ranger Station at 2:35 P.M.

Rangers Don Pledger, Pete Nichols, and Carl Myers drove to the Spruce Mountain Lookout Tower and hiked into the scene that afternoon led by the horseback party. Meanwhile, the Tennessee Civil Air Patrol, the Civil Aeronautics Board, an FAA medical examiner (Robert Lash), and the family were all contacted. An army helicopter took Lash and other officials to a landing zone near the scene, and the investigators joined the rangers at the incident site.

The following morning Sevier County, Tennessee, and Cherokee, North Carolina, rescue squad units aided in the extrication and carryout of Crawford. His body was transported to Knoxville via helicopter, and his family was able to finally bring an end to the nightmare of waiting.

The Frustrating Koppert Search

Three seconds. That is the amount of time a spotter would have had to see the crashed Cessna 182 from the air. Because thick vegetation was hiding the wreckage, the search for N8973T continued without success for more than a year. The plane crashed into brush so thick that the ground team had to stand right beside the site to see the wreckage.

John Koppert of Columbus, Ohio, was a sales representative for a Columbus business firm. He left his home on Tuesday, February 11, 1969, in a Cessna 182 owned by the Central Ohio Flyer's Club. He departed the airport at Ohio State University en route to Asheville, North Carolina, with a stop in Knoxville. On Wednesday the twelfth, he took off from the Knoxville Downtown Island Airport at 10:05 A.M. en route to Asheville, a forty-five minute flight. His estimated time of arrival would have put him on the ground around 11:00 A.M. Once he was determined to have been "overdue" a search began.

Koppert was the sole occupant of the aircraft and was the object of a very lengthy and intensive search operation. Many organizations were involved in the search, including the Park Service, Civil Air Patrol, friends, family, the FAA, the Carolina Hiking Club, the Smoky Mountain Hiking Club, North American Aviation, the U.S. Navy out of Albany, Georgia, a naval squadron from Ohio, a photo reconnaissance group from Birmingham, and various local rescue squads and sheriff offices. It was eventually due to the skill and keen observation of a CAP pilot that the missing aircraft was found. Fifteen months after the disappearance of Koppert, the crash site was spotted, although it was likely that many persons had flown over the site several times.

From the beginning of the search, weather hampered the operation. With snow already on the ground, additional snow blanketed the region and clouds hid the mountains, making a productive visual search impossible. For two weeks after the crash, snow fell periodically throughout the region. A week after the search began, the deepest snow in three years fell in the Smokies, foiling any chance of locating the crash site. North Carolina CAP ground teams were reporting snowdrifts up to two feet deep.

Evelyn Johnson, a well-known flight instructor, airport manager, and CAP member was flying over the Smokies on Wednesday, May 28, 1970, and was in the right place at the right time (10:25 A.M.). A piece of metal reflected the sun for a brief second and caught her attention. She flew low enough to see "73T" on the fuselage of the downed plane and reported the sighting to the CAP and Park Service.[12]

On Thursday the twenty-ninth, another CAP plane flew over the site in order to pinpoint the location and guide a ground team into the area; however, weather again hampered the effort. On the thirtieth, a ground team consisting of three rangers and three CAP members hiked to Pecks

Corner shelter and attempted a search without success. After spending the night, they resumed their search and ended up spending another night in the backcountry. At daybreak on Saturday, the air search was halted again because of weather, but the ground search continued. That evening the team was joined by another ranger and members of the Sevier County Rescue Squad. On Sunday, June 1, a CAP plane with Ranger Hubert Penny on board was able to lead the team to the wreck. At 10:20 A.M. it was positively identified as the missing Cessna 182.

It had rested on the side of Mount Chapman in very thick brush, and, of course, Koppert's body had fallen victim to the elements and ways of nature. His body was carried out, and his personal effects were given to his family anxiously awaiting confirmation that Koppert had been found.

FIVE

The 1970s

A Search and a Rescue

On Saturday, January 27, 1973, a Cessna 182 piloted by Jens Petter Schmidt became the first of three aircraft to crash in the Smokies in 1973. It would be an abnormally busy year for the NPS, CAP, and other searchers. The Smokies claimed another flying machine and three lives but allowed one person to survive the crash. This is an incident with a search, a rescue, and a recovery.

The Cessna 182 is a powerful and popular light aircraft known to aviators as a "performer." Jan Petter Schmidt, the twenty-eight-year-old pilot, was flying a 182 owned by Air Transit, Inc., out of Kanawha Airport at Charleston, West Virginia. Schmidt was transporting three passengers from Charleston to Andrews-Murphy Airport in North Carolina when the tragic crash occurred.

On board the ill-fated Cessna were James W. Miller, forty-seven, of Charleston, president of the mining firm James W. Miller and Associates; Harry Adams Jr., also from Charleston, who worked for Miller; and Carl Long, who was a business associate of Miller's from San Marino, California. The passengers were en route to North Carolina to attend a meeting to deal with the joint operations of two coal-mining companies.

After Schmidt departed Charleston at 10:30 A.M. he landed at the Knoxville Downtown Island Airport around noon. There he took

Cessna 182 investigation with physician Robert Lash. Courtesy of Kent Higgins.

on fuel and waited for the overcast skies to clear. An hour or so later, the four men re-boarded the plane and departed. The ceiling, however, was still only eighteen hundred feet. James Miller was sitting in the back of the plane with Adams. Long was sitting beside pilot Schmidt in the front of the aircraft.

Approximately thirty miles southeast of Knoxville, Miller said the pilot thought he had enough altitude to make it over the mountains, but they all suddenly saw treetops rushing up beneath the plane, which was in level flight. At that point the pilot turned the plane sharply to the left to avoid a wooded ridge to the right but in the process flew into another ridge on the left. The plane hit treetops, and the propeller cut limbs from the trees. The front of the aircraft lodged in a tree, flipped onto its top, then fell to the ground. The aircraft landed on its right side with its tail section in the air at a forty-five-degree angle. The right wing was folded along the fuselage, and the engine was thrown about fifty feet beyond the wreckage.

The Cessna 182 crashed approximately one mile from the Appalachian Trail in very thick underbrush (the underbrush is still so thick that the authors were within thirty feet of the site before seeing it during a trip in 1990). Carl Long died instantly. Schmidt lived for a very short period of time, never regaining consciousness. Miller and Adams survived.

Miller began a fifty-six-hour survival quest still strapped into his seat, upside down. He loosened himself from his seat and talked to Adams. He could hear the pilot barely breathing. Miller found a hole in the metal fuselage large enough to crawl through and exited the airplane. Surveying his own injuries, he realized that the impact had fractured his ankle, wrist, and ribs and left him with several bruises and cuts. He used his necktie as a tourniquet to stop blood loss from a severe cut in his leg.

Schmidt soon died, and Miller's mind turned toward not only his own survival but also that of his good friend and business associate Harry Adams. Miller tried to crawl back into the hole in the fuselage, but because of his injuries, was unable. Adams managed to free himself from the seat belt but was still encased by the airframe and interior material. Miller tried without success to help him out of the plane. Miller stated that he tried to keep his injured friend as warm and comfortable as possible throughout the ordeal and spoke to him regularly.

Dressed only in a business suit and ill prepared for mountain weather, Miller used his knowledge as a Boy Scout leader and camper to survive. He was able to collect a briefcase that contained several items that might help him. He found lighter fluid, a cigarette lighter, a pack of mints, and almonds. He moved some twenty to thirty feet from the plane and used rolled-up papers and the lighter fluid to start a fire to warm himself and attract searchers. Miller was exhausted but did not sleep the entire time he was on the mountain. He concentrated on staying alive, watching for searchers, and trying to keep Adams alive. His bed that night was a thin pile of clothes laid upon a raincoat. Day one of the ordeal was over.

The manager of the Andrews-Murphy Airport, Edgar Woods, reported the Cessna overdue to authorities when it did not arrive as scheduled. A search began, Woods flying the route between Knoxville and his airport on Sunday, January 28, concentrating on the Great Smoky Mountains National Park. As he flew above Mollies Ridge, the weather began to close in again, but Woods spotted what he thought was a crashed airplane on a thickly wooded ridge. He was initially unable to make out specific colors or an identification number but relayed his information to the Park Service at 2:05 P.M.

A Civil Air Patrol aircraft flown by Maj. Dennis Sparks was able to fly into the area later on Sunday and determine that the wreckage was that of a white Cessna 182 with blue and red trim. The tail number was also readable. Sparks plotted approximate coordinates and radioed the information to the Park Service.

Cades Cove Subdistrict ranger Lowell K. "Kent" Higgins drove into Cades Cove and was able to watch the CAP aircraft circle over the wreckage. Higgins then established a compass heading from a point in lower Cades Cove toward the circling aircraft and marked the position on a topographical map.

By 3:00 P.M. Ranger Higgins had gathered a crew of five persons and enough supplies to carry out a "hasty search" on the mountainside. The plan was to try to locate the aircraft and possible survivors as quickly as possible and then radio for whatever resources were needed. Severe weather moved in before the downed aircraft could be located that evening.

When the search party was about half way up the very steep, difficult, and poorly defined Ekaneetlee manway, they encountered a severe thunderstorm with extreme lightning and heavy rain. Perhaps three inches of rain fell in an hour, drenching the searchers. Soon the temperature dropped and the rain turned into heavy, wet snow. Winds were between twenty and forty miles per hour, according to the search party. Before morning there would be ten inches of snow and deeper drifts.

By dark the searchers were nearly exhausted from their urgent response and heavy exertion on the slick and practically non-existent trail. From their exposure to the diverse and constant elements the men began to experience symptoms and signs of hypothermia and frostbite. For their own safety they decided to try to make it to the Mollies Ridge Shelter for the night. The five searchers were joined by two additional men a few hours later, and they all huddled around a wet, pitifully small, and smoky fire through the night.

As the temperature dropped into the teens, Miller crouched near his own small fire. The wind, rain, and snow slowly put an end to it, and Miller, with no shelter, no fire, and no way to assist his dying companion or himself, shivered through the night. Before Sunday ended, Miller became the only survivor of the crash. Harry Adams Jr. died as a result of exposure, his injuries, and shock. Miller was now alone but still confident that he would survive. Day two had ended.

By daylight on Monday, January 29, the snow and wind had ceased. North District ranger Alsen "Bud" Inman, Cades Cove ranger Higgins, and Abrams Creek ranger J. R. Buchanan took a compass heading from the Mollies Ridge Shelter toward the approximate location of the crashed aircraft. They began hiking cross-country off the main Smokies ridge through wet rhododendron and underbrush in ten inches of snow and thick fog. Every step left the searchers wetter and colder. With a sense of urgency, they struggled through the vegetation.

By 11:00 A.M. Chilhowee ranger Tom Henry led a hand-picked crew of three woods-wise park maintenance men from Cades Cove up the

Ekaneetlee manway and met the others on the ridge to be searched. In addition to park rangers, rescue squad members from Sevier, Blount, and Cocke Counties and other volunteers departed Cades Cove to begin their search. The deep, slick snowdrifts, freezing temperatures, and thick woods on steep mountain slopes combined to create miserable conditions for searchers looking for a white aircraft. Progress was very slow.

Just before noon the overcast layer of clouds began to lift and a request was made to launch another CAP flight. Edgar Woods also returned to the area and at 11:45 A.M. was over the crash site. He was only able to circle the scene three times before clouds once again shrouded the ridge. The ground teams realized they were still not very close to the aircraft.

At the crash scene, lonely Miller saw the sky clear and heard the search plane. Although he had high hopes that the Cessna would be spotted, he realized the snow had covered the plane to such a degree that it might not be seen from above. He took more of the business papers from the briefcase and decided to burn them to produce smoke. He measured the chance of success in signaling the search plane against keeping warm for the next night if he was not located.

At 1:03 P.M. Park Ranger Art Whitehead led the Blount and Sevier County Rescue Squads to the rangers already on the mountain. They had carried four Stokes litters and other supplies with them. This group of rescuers set up a staging area and prepared for a rescue or carryout as need would dictate.

The crews spread out and continued to comb the densely forested ridges. Search members were yelling back and forth to one another to keep in contact. Then a wonderful thing happened: Miller heard the searchers calling. He responded, "Over here . . . over here."

By this time a large group of searchers were all over the mountainside, but they had no radio contact with one another. Miller's shouts were heard, but the searchers thought he was one of their own because no one yelled "Help." Bud Inman and others began to smell the papers burning and called out. Miller again responded and led the searchers to the aircraft.

Near the top of a small ridge the searchers saw the outline of the aircraft through the thick rhododendron. Rangers Inman, Higgins, Buchanan, Henry, Glen Boring, Grady Whitehead, and Archie Whitehead came face to face with an obviously extremely distressed Miller, who was shivering violently on the ground.

Miller was found with his arms across his chest and his bare hands partially protected under his armpits. His first words according to Kent

On January 27, 1973, a Cessna 182 crashed on thickly wooded Mollies Ridge. One of the plane's four passengers died instantly, another died shortly thereafter, and a third died from exposure to the bitter cold. Only one passenger survived the ordeal. Pictured here is the team preparing to carry James Miller from the mountain. Photograph by Merrit "Mickey" Creager.

Higgins were, "Boys, you just saved my life!" Then Miller said, "If I can just get my head warm I think I will be alright." Higgins removed his own wool sweater and wrapped it around Miller's head and ears.

Quickly, the search turned into a rescue. The rescue squad members were summoned from the staging area to the scene with a Stokes litter basket. Miller was stabilized, placed into a rescue litter, and given his first food in three days. Rescuers applied bandages and splints to the injured man and gave him canned apricots, crackers, and tomato juice. A helicopter was called to lift Miller out of the mountains, but poor visibility canceled the flight. A carryout plan was initiated instead.

It was obvious that time was of the essence if Miller was to survive the ordeal. First, two teams were assigned to mark and cut an evacuation trail. Next, persons were specifically assigned to take care of medical issues along the way for Miller. The remainder of the rescuers on the mountain were stationed down the carryout route to assist in Miller's actual removal. Some of the men were too exhausted to assist in the rescue, so they walked slowly behind the rest of the team. Hypothermia and frostbite were taking their toll on everyone.

Rangers Whitehead and Henry begun the process of leading the carryout team down the mountainside. Thick underbrush had to be cleared and small trees cut. Ranger Dwight McCarter led a relief crew of eight men, including Robert Lash. They met the rescue party about half way in at about 6:30 P.M. "Doc" Lash examined Miller and administered pain medication to him. The relief crew wore headlamps and provided assistance and light for the next agonizing four hours. Once at Mill Creek the team had to cross the stream many times while wading in knee-deep icy water. Many large, blown-down trees also barred the way. At 9:00 P.M. three additional men arrived to assist in the carryout—just in time, for now even the relief team needed relief.

At 10:21 P.M. the backcountry rescue was completed. The weary but triumphant rescue team loaded Miller into a waiting ambulance and transported him to the University of Tennessee Hospital in Knoxville. At the emergency room he was treated for broken bones, bruises, cuts, and severe frostbite. He remained overnight in the intensive care unit and was transferred to a private room the next day. At first it was thought that Miller's frozen leg would have to be amputated from the knee down, but with expert care his leg was saved.

The rescue of Miller was completed on Monday night, but the recovery of his three companions was not completed until Wednesday the thirty-first. The army at Fort Campbell sent a Chinook helicopter to transport FAA agents, NTSB investigators, and park rangers to the scene. Since there was no place to land the very large, twin-engine helicopter, it was decided to lower each of the personnel by cable. While the helicopter returned to Knoxville for fuel, the men investigated the aircraft and prepared the bodies of Schmidt, Long, and Adams for transport. Within three hours the entire operation was completed. The men's bodies were brought to UT Hospital at 1:45 P.M. on Wednesday and from there sent to waiting families in California, West Virginia, and Norway.

For their work, the search-and-rescue personnel were described as "heroes" by their communities. Some of them were on the mountain from Sunday afternoon until late Monday night. Some suffered frostbite and hypothermia, and most dealt with exhaustion. A couple of rescuers were treated for injuries and also carried out. The carryout of Miller was very strenuous, according to Lash. "The men were so exhausted and it was so cold that six of us could carry the litter only about 50 feet before we had to rest," he said. "We sent two rescuers to the hospital and several men had to leave the group because of exhaustion. One man left but was so tired, we caught up to him where he had stopped and built a fire. Those were hardy, brave men who brought that survivor out."[1]

An Afghan Hound Survived

A twin-engine Piper aircraft was flying from Cincinnati, Ohio, over the Smokies and crashed onto the north side of Mount LeConte in a very rugged area. The wreckage burned upon impact, killing the occupants and quickly turning the once-large airplane into cinders. The plane cannot be seen from the air, and through the years souvenir hunters and the elements have made the plane all but disappear. This time the Smokies claimed a flying machine and four lives. Only a dog survived the fiery crash that occurred on Tuesday morning, April 3, 1973.

John Brandt, thirty-five, of Crescent Springs, Kentucky, piloted the twin Piper Aztec carrying three passengers: Bonnie Lou Frasier, eighteen, of South Shore, Kentucky; Linda Picklesimer, age seventeen, of South Portsmouth, Kentucky; and Thomas James Sueter, age thirty-nine, of Cincinnati. Sueter was an FAA controller at the Cincinnati Airport. Also on board that flight was John Brandt's dog, Khzin, an Afghan hound. The dog was thrown clear of the wreckage and later returned to the site. It was found six days after the crash and several days after the bodies had been removed.

Shortly after the crash, a hiker at the Cliff Tops on Mount LeConte spotted smoke and reported it to the LeConte Lodge staff. A lodge employee reported the smoke to the Park Service about noon. Later that day a search began for the missing aircraft, and a Civil Air Patrol plane was dispatched to the area. At approximately 2:00 P.M. the CAP plane discovered that the smoke was coming from a crashed aircraft. Two smokejumpers from the U.S. Forest Service were sent in at 4:00 P.M. to search for the plane, and two park rangers hiked in. They discovered the badly burned site just before dark. The four searchers spent the night waiting for additional help.

At 8:00 A.M. the next day, Wednesday, April 4, the Park Service closed Newfound Gap Road and set up a command post at a pull-off near Alum Cave Bluff Parking Area. Between seventy-five and one hundred persons, including members from the CAP, NPS, Explorer Post 888, and volunteer rescue squads, hiked with Robert Lash more than two miles into the drainage to do the recovery. The operation was completed at 3:30 P.M. The bodies were recovered and carried out to Highway 441, where they were transported to UT Hospital.

A week later, on Monday, April 9, a group of students from the Asheville School for Boys, led by Jim Hollingsworth, were at LeConte Lodge. In the afternoon the hiking party left the Alum Cave Bluff Trail and descended into the thick rhododendron forest below. They found the desolate crash site and spotted a hungry but uninjured Afghan Hound lying curled up at the site. The party led the dog out to the road and turned it over to the rangers. The Park Service then transported the dog to the Parkway Animal Clinic in Pigeon Forge for a checkup. After giving the dog a clean bill of health, veterinarian Irvin Rhodes gave the dog back to the Park Service, which arranged for it to be flown to Macon, Georgia.[2]

Noisy Creek Cessna 150

In 1973, nine people died and one survived as a result of airplane crashes in the Great Smoky Mountains National Park. These ten persons were involved in three incidents that included two Cessna and one Piper aircraft. The last of the three crashes claimed the lives of two local men. The historical records indicate that only half a dozen local flyers had been killed in Smoky Mountains crashes since 1920. Three were "working" aircraft that were doing something locally "for hire" when they crashed. On November 2, 1973, the Smokies claimed two local men and their aircraft on Noisy Creek near Cobbly Knob.

Jack Roberts, age thirty-six, was the president of Great Smoky Mountains Aviation based at the Sevier-Gatlinburg Airport in Sevierville, Tennessee. He was a well-known flight instructor and respected aviator. Roberts respected the mountains and seldom flew over them unless the weather was good and he was confident of his abilities. He and his wife, Peggy, had operated the airport and the flying service for years, and Peggy remained the owner-operator after her husband's untimely death.

On that Friday, Jack was flying N99PR, a two-person Cessna 150 that was white with gold and green stripes. He and Jim Yett, a thirty-year-old photographer also from Sevierville, were taking pictures of the Cobbly Knob area near Highway 321 outside of Gatlinburg when the crash occurred. The two left the Sevierville airport at 1:30 P.M. and were expected back mid-afternoon, as the flight en route was only fifteen minutes each way. The plane, however, could have stayed aloft until 5:30 without running out of fuel.

The exact cause of the crash has remained a mystery, but investigations revealed that the aircraft apparently developed engine trouble while over the Cobbly Knob Golf Course. Residents reported hearing the plane sputter. That sometimes happens when a pilot backs the power off in a descent. Whatever the problem, Roberts was flying just inside the national park when the plane lost power and he stalled it into the tops of some poplars.

The Cessna fell through the canopy of trees, and just before it struck the ground, it inverted and came to rest upside down almost perfectly intact. The left wing folded onto the right wing like a butterfly lying on its side. Roberts and Yett died immediately and remained strapped to their seats inside the aircraft.

By 4:30 Peggy Roberts realized that something was wrong. She decided to report the plane as overdue, and a search was begun immediately. The Sevier County Sheriff's Department and Rescue Squad began a ground search at 5:00 while the Sevier County Civil Air Patrol, other CAP squadrons, and Peggy divided the area for an aerial search. It being late fall, it was thought that if the plane had gone down, it would be easy to find.[3]

After the initial search failed to produce any clues and daylight turned into darkness, the search was expanded. Throughout the night persons along the flight route were contacted and back roads and open fields were checked. At 3:30 A.M. additional searchers were summoned. At 6:00 A.M. the Tennessee Highway Patrol sent a helicopter to the airport. By 6:30, just as the sun began to illuminate the East Tennessee mountains, the THP helicopter announced that it was hovering over the crash site of a small airplane matching N99PR's description.

Ground teams arrived at the mouth of Noisy Creek where it crosses under present-day Highway 321. An hour later the team located the slightly damaged aircraft lying beside a small creek. Inside, the searchers found the bodies of the two men. The aviator and photographer were placed on litters and carried out to the highway. The search was over, and the families of men could put the unknown behind them.

Friends and relatives gathered on Monday the fifth to say goodbye to the men. Jim Yett was buried at the Shiloh Cemetery. He was survived by his wife, Kathy Huff Yett, his parents, Mr. and Mrs. Claude Yett, and an uncle. Jack Roberts was remembered with a funeral service at Atchley's Funeral Home in Sevierville and was buried in Asheville at the Pisgah View Cemetery. His wife, four children, two stepchildren, and two brothers survived him.

For a number of years following the crash, the site was used by the Park Service and the Civil Air Patrol for practice searches. The wreckage was easy to walk to because it rested only twenty-five feet from an old road that follows the creek. The CAP and others have since removed the plane.

Trial at the Devil's Courthouse

In 1974 a lone aircraft incident in the Smokies was a spectacular one to say the least. What could have been a fatal tragedy for a family turned into a miracle in which all the occupants survived. It was a great boost of morale for the search-and-rescue community, considering the tragedies they had experienced in recent years.

Heavy snowfall. That is what attracts many persons to the Ober Gatlinburg Ski Resort each winter. The ski area is within a day's drive for most of the population in the eastern United States and is a convenient place to ski. Gatlinburg offers great restaurants and hotels, and the roads are usually plowed to allow the thousands of skiers to make their way to the slopes. The possibility of deep snow is what attracted a Mississippi family to the Smokies, and it is what almost took their lives.

On Saturday, February 16, 1974, seven persons were en route to the Sevier-Gatlinburg Airport from Pascagoula, Mississippi, flying in a single-engine Cherokee Six (N56508). Ray McCarra, age thirty, a contractor, piloted the plane. He had with him his wife, Phyllis, and their three children: Jonathan, three, Jeffrey, nine, and Joel, six. Ray's brother, Russell, age forty-five, and his wife, Zilla, also forty-five, residents of New Orleans, were also on board. The original plan was to fly to Chattanooga then over the Smokies before landing in Sevierville. Ray told a park spokesperson that the "weather looked good so he figured it would be no problem to fly over the Park to Sevierville."[4]

As they approached Clingmans Dome, the plane's carburetor begin to clog with ice from the cold, moist air. Carburetor icing causes a disruption of fuel flow into the cylinders, which in turn restricts power and the performance of the aircraft. Compounding the problem was a low ceiling and a strong north wind. The wind was approaching the Smokies' main ridgeline and spilling over like a waterfall into North Carolina, creating an enormous downdraft. As the aircraft began to lose power, therefore, it began to lose altitude. As the plane dropped like a rock, the pilot had to quickly chose between crash-landing the plane or trying to turn back. He chose to stall the plane and make a controlled crash landing onto the mountain.

The plane began to shake and bump as it hit severe turbulence, which is common over the mountains with the downdrafts. Ray and his brother Russell, who was also a pilot, reduced their speed and told everyone to tighten their seat belts. The two men timed the stall just right and dropped the plane into trees at the bottom of a large rock wall. "Both of us just grabbed the wheel and yanked it back and just pancaked it in," Russell told the *Knoxville News Sentinel*.[5] "The plane bobbed and buckled in the turbulence," Zilla recalled. "Trees and boulders rushed up at us. I shut my eyes, praying hard, 'God help us, help us! But Thy Will be done.'"[6] After the abrupt and violent stop, the scene was momentarily silent.

The crash site was inside North Carolina on Mount Buckley on a ridge named Devils Courthouse. It was a miracle that all seven persons survived. Not only did everyone survive, but no one seemed to have been seriously hurt, although later Zilla began to complain of severe pain associated with the landing.

The aircraft received minor damage considering what had happened. The entire nose section was demolished when it hit a large rock, but the remainder of the fuselage remained intact. In fact, when the plane was later airlifted off the mountain it was in one piece; both wings, the fuselage, and the tail surface were pulled out at one time. This is significant because in most crashes the plane is usually destroyed. In this instance, the plane became the survival shelter for the family.

Once everyone had been checked for injuries, camp was made for the night in hopes that searchers would try to locate them. It was 5:00 P.M., and the sun had nearly set. Snow began to fall, and the temperature dropped to below freezing. They built a fire and, with hopes set high, the seven stranded family members braced for a cold night of waiting. They had no water, food, or blankets. As the sun set, the family could see lights to the

An aerial photograph of the single-engine Cherokee Six piloted by Ray McCarra. In February 1974, McCarra made a controlled crash landing on a park ridge named Devils Courthouse. Remarkably, McCarra and his six passengers, all family members, survived the crash. Courtesy of Sevier County Civil Air Patrol Archive.

south; perhaps the lights were from a car, or maybe a home.

The next morning, Sunday, at 5:00 A.M., after spending the night inside the aircraft, they found icicles hanging from the ceiling. It was obvious to Ray that they could not survive very long, and to make matters worse no one even knew they were overdue. The radio did not work because the airplane's battery had been destroyed in the impact, so there was no way to call for assistance. After much discussion, Ray decided to walk out to seek help. Not knowing exactly where they were but seeing lights during the night, Ray kissed his wife and sons goodbye and began walking downhill through the underbrush, balsams, and firs. Phyllis at that time thought she might never see her husband again.

Ray was dressed for flying, not hiking. He had on low-cut street shoes but had salvaged a warm coat from a suitcase. He hiked downhill along Devils Courthouse Ridge and then into a drainage. During his walk for help he crossed small and large creeks, scaled a waterfall, had an encounter with a wild hog, and bushwhacked through thick rhododendron and other undergrowth. In the late morning he found Fontana Lake and a trail. After following the trail he came upon an intersection and a trail sign. The sign directed him to Clingmans Dome, a landmark he recognized and had previously visited. He knew that there was a road at the Dome trailhead, and where there are roads, there are cars. It was his best shot.

Throughout the remainder of the day Ray hiked back up the mountain. He apparently went up Forney Ridge Trail, which eventually took him within a mile of his family. He was tired, hungry, cold, and wet, but a few hours later he reached the Clingmans Dome Parking Area. Expecting to find people and cars he was disappointed to find nothing since the road was closed for the winter and was covered with seven inches of snow. Not giving up, Ray remembered that the road from the parking area ended at Newfound Gap. He hoped that there would be people there. With eight more miles of snow in front of him, he trudged on. Day turned into night and his thoughts were of his family. As they were preparing for another night in the desolate mountains, he was almost "out of the woods."

Arriving at Newfound Gap at approximately 11:00 P.M., his chances of finding anyone on a February evening seemed slim to none. Suddenly, however, he saw headlights. He waved down the college student motorist, who took him to a nearby ranger on road patrol once he convinced her of his story. His hiking had ended—all thirty-plus miles of it.

The ranger radioed park headquarters that he had an aircraft crash victim with him and that six of his party were still at the crash site awaiting rescue. At headquarters, Ray met with another ranger and told him the full story. The pilot plotted his estimated position, and the Park Service began their investigation. McCarra was taken to a local motel to clean up, rest, and eat. Now the search was in the hands of the National Park Service. Ray was glad he was out of the mountains but was very concerned for his family, knowing how unprepared they were for surviving the adverse conditions.

Cades Cove Subdistrict ranger Kent Higgins was at home and overheard the radio transmission. Thinking that he would be called to assist, he prepared his gear. At that time Higgins was the only (and first) "park medic" who was an emergency medical technician (EMT). Higgins called the park dispatcher, who in turn informed him that no one was seriously injured enough to require medical treatment and that the pilot had informed rangers that he thought every one could probably walk out on their own.

Maj. Glenn Fox, the director of emergency services for the Tennessee CAP was on call that evening and received a phone call at 1:00 A.M. from the Park Service explaining the incident. Major Fox quickly assembled a search management team with members of the Sevier County Civil Air Patrol. Capt. Bob McCarter was appointed search mission coordinator, and he assembled his staff to make formal plans and gather additional information.

Throughout the night the Park Service, CAP, and other agencies prepared their air and ground teams for a large-scale search-and-rescue operation. The knowledge that there were still six persons who needed to be located and brought out of the cold mountains gave their mission a sense of urgency. Cold, snowy weather was forecast, but everyone was ready to go by first light.

During the night, four rangers drove through the snow to Clingmans Dome and hiked the few miles to the Double Springs Gap Shelter. Along the way they looked and listened for any sign of the crash site. They stayed at the shelter until the sun rose in the morning, then began searching down the south side of the mountain.

Early Monday morning, Captain McCarter briefed his staff and search team members. At 8:11 A.M., as the sun rose over the horizon and the haze lifted, a Beech Baron piloted by two Sevierville brothers, 2 Lt. Jimmy King and Senior Member Danny King, departed the Sevier-Gatlinburg Airport for Clingmans Dome. Moments later the brothers were in the general search area and had their eyes peeled for the white aircraft. The McCarra family could hear the sounds of the Baron. They knew Ray had made it out.

As the ground rescue crews waited, the search plane continued along the main ridge between Clingmans Dome and Silers Bald. At 8:25 A.M., just fourteen minutes into the search, the Cherokee Six was spotted and positively identified. The brothers circled the crash site and were elated to see the family waving at them. Everyone had survived the cold night! The Kings radioed the mission base and gave an exact location to the mission coordinator, who in turn plotted it on a map. It was on Devils Courthouse Ridge, just two miles below Clingmans Dome on the North Carolina side of the mountain. The news was relayed to Ray McCarra.

The quick search turned into a long rescue. It began as the Baron arrived back at headquarters with two excited crew members. It was the first "save" for the squadron since it had been formed in 1966. Their thoughts then turned to getting food and blankets to the survivors with haste. McCarter contacted park headquarters with the details of the location and immediately the Park Service launched rescue crews to the area.

Higgins and a park photographer were on their day off and volunteered to hike in to join the ranger team already on the mountain.

The CAP developed a plan to drop a survival package to the family from the air. The CAP members packaged candy bars and sandwiches inside a duffel bag, along with blankets, a first-aid kit, warm coats, and orange vests. This bag was placed inside a bright orange U.S. Mail "air-mail" bag donated by a mail carrier and loaded it onto a Piper J-3 Cub. The plan was to fly the airmail bag to Clingmans Dome, find the crash site again, and drop the heavy bag through the trees to the McCarras.[7]

The J-3 Cub and crew flew to the area and spotted the family again. Flying low and slowly, Danny King and 2d Lt. R. L. Davis dropped the bag out of the plane to within thirty feet of the crash site. The stranded party emptied the duffel bag and hung the orange airmail bag in a tree to attract the attention of the searchers. The Cub returned to mission base and picked up Ranger Paul McCrary, also a CAP member, and they led the ground search crew into the crash scene by radio.

The ground crew left Clingmans Dome and hiked down the Appalachian Trail toward Double Springs Gap while the crew already at the gap hiked east on the trail to meet with the others. Making their way down the south side of the mountain, the contingent of searchers marked the trail with flagging ribbon to the crash site. In the meantime, rescuers were trying to determine the best way to get everyone at the scene off the mountain. Perhaps a helicopter could hoist or meet them at Mount Buckley. Once the searchers arrived at the scene, that would be determined.

By noon the rescuers had arrived on the scene and given everyone more food and a quick medical check for injuries. Phyllis, Jeff, John, Joel, and Russell were fine. It was Zilla who was in a more guarded position and could not walk out. She needed to be in a physician's care. While the search party was not fully equipped to deal with Zilla's pain and injuries, she was made comfortable, and the remainder of the supplies were left with her, her husband, and Ranger Guy Taylor until more help could arrive.

Meanwhile, the rescuers escorted Phyllis and the boys from the aircraft, down the ridge, and over a drainage to the Forney Creek Trail. From there they hiked up to the Dome parking lot, and by midnight they met Robert Lash, who gave them a medical exam and deemed that they were okay. They were driven off the top of the Smokies and joined Ray at the motel for a happy reunion.

Shortly after the first group was escorted away from the crash, Higgins and the photographer arrived on the scene. After asking some pertinent questions Higgins discovered the full range of injuries sustained by Zilla during the crash. She had not begun to deteriorate until several hours after Ray had left the wreckage. Severe pain persisted in her back, abdomen, and legs. There was a definite probability of internal injuries.

Higgins requested that an attempt be made to bring in a helicopter to remove her, but the weather did not cooperate and the type of equipment needed was not close at hand. Instead, Lash employed a Jet Ranger helicopter to dodge the clouds and drop another load of supplies to the scene. After sunset, but just before dark, the helicopter appeared just above the crash site and out came a bundled load of blankets, sleeping bags, medical supplies, and food. During the night Zilla was given pain medication and was made as comfortable as possible in a "bed" a few yards from the aircraft. The rangers and her husband made a fire to keep the group warm. Russell bedded down beside his wife to console her and encourage her throughout the cold, windy night. The wind began to howl, light snow fell, and the couple was about to spend their second night in the woods.

The carryout of Zilla McCarra from the Cherokee Six crash on Devils Courthouse. Courtesy of Kent Higgins.

During the night the rest of the family was reunited and the rangers planned two operations. The first was to have a helicopter hoist Zilla off the mountain in a rescue litter.

The second was a contingency plan: they would arrange a massive carry-out to the Clingmans Dome Parking Area if the first plan fell through. Search planners must always have a backup plan in their pocket, especially when trying to deal with Smoky Mountains weather and helicopters.

The following morning, Tuesday, January 19, the rescue crew at the crash site received word that a U.S. Army Chinook helicopter from Fort Campbell, Kentucky, would soon be on its way to make a hoist evacuation of Zilla and Russell. At the same time several rescue squad members from North Carolina and Tennessee were being assembled to cut a trail through the thick woods for an urgent carryout should the helicopter rescue fail. Their work began at once.

The weather cleared, and a helicopter left from Fort Campbell. As it approached the Smokies, however, one if its engines failed. The very large helicopter had to make a forced emergency landing. No one was hurt in the landing, but the air ship was out of action. A second Chinook was soon dispatched, but it was racing in front of a potentially harsh system.

By noon Zilla was feeling somewhat better because of the pain medication and sleep. She was in good spirits and called on her Christian faith to see her through. In the early afternoon the rescue crews could hear the distinct thundering sound of a loud, twin-engine helicopter in the distance. There is no mistaking the sound of a Chinook. It approached the scene from the direction of Fontana Lake and slowly moved up the slope at treetop level. Everyone was elated that the rescue was at hand. It would be a race against time because on everyone's mind was the clouds, which loomed over the top of the mountains.

The pilot made several attempts to get close to the scene, but time ran out as dark clouds engulfed the mountainside. Waiting, turning, hovering, and trying again, the green aircraft sought to get close enough and safe enough to lower a cable to the rangers. Soon it was obvious that the air rescue was not going to happen. The engines increased in volume and the helicopter turned away, disappointing the rangers, aircrew, search coordinators, the family, and, of course, Zilla and Russell. It was nearly 3:00 P.M.

As silence overtook the crash site again, the carryout crew prepared to expedite their role. As Zilla was already "packaged" in the Stokes litter, the first six persons lifted the stretcher and off they went on the first leg of a three-mile hike. A cleared area was prepared straight up Devils Courthouse Ridge to the Appalachian Trail, and eighty volunteers and rangers were stationed at strategic intervals along the route to carry Zilla to a waiting ambulance. This plan was established so fresh team members would be able to quickly carry the Stokes basket up the steep, slick, and overgrown slope.

During the operation the wind picked up and the temperature dropped. Snow continued to fall, and visibility was often less than twenty yards. This is one detail everyone who was part of the rescue recalls: freezing rain and snow alternated throughout the ordeal until everyone was wet, tired, and cold. The carryout progressed until everyone was safely out of the woods. Zilla made the painful trip without complaint.

After the crew arrived at the Appalachian Trail, Zilla was carried another mile to the Clingmans Dome Road, where she was placed into a warm ambulance. What a welcomed sight! Once it finally began, the entire operation was completed in three hours.

Zilla was met by Lash at the parking area and was prepared for a trip to the University of Tennessee Hospital in Knoxville. Her trial at the Courthouse was over. She won!

At the hospital, tests and X-rays revealed that Zilla had sustained several injuries as a result of the impact. She was treated for contusions on the lower back and pelvis, dehydration, bladder and bowel paralysis, a fractured spine, and internal bleeding. She stayed at the UT Hospital for several days before she was released and sent home to New Orleans on March 1. She had to wear a back brace for nearly a year but recovered completely from her injuries except for an occasional back ache.

Until just recently, the McCarras periodically traveled back to the Smokies and visited the rangers and medical staff who took care of them. Zilla was especially proud of Kent Higgins, who had responded to take photographs but ended up taking very good care of her. She has told Higgins that it was God who guided him to her in her time of need—and she has no other explanation.

Once the snow had melted and the weather was appropriate, the salvage operation to retrieve the airplane off Devils Courthouse Ridge began. St. Louis Helicopter Airways was contracted by the insurance company to airlift the plane from the backcountry to the Clingmans Dome Parking Area. The large and powerful orange-and-white Sikorsky helicopter was outfitted with a harness and a cable approximately two hundred feet long. It slowly approached the scene, and the cable was connected to the aircraft. Because the plane's left wing was damaged, the sling was attached to the tail and to the right wing. The plane was slowly pulled away from the ridge and carefully lifted to the western

The removal of the Cherokee Six by a skycrane helicopter. Courtesy of National Park Service.

edge of the parking lot. From there it was transported out of the park on a flatbed trailer. No wreckage remains at the scene.

Today, Zilla and Russell live in Mandeville, Louisiana, and have had no health problems related to the crash. Ray, Phyllis, and their children live in Pascagoula, Mississippi. In a February 2001 interview, Zilla had high praise for the CAP and NPS and wished to pass on their hearty "thank you."

Rutland's Cessna 172

"We turned into a canyon and it was sort of shaped in a 'Y.' I took the right leg and it turned out to be a box canyon. . . . I decided to climb out and as I applied power—well, I found out I didn't have any power. We just stalled into the trees."[8] That is what the pilot of a Cessna 172 reported to the *Knoxville Journal* regarding the last seconds before his crash into the Smokies on Wednesday, August 13, 1975.

Jerry Rutland, twenty-nine, of Columbus, Georgia, was the pilot of a 1967 Cessna 172 (N234FB). He was on a cross-country flight between Knoxville and Fort Benning. With him was Charles Morgan, twenty-nine, of Fort Benning and Nicki Dufort, twenty-three. They had departed at 9:00 A.M. on the thirteenth. The trio's plan was to fly to Knoxville, refuel, and return home by 9:00 P.M.

The Cessna left McGhee Tyson Airport around 3:30 P.M., and half an hour later it was over the Tremont section of the park. Without adequate altitude over the mountains, aircraft often experience low clouds and turbulence that sometimes will bring a craft down into trees. This is what happened to Rutland and his companions. They flew over the Tremont area and did not have enough power and altitude to make it over Derrick Knob. The plane crashed at 4:15 P.M. approximately two miles north of the Appalachian Trail on the west side of Sams Ridge near Shut-in Creek.

The plane dropped through the lush, junglelike canopy of forest resting on the ground in one piece. Jerry, Charles, and Nicki found that no one had received serious injuries, only minor cuts and bruises. Not knowing exactly where they were, they decided to stay put. Rutland hoped that the plane's emergency locator transmitter (ELT) was broadcasting a distress beacon. The ELT was not operating, however, so no one knew they were down. As the evening progressed the three survivors thought that someone, somewhere would be looking for them. The plane was reported overdue when it failed to show at Fort Benning on time.

On Thursday morning at 9:00 A.M. the three decided to leave the plane and find their way out. They hiked uphill through rhododendron, creeks, and underbrush until they reached the Appalachian Trail, where they came upon a hiker. The hiker told them where a ranger's jeep could be found, and they walked to it. The hiker later found some Park Service workers and explained the situation to them. They, in turn, hiked back to the jeep, met the crash victims, and radioed to headquarters information about the incident.

Once the three arrived at park headquarters a helicopter was waiting to transport them to the University of Tennessee Medical Center, where they were all treated for the minor injuries received in the crash

A skycrane with Jerry Rutland's recovered Cessna 172 in the background in the Cades Cove fields. Courtesy of National Park Service.

and released. A salvage company later removed the aircraft from the park. It was lifted out of the forest by a helicopter and loaded onto a flatbed trailer at Cades Cove.

That Others Might Live

The next three case studies are the most memorable to searchers of the past few years. All three involved life and death and a search and a rescue. Between December 1, 1977, and February 11, 1979, the search-and-rescue skills of air and ground crews were put to the test. Each will be explained separately, but while reading, try to put yourself in three roles: that of a searcher, a waiting family member, and an occupant of a crashed aircraft.

Of all the stories in Smoky Mountains aviation lore, this one takes the prize. The story of how two small children survived a crash that killed their father and older sister is indescribable, but some sort of description will be attempted here.

Tom Shrewsbury of Ann Arbor, Michigan, a thirty-four-year-old marketing representative for the IBM Corporation in Detroit, was also a pilot. He had recently separated from his wife, Carole, but maintained a close relationship with his children. He leased a Cessna 172 from a flying service in Michigan to take his three children—Laura, eleven, Jeff, ten, and Jennifer, eight—to see their grandmother, Anne Shrewsbury, in St. Petersburg, Florida. They were returning to Michigan on Thursday, December 1, 1977, when the accident occurred.

After eating their Thanksgiving meal and opening early Christmas presents the family packed the aircraft and began their flight home. They departed St. Petersburg on Tuesday, November 29, and stopped in Valdosta, Georgia, for fuel and a break. Tom loaded the kids into the plane and continued flying north until the weather began to deteriorate. Tom landed at the Blairsville, Georgia, airport, and after considering the weather, decided not to continue the flight. For the next two nights and three days the foursome rented a motel room and watched the rain and clouds.

On Thursday, December 1, the dad and kids had breakfast, packed, and headed for the airport to continue their journey to Michigan. Jeff recalled climbing a tree behind the motel that morning and ripping a pocket of his coat; it would be a problem for him in the next two days. After an argument between Jeff and Laura about who was going to sit in the front seat with their dad, Laura played the "I'm older" trump card and Jeff ended up sitting in the back seat with Jennifer (later Jeff would say he lost both the seat and a sister). At 9:30 A.M. the Cessna departed Blairsville, heading north.

During an interview in February 2000 the Shrewsburys mentioned that there were scattered clouds just above the altitude they were flying and dark storm clouds to the west. Jeff and Jennifer recall flying over a lake (probably Fontana) and approaching the mountains when the trouble began. For about three minutes the Cessna, flying at about forty-five hundred feet, started bouncing, shaking, and violently losing and regaining altitude. Jeff said it felt like hitting bumps on a rough road. They described the next few minutes as scary but not terrifying. The plane began to rise and fall as it rode the invisible tidal wave of air. "The plane began to shake, and dad said that everything would be okay," Jeff recalled. "I noticed a high ridge to our left and right and one directly in front of us. He was trying to stay below the clouds and away from the trees. I noticed that the trees were right in front of the plane and how weird it was that when he was trying to make a turn to the left, the plane turned upside down and the horizon looked funny."

As the plane inverted, it fell quickly to the ground, clipping a few treetops on the way. The aircraft came to a rest upside down but very much intact. Jennifer said that "it felt like things were going in slow motion. Just before we flipped, Dad said that things would be fine. As the plane was going down, I blacked out." Then it happened. The plane hit the ground and Tom and Laura were killed instantly. The force of the crash against Jeff tore his seatbelt, slamming him against the ceiling of the plane. Jennifer remained in her seat but hung upside down by her seatbelt. Both children were unconscious for an undetermined amount of time. Then came the quietness.

After the traumatic and violent impact the mountain became still, except for the moaning of the brother and sister who were now alone on the side of Long Hungry Ridge. The crash occurred approximately two hundred yards south of the North Carolina–Tennessee state line, just east of popular Gregory Bald.

Once Jeff regained consciousness he realized what had happened. He was laying on the ceiling covered with suitcases and Christmas presents. Immediately he was aware that he could not feel his new Nike tennis shoes on his feet. He tried to move his legs and nothing happened. "It was like my legs had fallen asleep," he said. "You know, that funny tingly feeling."

As Jennifer woke up she was looking down at Jeff in front of her. He reached up and pulled Jenn's buckle, releasing her body. She

Jeff Shrewsbury (seated) with the author, Jeff Wadley, during the 2000 interviews with Jeff and Jennifer Shrewsbury. Courtesy of David Wadley.

fell on top of him, and they looked and saw their dad and sister in the front seats. Jeff knew that they had died. Reassuring Jenn, Jeff calmly told her that they would be okay. He took one of Jennifer's shoes off and beat against the back window of the crumpled aircraft. After a few moments the plastic glass broke and Jeff crawled out the hole. He fell out of the plane and landed beside a log, where he would remain for the next day and a half.

The ten-year-old brother told his sister to stay in the plane. It was warmer, and every time she moved her back was in excruciating pain. The two had no food or drink except for a few pieces of chocolate candy their grandmother had given them for their trip. Neither could get into a position to see each other, let alone try to start a fire to stay warm. Jeff said that it never entered his mind to try to start a fire. The overnight low temperature recorded at park headquarters was twenty-seven degrees Wednesday morning; it was much colder where the plane had crashed.

Along with other injuries, the two survivors were dealing with hypothermia, which often results in death if the body is not warmed. Frostbite was also a problem for both children because neither was able to move around or adequately cover themselves.

Jeff's injuries were very serious. The impact of the crash resulted in a transected spine. His injury was to the thoracic number ten and caused paralysis from the waist down. He also had suffered scrapes, bruises, cuts, and internal injuries. He was, he later said, in a great deal of pain and discomfort during the whole ordeal.

Jennifer also suffered spinal trauma but experienced no paralysis. She also had numerous injuries and was in great pain. Both children suffered from frostbite, mainly to their toes, fingers, and ears. Jeff's torn coat pocket prevented him from keeping his hands warm. It would be a long, cold, scary day and night for the siblings. What goes on in the mind of someone who is very young, injured, and waiting for help in the cold and dark mountains?

The two stated in an interview that they were never really scared during their time on the mountain. Jeff commented that he never thought they "would die out there." They did not realize, he said, that they were in real trouble. Jennifer recalls Jeff talking with her, even though she could not see him. They faded in and out of consciousness during the day and actually slept most of the night. Jeff remembers having "crazy" hallucinations, such as seeing "a cabin nearby with smoke coming out of the chimney and having a cup of coffee on my head."

Jennifer recalled needing to go to the bathroom and wondering how long they would be there.

What a couple of brave children! They never knew the danger they were in. Even more disturbing was that no one else knew the plane had crashed.

When the Shrewsburys' plane did not arrive in Michigan, Carole Shrewsbury reported it overdue. The Michigan Civil Air Patrol set up a command post at Carole's home and began the investigation. First, phone calls were made to airports between Blairsville, Georgia, and Plymouth, Michigan. A call to the airport in Blairsville revealed that the airplane had left there around 9:30 A.M. but had not been heard or seen since. At least they had a starting point. It was labeled as the "last known position."

The Air Force Rescue Coordination Center (AFRCC) issued mission number 4-1460 to the Civil Air Patrol at 5:30 P.M. that day. The Georgia, North Carolina, and Tennessee CAP wings were notified first. During the night plans were made, CAP members packed their gear, and aircraft were readied. People were biting at the bit for the sun to rise.

The next day, Friday, December 2, an air search began with aircraft and ground crews dispatched along the route looking for

The Cessna 172 piloted by Tom Shrewsbury. The plane crashed in bad weather just east of Gregory Bald in December 1977. It landed upside down, killing Tom and his eldest daughter. His two younger children miraculously survived the accident. Courtesy of Kent Higgins.

wreckage and listening for the ELT beacon. All civilian aircraft, by law, must have an operating ELT on board for such an emergency. Although Tom had one in the aircraft, the signal was not being heard because it did not automatically turn on at impact.

Maj. Jack McGivney, a member of the Tennessee Civil Air Patrol, was contacted about flying the mission. He was asked to fly the proposed route of the missing Cessna 172 from Blairsville to Knoxville. He and Capt. Jim Oliver flew to Blairsville on Friday morning and left from there at the same time of day Tom Shrewsbury had left. They calculated the winds that Tom would have experienced (estimated to have been more than sixty miles per hour at that altitude) and plotted a probable flight path.

While flying the route, the two men noticed the mountains towering in front of them and decided to carefully search the peaks. At 10:30 A.M. near Forge Creek Gap, about two miles east of Gregory Bald, the crew spotted something that was in contrast to the terrain. Through the leaf-less tree limbs they could see a white aircraft with a dark stripe but no signs of life. Jeff and Jennifer said that they do not remember seeing or hearing the circling CAP plane (which stayed over the crash site to lead in the helicopter and ground team). McGivney and Oliver's commander, Col. Bill Tallent, remarked later that "they were right on the money."[9] They had found N8821Z.

When McGivney and Oliver reported their find, excitement filled the mission base. The geographic coordinates of the crash site were relayed and plotted by the Civil Air Patrol mission coordinator and then given to the Park Service. The rangers and Robert Lash and his medical team were flown to Gregory Bald in a UH-1 Huey from Fort Campbell, Kentucky. The pilot was Capt. John Dunnavant (who died in a helicopter crash four weeks later on another search-and-rescue mission in the Smokies). After landing on the bald, they had to walk two miles to the air-plane crash. Little did anyone know what was to be found at the scene.

When searchers are called to duty, various thoughts and emotions run through their minds and hearts. Everyone desires a "happy" ending and everyone dreads a fatal scene. House fires, automobile accidents, and murders are examples of incidents where rescuers experience "critical incident stress." Whenever the phone rings to call these professionals to work, critical incident stress is a part of the event. With this particular incident, the searchers and rescuers had only a small indication of who was on the plane. Not many people can prepare themselves to deal with trauma, especially that of a child. The searchers on the Shrewsbury search were preparing themselves for a disappointing scene—the possible death of a father and his young children.

The thought of finding someone alive is the driving force behind most rescue workers. The men and woman who served on this mission would all agree that even though there were fatalities, finding Jennifer and Jeff alive and helping them to safety was probably the icing on the cake of their search-and-rescue careers.

In urban accidents, rescuers speak of a "golden hour," the time between the accident and when that person should be stabilized in a hospital. In the backcountry it is referred to as the "golden day." Most victims of backcountry incidents are fortunate to be stabilized in a day's time. Aircraft crash victims do not have a good chance of surviving the initial impact, let alone surviving with injuries. Poor weather and a desolate location just increase the trauma. As the first twenty-four hours transpire, chances of finding injured persons alive become very slim.

The rangers and medical personnel hiked into the site expecting the worst, but as they approached, Jeff and Lash's eyes met. The team heard the most wonderful sounds—those of children! Jeff was found near the aircraft and was tended to by some rescuers. After a door was removed from the airplane to get to Jennifer, she was carefully removed from the twisted metal airframe. The rescuers realized immediately that the children

Rescuers on Gregory Bald preparing their gear for the Shrewsbury rescue. Courtesy of National Park Service.

had had to deal with the death of their father and sister alone for more than thirty hours. Lash and nurses Jo Ann Cornelius and Peggy Vesser gave immediate attention to the two injured patients. Jennifer remembers someone giving her warm orange juice. "That was the best drink I have ever had in my life," she said. "Whoever gave that to me . . . thanks!"

The mission staff and family members were saddened over the fate of Tom and Laura but were ecstatic about the survival of the younger children. Now another problem existed: How were the rangers and medics going to carefully extricate the two survivors from the mountainside without further injuring them? A carryout would be very painful, would take a very long time, and would involve dozens of people. The temperature was extremely cold and exposure to the elements was a concern for the two patients and all the workers. Lash and the Park Service agreed that the best method of transport would be by a helicopter hoist. "The location of the wreckage just made it impossible for us to get those kids out of there by trail before nightfall," explained Lash in the *Knoxville Journal.*[10]

Rangers and CAP members began to cut trees near the crash site to open a small clearing in the vegetation. A cable was lowered from the rescue Huey into the scene and was connected to the two Stokes litters. The rescuers explained to Jeff and Jennifer what was going to happen, and their soothing voices comforted the kids. Jennifer recalled being mesmerized by the loud engine of the helicopter and the weird feeling of being lifted from the ground into the cabin of the helicopter. "As I watched the rotor blades swing around," she said, "I hoped I stopped before I got there." She put all of her trust in the rescuers.

The helicopter then winched Jeff and Jennifer up from the crash site and flew them to the University of Tennessee Medical Center. The children were seen in the emergency department first, then taken to surgery and transferred to the intensive care unit. Within the week they were put in the same room with their beds pushed together. After the initial treatment Jennifer showed no signs of circulatory, motor, or sensory loss in her extremities. She did not require surgery. "They set my back and put me in a body cast," Jennifer recalled.

Jeff was not so fortunate. He could not move his legs and had sensory deprivation below his waist. The two were also treated for frostbite on their feet and fingers. Jeff's back required a reduction and a bone graft to strengthen his bones. The fusion was expected to provide hope that one day he might walk again. Edwin Schaumburg, an orthopedic surgeon at UT Hospital (who, by the way, is still practicing medicine), operated on him. "Lots of people are walking around with fusions," stated a hopeful Lash.[11]

While at UT Hospital the children and family members were overwhelmed by the kindness of people from East Tennessee. Clara Stevenson, Carole's mother, stated, "You hear so much these days about people not caring, but they do care. One of the girls at the hospital did my laundry."[12] The family was swamped with two hundred get-well cards and lots of gifts. They were especially impressed with and thankful for all the searchers, rescuers, and hospital staff.

After the joyful task of rescuing the children had ended, the sadness of removing Tom and Laura's bodies began. Later in the day the rescuers carried the father and daughter from the scene. Loved ones could now begin to try to put their lives back together.

A representative of the AAA Flying Club in Detroit arrived in Cades Cove on December 11 to authorize the salvage of the crashed aircraft. John Gilbert of Executive Helicopters was hired to remove the wreckage. He used a Hughes 500C to first remove the engine and then the airframe. Both were placed on a truck and trailer in Cades Cove. There is nothing remaining today at the scene.

On December 17 Jeff and Jennifer were well enough to leave Knoxville to continue the trip they had begun sixteen days earlier. Jennifer received additional treatment in Ann Arbor and soon returned to school as a fourth grader at Isbister Elementary School. She had to wear her bathing suit–shaped body cast until February and a back brace through March. Jeff went through more surgery to correct problems with his feet, a skin graft, and other treatments to restore his health. He was able to return to sixth grade at Pioneer Middle School in April.

The two children had a lot of adjusting to do. Jeff, confined to a wheelchair, had to change his entire life-style. He had to learn again how to do simple things such as dress himself and take baths. He was no longer able to play football, baseball, soccer, or basketball. "I've been very impressed with the way he's handled himself through all of this," said Mrs. Carole Shrewsbury a year after the crash. Jeff said, "I have no dreams or nightmares about the accident. I'm just happy to be alive."[13] In our recent interview with Jeff he mentioned that he did not have a lot of psychological problems until a couple of years after the accident, and most of that was centered around things he would have had to deal with anyway as an adolescent. Jennifer suffered no paralysis and adjusted well. She told us that this whole ordeal has made her a better person.

Meanwhile, the Knoxville community was proud of its "heroes." Maj. Jim Oliver was recognized by the Civil Air Patrol and several organizations for his part in the search. The Great Smoky Mountain Council of the Boy Scouts of America, an organization in which he had invested much of himself, gave Capt. McGivney the Medal of Merit. The citation read, "Mr. McGivney was instrumental in pinpointing the location of the wreck, a feat similar to locating a needle in a haystack, and thus led rescuers to the scene in time to save the two children's lives. Capt. McGivney's skill and concern reflected much credit upon him and were in Scouting's best traditions."[14]

Lash and his team were recognized, as were the rangers and the other volunteers. Their greatest award, however, came in the form of Jeff and Jennifer's smiling faces, and in the knowledge that the two would live long, happy lives. "I know I owe a lot of people letters," said Carole Shrewsbury. "It is unbelievable how great Knoxville and East Tennesseans have been to us."[15]

What are they up to now? Where do they live? What has happened in their lives since 1977? Many people have asked us about Jeff and Jennifer, and after an interview in February 2000, we now know the rest of their stories.

Jennifer, who was eight at the time of the crash, is now thirty-two years old and lives near Charlotte, North Carolina. Her mom married Bill Mathers in 1980, and the family moved to Charlotte the following year. She graduated from South Mecklenburg High School in 1987 near the top of her class and graduated from Elon College with a bachelor's degree in economics in 1990. In 1996 she married Ben Adelman, and in May 1999 she and Ben welcomed their daughter Hannah into the world. Since then, Jennifer has elected to be a stay-at-home mom after working in the mortgage banking industry for a number of years. She is a very kind person with a contagious personality. When asked about future plans, she indicated that her main objective was to spend a lot of time with her husband and baby. She still does not understand why so much "hype" surrounds the crash. "I am just an ordinary person who had an accident," she said. Jennifer, you are an *extraordinary* person!

Being ten years old at the time of the crash, Jeff is now thirty-four, and he too lives in Charlotte. Jeff graduated from South Mecklenburg High School in 1985, then attended the University of South Carolina at Columbia. In 1989 he earned a bachelor's degree in journalism and had aspirations to become a sports writer for a newspaper. During his senior year he became editor of his college newspaper. His career has taken him to Augusta, Beaufort, and Columbia working at news companies. He is currently working on his senior master's thesis in journalism. He is employed by an Internet company in marketing and would some day like to earn a doctorate in teaching and journalism. Despite his back injury, Jeff is able to compete in distance wheeling, tennis, basketball, and other track and field events in his wheelchair. The chair has not stopped him from enjoying life, it has only made him adjust to doing things differently. He has experienced half a dozen surgeries and more hospital stays due to the injuries in the crash.

Both Jennifer and Jeff say their lives are "normal." When people find out about their accident, they often become very sympathetic, but the two survivors shrug it off. "When you are on a journey, you take small steps and celebrate how far you came," Jeff said. "This is the process for life. It's a never-ending process of how I . . . all of us . . . live. You just do it. I do not feel different after the crash. The most traumatic part was for the people who have to wait at home by the phone, waiting for word. That is the most traumatic thing anyone could go through. That's what our mom had to do . . . wait. I did nothing. I just survived." Jeff, we celebrate with you!

What an incredible story of courage. Although the Smokies claimed two precious lives and another flying machine (which has been completely removed from the mountain), two children beat the odds on December 1, 1977—and every day since.

Parsons Bald Crash Kills Nine

The last time a Smokies rescue worker died while on an aircraft search mission was in 1964, when Frank Shults of the National Park Service suffered a heart attack near Sheep Pen Gap. He was with a team of searchers looking for a Twin Beechcraft that had crashed on the west side of Parsons Bald. In 1978 more rescue workers died on a search-and-rescue mission. In this case a U.S. Army UH-1 Huey helicopter fell to the ground while maneuvering for a rescue near a crashed Cessna 421. In two days nine persons died and four were injured.

On Tuesday night, January 3, the Sevier County Civil Air Patrol was conducting their first meeting of 1978 in Sevierville. The phone rang at their headquarters building; it was the AFRCC at Scott Air Force Base calling. The CAP was asked to immediately begin a search for a suspected downed aircraft. The details were explained, and the unit quickly responded. It was USAF mission number 4-013A, which began at 9:00 P.M. Truett Frazier was the mission coordinator for the CAP.

The search was for a white Cessna 421, Golden Eagle, registration number N41037. It was an eight-seat, twin-engine airplane capable of a cruise speed of 172 knots. On board were five people and a small dog. Piloting the aircraft was Fred Philip, age twenty-seven, who owned a roofing company in Illinois. His parents, Thomas and Elaine Philip, were on board with him. Thomas was the chief officer of the Talisman Development Corporation in Chicago. Also on board were Fred's ten-year-old brother Tim and Fred's girlfriend, Mary Yates, a twenty-two-year-old school teacher. All were residents of Matteson, Illinois.

The plane was en route to Chicago from Fort Lauderdale after a Christmas vacation visit with Thomas and Elaine's daughter Mara and Thomas's mother. On January 3 Fred filed his flight plan, which included a scheduled refueling stop in Knoxville, with the Miami Flight Service Station.

The group departed Florida at 4:00 P.M. on an instrument flight rules flight plan. Near Macon, Georgia, Fred canceled the IFR plan and switched to a VFR, or visual flight rules, plan. On IFR, Fred was flying using his instruments to guide him along the route and was always on radar and talking to an air-route traffic controller. This procedure is similar to a car operating on an interstate system, where the driver stays on a particular prearranged route and is not driving into the path of oncoming vehicles. Pilots usually change from IFR to VFR if the weather is clear, they are familiar with the area, or they want to alter their course to see something special.

Knoxville tower had radar and radio contact with N41037 several miles south of the McGhee Tyson Airport. Just as the tower told the pilot to "proceed for a left turn into the airport," the crash occurred.[16] While on approach to land, at 7:20 P.M., the "blip" that represented the plane on the radar suddenly disappeared. Radio contact was also lost. It was apparent to the air controllers that an accident had occurred in the Smokies.

At 9:00 P.M. the Air Force put the CAP on "mission" status. The Park Service was contacted because the plane appeared to have gone down in the park. A search that would turn out to be disastrous began.

As soon as the various agencies were alerted, they began to assemble and prepare for a search-and-rescue mission. Assistant Chief Ranger Bill Wade was appointed search manager. He established a makeshift command post in a pasture near Sparks Lane in Cades Cove along with a helicopter operations area. Park rangers were soon joined by the Sevier

County CAP, Sevier and Blount County Rescue Squads, the Tennessee Emergency Management Agency (at that time it was referred to as Civil Defense), and members of the Knoxville Fire Department. Other groups were requested to arrive by 6:00 A.M. The CAP dispatched an airplane into the night sky and began to monitor the 121.5 MHz. ELT frequency. Soon after departure from Knoxville, the CAP plane began to track an ELT signal. At 11:30 P.M. the plane homed in on the beacon and circled the area where the signal was the loudest. The location was narrowed to the western edge of the park, just southwest of Parsons Bald. In the darkness, the CAP team could not make visual contact with the wreckage but had a very good coordinate of an intermittent ELT signal.

At 11:55 P.M. fourteen vehicles were stationed in the field off of Sparks Lane to illuminate a landing zone for an oncoming fleet of helicopters. A Tennessee Army National Guard fuel truck arrived and positioned itself. By 12:16 A.M. two U.S. Army Hueys from Fort Campbell, one

Fred Philip's Cessna 421 Golden Eagle. It was during the search for this Cessna in January 1978 that a number of rescue workers were killed and injured. Courtesy of National Park Service.

Tennessee Civil Defense (CD) Huey from Nashville, and one city of Knoxville Bell Jet Ranger had landed safely at Cades Cove. With the information plotted from the CAP aircraft, Capt. John Dunnavant flew his Huey and crew to the coordinates. It was Captain Dunnavant and crew who had rescued the Jeff and Jennifer Shrewsbury a month earlier. Their mission was to go to the coordinates and illuminate the mountainside with the aircraft's searchlight to locate the missing aircraft.

In the Civil Defense Huey were state CD director Jerry McFarland, Robert Lash, and Ranger Kent Higgins. Their job was to locate the crashed aircraft and, if possible, land on Parsons Bald and hike to the site. Until 2:30 A.M. the CAP airplane and the two helicopters continued their air search while ground teams were forming and getting their briefings. By 3:30 A.M. it was decided to suspend the search until daylight because none of the aircraft reported seeing the missing Cessna. The temperature dropped to six degrees, so the command post was moved into the Cades Cove Maintenance Building.

Although the air search was suspended at 3:30 A.M., the CAP and Park Service were confident of the coordinates of the crash site. They had a radar tracking readout of the plane's flight path, which ended where the CAP had picked up the ELT signal. Plans were made to continue the search at sunrise, to determine from the air the best way to lead rescuers into the crash site, determine team composition, plan for a possible rescue of injured patients, and prepare for fatalities.

Arriving at the command post before the morning operation began were three additional doctors and six nurses along with more emergency medical technicians and rescue squad members. As the day progressed, more than two hundred individuals had gathered for the search.

The few hours of waiting for the sunrise weighed heavily on the searchers. They had on their minds the Shrewsbury children who were found alive after spending a cold night injured only three miles to the east. That incident was barely one month old. What would they find at this Cessna?

At 7:00 A.M. the Cove once again turned into a busy place. The crews were formed and each was given a job to do. The engines were fired up, and all started except for the Jet Ranger. The cold night had pulled the battery power too low. It sat at the command post for the early morning operation (the "Rescue 1" helicopter was precursor to the current-day "Lifestar," which is operated by the University of Tennessee Medical Center, thanks to the interest of the search-and-rescue community, the vision of trauma care, and Lash). One UH-1 would transport searchers to the approximate area of the crash to try to locate the wreckage while another was to go to Parsons Bald and drop off a rescue team that would hike to the site. Lash, McFarland, Higgins, an EMT, and a crew of four were dispatched on the CD helicopter directly to the mountaintop. It was going to scout the area in hopes of getting a close view of the plane crash from tree top level, and, if needed, the crew would rappel into the scene.

On Captain Dunnavant's Huey were Rangers Dave Harbin and Bill Acree and CAP officers Ray Maynard and Phil Thurlow. The aircraft was flying directly to Parsons Bald, where it would land and drop off the crew for their hike to the crash site. At 7:33 A.M., just after sunrise, the two army Hueys and the state Huey departed the staging area to resume the search for the missing Cessna.

As the sun rose over the mountains, the CAP search aircraft was already in the air looking for the downed Cessna. At 7:40 A.M. the CAP aircrew located the wreckage and radioed their report to the Park Service command post. The CAP members reported that the ELT would transmit then stop and start again. This made the Coordinators believe that it was being manually switched on and off. Maybe someone was alive after all!

Rescue workers, including park rangers, the Sevier County CAP, the Sevier and Blount County Rescue Squads, the Tennessee Civil Defense, and members of the Knoxville Fire Department, gathered at this CAP command post in Cades Cove to search for the missing Cessna 421. Courtesy of Civil Air Patrol Archives.

Quickly, the three helicopters, loaded with teams, departed Cades Cove. At approximately 8:00 A.M., the two Hueys also located the Cessna 421 crash site, and each helicopter made a pass over the site. One Huey turned to land at Parsons Bald to unload its crew, and the other Huey, HEL 218, was behind it preparing to approach the bald. The state Huey was observing the other two helicopters and was preparing to lead the ground crews through the woods to the wrecked aircraft. It was decided that rappelling into the scene was too risky; they would drop off the crew on Parsons Bald.

HEL 218 was flying at approximately five hundred feet above the terrain when it developed engine trouble. The two other aircraft did not notice anything out of the ordinary until HEL 218 dropped to the ground. "Jesus, we've got an engine out," cried Capt. Terrance Woolever, one of the pilots of the helicopter.[17] Capt. John Dunnavant and Woolever tried to find a clear place to land but could not make it to Parsons Bald.

Lash, who was flying about one thousand feet above HEL 218, said, "I saw him dip to the right, when I looked back, he was down. It was obviously too steep and too right a turn for it not to be in trouble." Lash was looking out the left window of the helicopter when he saw HEL 218 make a sudden U-turn and disappear into the woods below. The helicopter sunk into the treetops, and the rotors began to slice limbs and branches. It stalled, hit a large tree, flipped over, and dropped hard to the open forest floor. "It was hovering and then I looked away and didn't see it actually start down," stated a crew member of the other UH-1. "When I saw it again, it was going into the trees. It just went down. I do not know what happened."[18]

Christopher Wyman, an army paramedic on the helicopter that crashed, described the scene to a *Knoxville Journal* reporter: "Capt. Dunnavant took over the controls and got out about four 'maydays' before we hit. I went to the back of the bird and told two of the guys to get into the 'hellholes.' Then I hooked my monkey suit to one of the rings on the side of the chopper and braced myself for the impact. Next time I looked down, the trees were coming right up at us. A tree with a V-shaped limb grabbed the rotors and stripped it off the bird."[19]

According to many reports and an interview with Ranger Kent Higgins (December 2000), the helicopter was flying about five hundred feet and moving up the drainage toward Gregory Bald with Parsons Bald on the left. As the aircraft gained altitude, the crew heard a loud "pop" and the engine lost lift, although it was still operating. The pilot made a sharp U-turn to the left so as to glide down the mountain, but the heavy aircraft quickly became tangled in the trees.

Everyone must have known that at that point the helicopter was going to crash. In the few seconds between the "pop" and the impact, the helicopter's crew chief, Sgt. Floyd Smith, yelled for everyone to assume a crash position. Dunnavant broadcasted "Mayday, Mayday," the men braced themselves and tightened their seatbelts, and Sgt. Thurlow gave Lt. Col. Maynard the "thumbs-up" sign. Then the ground came up very fast as the aircraft lost its ability to glide.

They heard the rotor blades hit the trees as the pilot raised the nose of the Huey to put the tail into the trees first and reduce their speed and impact. The next two or three seconds were a blur of leaves, branches, metal, glass, and other debris. As the large helicopter grinded, ripped, and fell to the ground, it turned onto its top and with an abrupt halt came to rest inverted, its nose buried somewhat in the ground. After the initial impact, the occupants were disoriented, confused, and in a great deal of pain. To make matters worse, the jet engine was still running, so the scene was also very loud.

As the Huey lay upside down near a rhododendron thicket, the state helicopter hovered over the site to look for signs of life. From one hundred feet off the ground it did not look like anyone was stirring. The command post was contacted, and through the broken radio traffic and confusion the incident commander realized that he had a major disaster on his hands. On everyone's mind was the well-being of their fellow searchers. "Is everyone okay?" "Do we know if they all survived?" The searchers, the news media, and bystanders all felt great concern and sadness. Now their attention turned to the occupants of the rescue helicopter.

The other UH-1 flew on to Parsons Bald, which was a little over one mile from the crash site. The state Huey followed and also landed. Some of the crew were dropped off and literally ran down the trail and through the forest toward the downed helicopter.

In the meantime, survivors of the crashed Huey began to move around in the compacted airframe. Dazed but conscious, four out of eight crew members called to each other with moans and cries for help. Sgt. Christopher Wyman and Sgt. Phil Thurlow lived. The two park rangers, Bill Acree and David Harbin, also emerged alive.

U.S. Army helicopter pilot Capt. John Dunnavant, age twenty-six, army copilot Capt. Terrance Woolever, age thirty-one, army crew chief Sgt. Floyd Smith, age twenty-seven, and Lt. Col. Ray Maynard, age sixty-two, of the Tennessee CAP occupied the four forward seats in the helicopter and were killed instantly.

Once again the crew on the state helicopter prepared to rappel into the forest, but the trees and underbrush, which were very thick, created an unsafe condition. Instead, it was decided that army paramedic Richard Collier on board the other army Huey would be lowered into the scene with a jungle penetrator. When that decision was made, the state helicopter flew to Parsons Bald, where the crew disembarked and ran toward HEL 218.

Two other search personnel hiked to Parsons Bald to assist in the search for the Cessna 421. They were met by Ranger Higgins, and they hurried down the trail to check for survivors.

Cosby Subdistrict ranger Bill Acree, age thirty-three, seemed to be the less dazed, even though his injuries were more severe and more extensive. After the crash he was the first to react. He realized the helicopter engine was still running and that there was danger of a fire or explosion. Rangers Acree and Dave Harbin talked to each other to determine each other's injuries. Harbin had been cushioned somewhat by Acree's body during impact.

The army UH-1 helicopter that crashed near Parsons Bald in the attempt to rescue the occupants of Fred Philip's Cessna 421. Photo by Dwight McCarter.

Acree knew that his lower right leg was fractured because his foot was pointed the wrong way. He also knew his right collarbone was fractured because he could feel the ends grating together as he tried to move. He would soon find out that he also had fractured ribs and a punctured lung.

In order to escape fire or an explosion the survivors knew they had to extricate themselves immediately from the crumpled wreckage. Acree found that he was the first one who needed to get out, as he was blocking the only clear way out of the cabin. To complicate matters, Wyman's foot was in his face. He asked Wyman to move his leg. He could not; his right femur was broken. He was in indescribable pain. Acree reminded him of their predicament and told him that he would *have* to move it! Wyman, with a great groan of pain and effort, moved his now swollen leg out of the way, and Acree began his excruciating crawl between the support strut and the door. He crawled through the forward broken window in the side door and continued dragging himself away from the helicopter.

Next came Abrams Creek ranger Dave Harbin. He was the least injured of the survivors, but his injuries were very painful and limited his mobility. He had incurred a fractured rib, lung laceration, torn ligaments and dislocation of his right shoulder, torn muscles, a chipped bone in his right elbow, and numerous bruises and cuts. Harbin worked his way past the support strut where Acree had so much trouble, then assisted Wyman out of the broken window in the side door as well. Wyman instructed Harbin how to shut off the engine, however, he could not find the fuel shut-off valve among all the levers and switches in the crashed cockpit. Ranger Harbin then started splinting Wyman's upper leg. Once the leg was somewhat secure, the two crawled up the slope above the helicopter to safety.

Civil Air Patrol liaison officer Sgt. Phillip Thurlow, age thirty-one, had no trouble getting out of the other side of the wreckage because his side door had been ripped off during the crash. He was dazed and had suffered injured lungs, five fractured ribs, a fractured collarbone, a head injury, and multiple cuts and bruises. Even with his injuries he tried to help Harbin move Wyman away from the wreckage. Do not forget that during all this time the jet engine was still very loud and hot. Harbin returned to the wreckage and attempted to drag Acree farther from danger. Harbin found there was too much pain and he had no strength left in his arms. He was unable to help his friend. Acree was in such great pain that he did not want to be moved anyway. Acree knew that there was nothing anyone could do for him without equipment and manpower so he sent Harbin back to attend to Wyman, even though he was much too close to the danger of fire.

About that time, the other army helicopter had prepared itself for the task of lowering paramedic Collier to the scene by way of a jungle penetrator. On the way through the thick trees, several limbs stuck and hit the rescuer. Near the end of the operation, when he was about ten feet off the ground, the cable dropped him to the ground very quickly. He became an injured rescuer. His back was hurting a great deal, but he knew he had to complete his mission. Even though he and Harbin were both injured, they returned to the wreckage and worked Acree onto a broken stretcher that was on board the crashed helicopter. The two men dragged the stretcher up a slope as far as they could, hoping that they would be out of harm's way.

Once everyone was positioned in as safe of a place as possible, Collier went around to each man and assessed the extent of his injuries. First he splinted Wyman's broken bones and began to treat him for shock. He then gave immediate help to the rest of the men and tried to develop a care plan. At this time he had no idea who or what help was on its way. Harbin located Acree's handheld radio and tried to call for help. No one responded. He walked farther up the side of the mountain until he could make radio contact with the command post. He proceeded to detail the grim situation: four dead and four injured—five counting Collier.

Soon after, Lash and the civilian paramedic arrived on the scene. They, too, began their physical exams of the men and formed a plan. With limited supplies on hand, Acree received some pain medication and refused IV fluids, insisting that Wyman receive them instead. At this time Wyman was in a serious situation. The four survivors of the helicopter crash were stabilized and prepared for evacuation. Medical supplies, Stokes litters, and other equipment were lowered by cable to the scene from the other helicopter. A chain saw sang through several trees to prepare an area to winch out the injured men.

In the midst of the stress, pain, sadness, unbelief and confusion, Ranger Higgins and two volunteers arrived at the crash site of the Cessna 421. The time was 9:00 A.M. They found a trail of aircraft parts and scattered suitcase articles strewn through the trees. The aircraft was fairly well intact, although the front and top of the cockpit area was crushed. There was considerable evidence of a terrific high-speed impact and no question remained that the occupants had been killed instantly. At 9:09 A.M. Higgins radioed the command post and informed the staff that no one survived the plane crash.

Once a preliminary investigation of the scene was completed, Higgins departed for the helicopter crash and left the two volunteers to guard the Cessna. He and another doctor met at the top of the ridge at a trail and carried some requested equipment down the slope to Lash.

As the news spread about the original search and the new rescue, the operation began to experience interference from non-official aircraft. Sightseers and the news media began to fly over the area to get a look at the two crashes and the rescue. The Park Service and CAP requested that the area be off limits to all but official aircraft, and eventually the request was honored. The airspace was restricted below ten thousand feet and within a ten-mile radius of Parsons Bald.

At about 11:30 A.M., Ranger Acree, the most injured, was winched out and taken to Cades Cove, where he was loaded onto the now-operational Jet Ranger helicopter and airlifted to University of Tennessee Hospital. At about noon another of the injured was brought to the Cove and transferred to UT Medical Center. The third patient was winched out at about 1:00 P.M., and at 2:30 the last patient was brought to Cades Cove and transferred to the UT Medical Center. At last all four survivors had been plucked from the deadly scene. All the while the crashed UH-1's engine was still on, and its lights flashed until the fuel supply finally exhausted. The woods became silent.

The death of firefighters, police officers, ambulance workers, and other emergency personnel is traumatic not only for the their relatives but also for fellow laborers. In this situation, there was no way for rescue workers to prepare for a casualty of one of their own. Prior to the winch rescue, Faye Maynard, Ray's wife, heard about the accident in the mountains, and when her husband did not call her as promised, she became worried. Faye's son-in-law drove her to Cades Cove to talk with Truett Frazier of the CAP to see if he had heard from her husband. At the time, communications were marginal between the command post and the scene, so there was no way for anyone to know who had survived or died in the crash.

When the last survivor was brought to the landing zone in Cades Cove, everyone put two and two together and realized who the fallen comrades were. The CAP members at the headquarters determined that Ray had died, and Frazier informed Faye of his death. Everyone was in total shock. *Why did this happen? Are you sure there are no other survivors?*

The crash of the Huey took four lives. Lt. Col. Ray Maynard of the Tennessee Civil Air Patrol was sixty-two years old. He was a World War II paratrooper and pilot. Maynard had been a CAP member for sixteen years and was the logistics officer for the wing. He had been very active in emergency services in the CAP and was always ready to go on a search at a moment's

Chinook hovering over crashed Huey. This is a photo taken from a helicopter of a helicopter during a recovery for victims of a helicopter crash. Photo by Dr. Robert Lash, in the possession of Dwight McCarter.

notice. He was survived by his wife, four daughters, ten grandchildren, five sisters, and two brothers. "I have never seen a more dedicated and loyal man than Ray Maynard," stated Col. Bill Tallent, the CAP's wing commander.[20]

Also killed in the crash were the pilot, Capt. John Dunnavant, age twenty-six, of Lynnville, Tennessee, Capt. Terrance Woolever, age thirty-one, of Mount Pleasant, Michigan who was the division's surgeon, and Sgt. Floyd Smith, age twenty-seven, of Madison, Alabama. He was the helicopter's crew chief. These three were attached to a medical battalion from Fort Campbell, Kentucky. Park Service rangers enjoyed working with this crew, and they learned a great deal from one another.

The day had ended with a total of nine people dead and four injured. Five were actually injured, if you add the paramedic who was injured after falling through the trees while in the jungle penetrator. Once the survivors were stabilized at UT Hospital, several things began to happen at the mission base. The CAP, army, Park Service, and other rescue personnel were mourning the loss of four friends, the two crash sites were being readied for Thursday investigations, and nine bodies were being guarded by rangers and friends.

Ranger Bill Acree, the most severely injured survivor in the crash of the army UH-1 helicopter, was lifted to safety in a Stokes litter from the deadly scene of the crash. Courtesy of Kent Higgins.

The National Park Service scheduled a briefing led by Bill Wade, the assistant chief ranger. In attendance were state Civil Defense director Jerry McFarland and the Civil Air Patrol and various rescue squad representatives. The subject was a discussion regarding the evacuation of the nine bodies and the transporting of FAA and army investigators to the sites. The approximately 240 search personnel rested, ate supper, and collected their thoughts throughout the night.

On Thursday morning, January 5, teams were flown to Parsons Bald for the difficult work that lay ahead. Workers cleared a large area of trees and underbrush near the Cessna 421 and the Huey. The bodies were prepared for transport and moved to these two areas. A twin-engine army Chinook helicopter from Fort Campbell was brought in for the task of airlifting the nine bodies from the two scenes. The three army personnel were airlifted to Fort Campbell, and Ray Maynard along with the five victims of the Cessna 421 crash were taken to UT Hospital by Thursday afternoon.

After all nine bodies had been removed and most of the rescue workers had left the mountain, a crew stayed behind at the Huey and the Cessna 421 to investigate the incidents. By the end of the day on Thursday, the helicopter was pulled out of the mountains by another helicopter and was taken to Sparks Lane. Returning to the site in 1996, Dwight McCarter stated that 100 percent of the aircraft was removed. Not even a small piece of metal or glass remains.

The Cessna 421 was also removed by helicopter shortly after the investigation. Some of its parts dropped from the cargo net, and in 1999 a piece was located by a Park Service Resource Management specialist near Parsons Branch Road. All that remains at both sites today are the horrible memories of death and suffering. The mountains have even healed from the marks of chain saws that cut two large openings in the trees to make the recovery.

It was a disastrous search-and-rescue mission that no one would soon forget. It sent shock waves throughout all of the search-and-rescue community. Let it never happen again.

Missed It by about Fifty Feet

A year and one month after the terrible tragedy on Parsons Bald, another aircraft incident occurred in the park. This time, the lone occupant of a Piper Tri-Pacer lived through a crash near Silers Bald.

Bill Bruning, age thirty-three, of Jonesboro, Georgia, had had his pilot license for only five months. He worked for the Bendix Corporation as a sales representative, and on Monday, February 12, 1979, he was on a flight to Knoxville from Jonesboro (just south of Atlanta) when he crashed in the snow-covered mountains. Bruning had an adequate altitude for flying over the Smokies but he developed an icing condition at 2:10 P.M. He was south of the Smokies and was talking to the Knoxville tower as he began to fly through clouds that were freezing to his aircraft. The additional weight and drag of the ice combined with the lack of additional power required to keep the plane aloft put Bill in a dangerous predicament.

The Piper battled for thirty minutes to stay aloft. "It took about two seconds for the windshield to ice. Then I started to lose altitude," Bill recalled. "I would hit a warm pocket, climb, then it would ice up again." He had to apply carburetor heat, hope that the control surfaces were not hampered by ice build-up, and pray that he could make it over the mountains to descend into Knoxville. What a job! "I could have turned around at the onset and gone back," he said. "But I figured at that location and altitude I could have cleared the ridge. I only missed it by about 50 feet."[21]

At 2:40 P.M. Bill announced that he was going down. He said he was at fifty-five hundred feet and 123 degrees off the Knoxville VOR navigational beacon. He prepared for the inevitable and crashed his plane into the Smokies. Remarkably, the aluminum frame, covered in taunt fabric, was not destroyed. If he had been traveling very fast and hit a lot of trees he would not have been so fortunate. The aircraft missed several large-diameter trees, but the wings caught two trees, slowing his speed. The plane came to a rest on a five-foot-deep snowdrift that cushioned his impact.

Bill had suffered only minor facial lacerations but was not prepared for a stay in the cold, wintry mountains of North Carolina. He had great presence of mind, however, and did not panic. He knew his plane was equipped with an ELT, so he crawled into the back of the small plane to make sure it was on. Bill's crash had not destroyed the airplane's battery, much to his amazement. He realized that his aircraft radio worked, and by chance, he keyed the transmitter button and it transmitted. However, the crash through the trees broke off the antenna so he waded in the snow and created a makeshift antenna.

Bill switched the radio to the McGhee Tyson approach frequency, exclaimed, "Mayday! Mayday!" and, to his comfort, a controller answered him. He explained his predicament and informed the controller that he was physically all right but needed help.[22]

The tower quickly made the determination that Bruning was in fact on the ground and needed assistance. The incident was reported to the National Park Service and Civil Air Patrol. The Tennessee Air National Guard was alerted at 3:30 P.M. and immediately launched two UH-1s, which were airborne at 3:35. The CAP began to alert their flight and coordination crews, and the Park Service chose personnel to manage the mission. The Blount County Rescue Squad and Sheriff's Department gave their availability report.

Robert Lash, the well-known FAA medical examiner and founder of UT Hospital's Aeromedical Service, was transported to the search area and determined that there was no way to spot the small aircraft amid the snow-covered trees without assistance. At 4:34 P.M. he requested that the CAP send a plane immediately to Clingmans Dome to do a search for the ELT signal.

The AFRCC, supervised by Major Hyman, opened mission number 4-0139 at 4:47 P.M. at the CAP and Knoxville tower's request. Maj. Dennis Sparks of Maryville was appointed mission coordinator, and the search mission officially began. They knew that the single engine Piper PA-22 was red, white, and blue and displayed N3649Z as its tail number. They knew one person was on board. The supervisor at McGhee Tyson said the last contact with the plane before it went down was around three miles west of Clingmans Dome on the 123-degree radial of the Knoxville VOR navigational beacon.

At 5:00 P.M. McGhee Tyson was again talking with the missing pilot via the aircraft radio. He was told that help was on the way. In fact, the CAP Cessna 182, N2911F, was dispatched from Downtown Airport in Knoxville at 5:08 P.M. to track the ELT. The thirty-mile flight took about twenty minutes, and the aircrew (Sparks, Bob Davis and Tim Berry) was able to home in on the beacon. At 5:50 (forty-two minutes into the search) the CAP aircraft located the crash site at 30.6 miles and 140 degrees off the Knoxville VOR.

Within a few moments of being airborne the CAP plane was not only over the crash site but also began to have the same weather problems Bill had experienced. In fact, Sparks indicated that "within two minutes we had up to ¾ of an inch of ice [built up on the aircraft]. Some of it began blowing off and we could hear it hitting our tail surfaces. We were losing altitude fast, so we had to get out of there."[23]

Once they pinpointed the ELT signal, established the coordinates of the crash site, and spoke with the survivor of the crash, they switched to an IFR clearance at 6:04 P.M. They landed safely at the airport in Sevierville at 6:36 P.M. to "defrost" the plane. They were unable to visually spot the wreckage but were certain of the location because of the ELT signal. Due to darkness and freezing temperatures, the UH-1 also returned to the base.

The coordinates were reported to the command center at park headquarters. Bill Wade, the incident commander, plotted the site to be east of Silers Bald and just west of Double Spring Gap Shelter. That put the site a few hundred feet inside North Carolina and very near the Appalachian Trail. If Bruning had known exactly where he was at the time of the crash, he could have walked less than a mile to the backcountry shelter and been met by rangers later in the night, but he did the best thing by staying in the fuselage of the plane.

Lash spoke with Bill at 11:00 P.M. and periodically throughout the night. Bruning was instructed to literally tear the inside of his airplane apart and stuff anything he could find into his clothes for insulation. He put on an extra set of clothes, wrapped himself in plastic bags, pulled an extra shirt over his head, and used air charts and the plane's interior lining to provide insulation. He made himself stay awake during the frigid night, cocooned in the small fuselage of the plane. His companion was the whistling wind and occasional radio contacts with the tower.

While the air search was on, ground teams were preparing for a long, cold night. The CAP put a small team together, but it was decided by both organizations to only insert the Park Service team during the night. The CAP brought their ELT beacon locator to park headquarters at 6:13 P.M. and gave the rangers a short course on its use. The unit was an old orange "B-Line" receiver that was "state-of-the-art" equipment in 1979. At 8:00 P.M. the rangers began their trek up the frozen Newfound Gap Road toward the Clingmans Dome Parking Area.

Things were going well for the Park Service ground team as they slowly followed a snowplow up the mountain. About half way up the Clingmans Dome Road the all-terrain vehicle in which they were riding bogged down in the snowdrifts. The team then had to don snow shoes and carry their equipment on their backs for the next three and a half miles. Their walk began at 10:00 P.M. "The wind was blowing strongly and when you'd sweat, the sweat would freeze on the outside of your parka," said Ranger Dwight McCarter. "I had ice all over my beard and my hair."[24]

At midnight the rangers tried to hear the ELT but were unable to get a good, strong signal. This was occurring as the pilot was making his radio contact with the tower in Knoxville. By 2:00 A.M. another radio contact was made, and the rangers tried to see the airplane's strobe light in the snowy, cloudy darkness or hear the ELT. The searchers made their way to the rest room at the Dome parking area and were able to sleep for a couple of hours. Fatigue from the day's hike, the stress of not being able to find the plane, and the extreme cold mandated the break. The searchers knew that Bill was all right, and if they pushed themselves harder, there could be additional casualties.

Bill spoke with the tower again at 3:00 A.M., 5:00 A.M. and at 5:55 A.M. He was still doing fine but reported that he was getting cold. His feet were becoming frostbitten; however, he maintained a positive attitude throughout the ordeal.

At Newfound Gap, the Park Service and Tennessee Civil Defense set up a communications staging area early Tuesday morning after plowing through the deep mountain snow. Also on hand were the news media, CAP, rescue squads, and other officials. The weather looked promising and everyone was waiting for the sun to rise in order to get aircraft in the area.

Finally it was 6:00 A.M. That was when the air national guard was going to have a briefing and attempt to fly a UH-1 as close to Bill as possible. The landing zone was going to be Silers Bald, an open field on top of the mountains that in pre-park days was used as pasture for cattle and sheep. With no trees to be concerned with at the bald, the UH-1 could easily land there, drop off a medical crew, and wait to see what assistance was needed for Bruning. On board Army Guard 363 was pilot Capt. Larry Shelton, Capt. Danny Norman, Crew Chief Billy Batson, and paramedic Sgt. Billy Clark. Lt. Col. Hayes W. Cathy, commander of the army's Aviation Support Facility, coordinated the efforts of the guard.

At 6:06 A.M. the CAP was ready to launch a Cessna to once again track the ELT, lead the UH-1 to the site, and watch to make sure everything went all right. The last search and rescue involving helicopters in the park, in January 1978, had killed four crew members and injured four others. The CAP plane along with another UH-1 was planning to orbit the area in case another accident occurred.

As the aircraft drew near to the Smokies, a bright sunrise with a clear, blue sky welcomed them. The mountains below were blanketed in snow, and the ELT signal was still transmitting. By 6:45 A.M. the UH-1 and the CAP were over the crash site, and the UH-1 dropped some food, blankets, and clothing to Bruning.

While the Cessna flew overhead, the UH-1 flew to the Clingmans Dome Parking Area and landed. There they picked up the rangers and transported them to Silers Bald at 8:05 A.M. The fatigued rangers who battled the mountain were Terry Darby, Tom Robbins, Bill Cook, Bob Grant, Dwight McCarter and John Batzer. Once the UH-1 landed at Silers Bald, they again put on snowshoes and hiked three-quarters of a mile east on the Appalachian Trail to where they had to go cross-country. As the searchers began to yell, Bruning heard them and they met at 8:20 A.M. They outfitted Bruning with snowshoes and began the walk to Silers Bald nine minutes later.

Searcher Darby stated that the pilot was in "really good spirits" and "was warmer last night than we were."[25] Bill boarded the rescue helicopter at 8:56 A.M. with Ranger Bill Cook, and it lifted off a minute later. By 9:15 Bill Bruning was thawing out at the emergency room at UT Hospital and being treated by Lash and CAP member/nurse Jo Ann Cornelius. During his checkup he stated, "Faith gave me the peace of mind. I wasn't worried about dying." A nurse told him, "You're the first crash victim I've ever treated. . . . All the others were dead."[26] Bruning was lucky to be alive.

Meanwhile a helicopter at 9:45 A.M. picked up the ground crew at Silers Bald, and the CAP aircraft left the scene at 10:20 A.M. Once all the aircraft were on the ground in Knoxville and everyone was home, the AFRCC mission was closed at 12:00 noon on February 13. CAP flew a total of five and a half hours on the search and had thirty-two members activated. The NPS, state Civil Defense, medical teams, and army guard logged in fifty people active on the search and rescue.

Truett Frazier of the state CD noted that "the cooperation has never been better between the National Park Service, the Civil Air Patrol, the Civil Defense and volunteer agencies."[27] In general terms, the search and rescue was a huge success and was a positive boost to the search-and-rescue community.

The Park Service guarded the Piper until the NTSB could do an investigation. The aircraft's engine, interior, instruments, ELT, glass, and fabric were removed. Through the years several persons have looted the plane, and all that remains now is the frame, which is being slowly covered by briars and other undergrowth. The plane is close to the Appalachian Trail on the North Carolina side between Double Spring Gap and Silers Bald but very hard to see until you are within twenty-five feet or so of it.

The 1970s ended on a positive note for search and rescue. The next crash would not happen until July of 1980, and what an interesting incident it would turn out to be.

SIX

The 1980s

Polynesian-Mountain Balloon

In the early evening of Wednesday, July 2, 1980, severe thunderstorms and the possibility of tornadoes were threatening the East Tennessee area, as a hot air balloon was seen flying over Pigeon Forge in a easterly direction. It was used for advertisement and rides for Porpoise Island, a Polynesian tourist attraction just outside Pigeon Forge (the old Porpoise Island property is near the "Track" and Beltz Mall).

Alan Postelnek, twenty-eight, was the balloon's pilot. He was a newcomer to the area from Las Cruces, New Mexico, and flew for Porpoise Island. On this day he was planning a flight in the Pigeon Forge–Gatlinburg area, but the winds that were bringing the storm also took him into the Greenbrier section of the Smokies.

The balloon's crash was not actually a crash in comparison to other incidents in this book. It was more of a forced landing. Postelnek saw the main ridge of the Smokies looming in front of him, but he knew that to gain altitude and cross it meant a long and dangerous attempt. He chose to set the balloon down instead of chancing a flight into North Carolina. "He's a level-headed, experienced balloon pilot," said Peter Rogers, manager of the now-closed tourist attraction. "There's no reason for us to believe that he's hurt. Balloons don't fall rapidly."[1] Search managers termed this a "low urgency" search after weighing all the factors.

The black, yellow, and orange nylon envelope was attached to a gondola that contained the fuel bottles and regulator. Alan was alone in the basket as he made his flight. The aircraft identification number was N563S. Once located, Allen told officials that he ran out of fuel and had tried to find somewhere to land safely. His only fear was being dumped out of the basket should it snag on the top of a tree or overturn on the way through the branches of the thick canopy.

He was last seen by a private airplane from the Sevier-Gatlinburg Airport at about 9:00 P.M. over Greenbrier. The twelve-thousand-dollar balloon was flying low, and it was getting dark in the mountains. The plane turned back just after 9:00 P.M.

During the night, heavy rains fell and high winds whipped through the mountains. Trees were blown down and lightning lit the sky. Postelnek was drenched with rain and was cold. He survived the forced landing and was trying to make it through the night, hoping that someone would find him or that he could find his way out of the mountains in the morning. He had neither food nor adequate clothing.

When Rogers decided that Postelnek was definitely in trouble, he contacted the Park Service and the Sevier County Sheriff's Department. Both organizations tried to look for the missing aircraft from the roads but were unsuccessful. During the night the Park Service requested that the Tennessee Civil Air Patrol be assigned to the search. Lt. Col. Dennis Sparks was notified of the incident and a mission number was issued.

Capt. Gary Green, a well-known ham radio operator and radio technician in Sevierville, was assigned the role of mission coordinator. He operated out of the CAP headquarters at the Sevier-Gatlinburg Airport with his mission staff and aircrews. The AFRCC mission number was 4-814A. The mission was opened at 8:30 A.M. on the third (Thursday morning). By 9:20 the mission staff had been briefed and an aircraft was en route from Knoxville to begin the search.

Capt. Roy Bearden and Capt. Eddie Woodrick flew a Cessna 337 Skymaster from Knoxville into the search area, which was generally the drainage of Big Greenbrier, south of Highway 73 and north of the state lines. Almost as soon as they arrived, at about 10:00 A.M., the large, collapsed balloon was spotted. The pilot was seen walking near the balloon, waving at the search plane. The crash site was located on Bald Top Ridge near the split in the Greenbrier Valley Road.

A helicopter was also in the area, and its crew dropped food, drinks, dry clothes, and a Citizens Band walkie-talkie to Allen. He opened the package and spoke with the helicopter, informing them that he was physically fine but needed help in finding his way out to a road. The helicopter hovered overhead to lead Allen to a small stream. From there he began a journey through creeks and rhododendron. Meanwhile, the CAP was asked to fly over the area while the helicopter was operating in case a problem developed.

At 12:52 P.M. the helicopter and the CAP plane left the area as the missing pilot arrived at the gravel road in Greenbrier with back-country rangers. At 1:05 P.M. the aircraft were on the ground at their respective airfields, Postelnek was eating lunch, and by 1:45 P.M. the mission was closed with a happy ending. The balloon was later removed from the site.

Fatal Flight of the Phantom

Four hundred and fifty miles per hour. That was how fast two U.S. Air Force crewmen were flying on Wednesday, January 4, 1984, when their F-4 Phantom II struck Inadu Knob. They probably never knew what happened.

Ranger Larry Barnett was at home near the Cosby Campground when he heard what "sounded like a sonic boom" at 7:12 P.M. "I felt the shock waves. We heard the jet. It sounded low. Then we thought we (heard) a sonic boom. I told my wife, 'They just broke the sound barrier.'"[2] It was a common sound in the mountain community; military jets fly low and fast all the time. But seconds later he heard and literally felt an explosion. Five miles away was a smoldering aircraft on the side of the 5,930-foot Inadu Knob.

Striking the Smokies literally on the Snake Den Trail just below the intersection with the Appalachian Trail, the aircraft tore off tree tops 150 feet below the summit. At 80 feet below the summit, it hit the ground. Debris was scattered in all directions from the impact zone, creating the largest crash site in the Smokies—almost twenty acres. It can still be seen as one hikes along the Appalachian Trail today on both sides of Inadu Knob.

One of the five RF-4Cs in the air force, this one was considered highly valuable. It had infrared side-viewing radar, a maximum speed of 1,650 miles per hour, and could fly under radar undetected. In Vietnam, the aircraft was used for photo reconnaissance. "It took photographs of the enemy, of possible targets and of the results of bomb strikes," Sgt. Mark Goldstein, the public affairs officer for Shaw Air Force Base, told a *Mountain Press* reporter.[3] Canisters of this type of film were found weeks after the investigation hundreds of feet away from the crash.

The story began at Shaw AFB earlier in the evening. Assigned to the 363d Tactical Fighter Wing at Shaw in Sumpter, South Carolina, the $3.6 million McDonald Douglas Corporation RF-4C reconnaissance jet was on its way home from a twenty-six-minute filming practice mission when the accident occurred. Capt. David F. Greggs, twenty-six, of Montgomery, Alabama, was the ill-fated pilot. He had accumulated 1,326 hours of flight time with 253 hours in a RF-4C jet. Riding as navigator was Capt. Scott A. Miller, thirty-two, of Irving, Texas. Their call sign was "Best 43." They were found dead 350 feet and 650 feet, respectively, from the point of impact.

Flying a predetermined military training route at night, the pilot contacted the radar traffic control in Atlanta at 7:05 P.M. and requested to climb one thousand additional feet. The controllers gave permission for the altitude change, but the jet disappeared from the radar screen as it struck the mountain. Soon after the crash, residents in Cosby saw a red glow on the mountaintop, and after a few minutes clouds covered the mountain. Rain began to fall and the temperatures dropped turning the rain into snow.

While Atlanta was trying to determine if the plane had actually gone down, the dispatch desks at the Sevier and Cocke County Sheriff Departments were flooded with reports from residents. McGhee Tyson Airport began to get dozens of calls that confirmed Atlanta Center's fears: a military jet had crashed in the Smokies.

This is one of the largest pieces of the RF-4U which crashed on a routine training flight and exploded. Photo by Dwight McCarter.

The Air Force Rescue Coordination Center was briefed of the incident, and the Tennessee and North Carolina Civil Air Patrols were put on mission status. Mission number 4-025 was issued and search planning was initiated. The McGhee Tyson Army National Guard Unit was activated and sent a helicopter to the last known position to do a preliminary aerial search. On board was CAP member Ed Cate, who was also a national guard crew member. "Snow was falling so thick up there that you couldn't spot a black dot," Cate said of the search that evening.[4] They also failed to hear an ELT signal on 121.5 or 243.0 MHz. The aerial search was put on hold at 9:00 P.M. due to the heavy snow and darkness. Cosby Ranger Station also began to get phone calls, as did park headquarters in Gatlinburg. The AFRCC informed the dispatcher that more than likely the crash site was in the bounds of the park, and it was determined that along with the air force, the Park Service would assume control of the search operation.

Many residents of the area had similar stories to describe the event. "We heard a low roar like something had gone bad with an engine, then it went ka-boom," said Nina McMahan, who lives near the Cosby Post Office.[5] "It was like a ball of fire. About half the sky seemed to light up," described Sonny Perault of Gatlinburg.[6] Apparently, two residents attempted their own search by hiking into the mountains during the night. A pack was found hanging from a tree, which, combined with tracks left in the snow, threw searchers a curve.

By midnight a barrage of USAF police, medical staff, and commanders had arrived in Cosby. Rangers were assembled and briefed in conjunction with the Civil Air Patrol, sheriff departments, USAF, national guard, and the governor's office through the Tennessee Emergency Management Agency. Plans were established through the late evening as to who would be on what team, what aircraft would be used, communications, airspace restrictions, horse teams, food, finance, and other logistical concerns.

The next morning two ground teams with five CAP members and one ranger each began the ground search. Forty other CAP members assisted with an aerial communications platform, mission base logistics, and other duties with other park staff and the air force. An equestrian search team was also used. After the early morning fog burned off, the national guard helicopter was joined by two CAP aircraft and a Tennessee Highway Patrol helicopter.

During the night nearly six inches of snow had fallen on the higher elevations of the Smokies, covering the scattered wreckage. To make matters worse, the F-4 was painted in camouflage colors. The ground and aircrews were in for a hard task.

CAP units arrived on the scene from Sevier, Blount, Anderson, and Knox Counties. Lt. Col. R. L. "Bud" Maples Jr. coordinated the efforts of the Sevier County team, and Maj. Dennis Faircloth coordinated the Blount County team. As mission coordinator, Lt. Col. Dennis Sparks coordinated the efforts of the Knox County CAP.

The search began early in the morning. Ground teams and the horse unit started their long, cold hikes into the backcountry. Aircrews tried repeatedly to enter the area, but intermittent cloud cover made air searches hazardous. Finally, at midmorning, aircrews were asked to try again. At noon, the energy level of the search base heightened as a helicopter called in a possible sighting. Once the coordinates were plotted, it was determined that the aircraft seen was that of a twin-engine Cessna that had crashed in 1962.

Ranger Mike Sharp was leading a CAP ground team consisting of 2d Lt. Scott Swabe and Cadets Judith Jambor, nineteen, Robert Whiton, seventeen, Dann Carlson, sixteen, and Anthony Rinderer, seventeen. They were hiking the five-mile Snake Den Trail and beginning to smell a heavy odor of kerosene when Ranger Sharp "slipped" on a piece of snow-covered wreckage at 2:01 P.M.[7] He literally slipped and fell onto a piece of the wreckage. The elevation of the impact site was at 5,850 feet. Once the team realized they had found the crash site, radios began buzzing at mission base and everyone had only one question on their minds: Was anyone found alive?

The ground team radioed their position to mission base and the members did a quick survey to find the cockpit and/or the two missing airmen. Much to their disappointment, there was not many large pieces of airplane to be found. Yellow signal flares and colored smoke were activated to signal to the aircrews the exact location of the site. The air force wanted the site secured, so the CAP members roped it off and stood by until other rangers and air force personnel arrived to guard the scene from curiosity seekers and looters.

A Tennessee Highway Patrol helicopter quickly flew to the coordinates with Sevier County Emergency Management Agency's Jeff McCarter on board. Within minutes of the announcement that a ground team had located the crash, the pilot, Mike Dover, and McCarter sighted the crash from the air. From that time local sightseeing aircraft and media helicopters tried to capture a glimpse of the tragedy.

Jeff McCarter of the Sevier County Emergency Management Agency (EMA) stated, "You really could not tell anything had happened from the helicopter" because the snow had covered the undergrowth.[8] Even with the fireball at the time of impact, the weather cooled the crash so thoroughly that snow laid on it during the night.

Other rangers and ground team members were sent into the area, and together they tried to find the missing crew members. "There wasn't much hope going in," said Lt. Col. Bud Maples, commander of the Sevier County CAP squadron. "When those aircraft hit the mountains there's just not much left."[9] He was correct. Days later, when the snow melted, investigators found the two bodies.

Col. Jerry Daniel, vice commander of the 363d Tactical Fighter Wing, began the incident investigation on Friday the sixth. Evidence was gathered and photographs were taken. Up to twenty investigators combed the snow-covered mountaintop, marking and identifying the small pieces of wreckage and the fuselage. A part of the investigation was to determine why the plane was off course. Usually, military training flights fly over Low Gap, but the F-4 was flying five miles to the west.

The investigation revealed the men never knew they were flying too low.[10] The aircraft and scene was thoroughly examined, and there was no evidence of ingestion, in-flight fire, or other mechanical malfunctions. Voice tapes revealed no discussion on the radio transmissions that anything was amiss. It was determined from the radar footage that the plane had not started its requested assent of the additional one thousand feet. It was in straight and level flight. Records showed that in the ninety days prior to the flight there were a few minor problems associated with the plane, but none were seen as "significant" enough to the cause of the crash.[11] To the families of the two men, this was a tragedy with questions that no one can ever answer.

Into the Hands of Scouts

If crashes could be planned, no one could have planned better than Patrick Hughes. Despite his accident, Hughes was a very lucky man because he crashed into the hands of the Boy Scouts of America.

Aircraft N8855B ended the 1980s' aviation incident history on a positive note. The 1980s, a relativity quiet decade for aviation accidents in the national park, had claimed five aircraft and two lives. This particular incident received a lot of press due to the remarkable, quick response for a backcountry search and rescue. Considering that his ELT did not work, that he was not on radar, and that he crashed in the wilds of the Smokies, Hughes was extremely lucky to have received help within minutes. He gave all the credit to the Boy Scouts.

The rented white, beige, and black 1958 model Cessna 172 was carrying a lone occupant on a trip from Luran Airport in Dayton, Ohio to Macon, Georgia, on Tuesday, July 11, 1989. Hughes was a thirty-eight-year-old agricultural technician with the Monsanto Company in Dayton with approximately one hundred hours of flying time. He was flying the Cessna, with its six-cylinder Continental engine, on a trip to see his seventeen-year-old daughter. He departed Dayton at about 8:00 A.M. on the eleventh and landed at Knoxville's Downtown Island Airport due to poor weather. While on the ground, he refueled and checked on the weather from Knoxville to Macon. He departed Knoxville for a direct flight to Macon but ended up sitting upside down in the Smokies a few minutes later.

As he was flying south, he noticed that the highest peaks were covered by clouds and that above the mountains were cumulus clouds building their energy. Trying to find a hole in the layer of clouds, he noticed a gap in a mountain that he estimated he could fly through without getting into trouble. Quickly, the clouds closed in on the pilot and without warning the mountains popped up to greet the aircraft. "I was flying through a mountain pass, and before I could get through, clouds rolled in and blocked my way," said Hughes. "I made a U-turn to try to find another route. Before I could complete the turn I hit the top of a tall tree and crashed."[12]

Hughes saw the impending danger and performed an evasive maneuver, trying to save himself and the plane. He banked and tried to turn away from the ridge, but it was too late. The aircraft's landing gear and propeller struck treetops, and for a few quick seconds the plane tore into the trees, creating a 100 foot swath of broken branches. The plane suddenly caught the top of a large tree and nosed straight down; it rolled to the right, flipped onto its top, and dropped through the canopy of hardwood trees, coming to a rest upside down. The aircraft's noisy crash sequence ceased and the forest was quiet again, except for the moaning of an injured pilot deep in the backcountry.

The plane was east of Sams Gap and west of Derrick Knob Shelter. It was only a few hundred feet north of the trail, but on a heavily wooded and steep hillside. The plane was not badly damaged except for the engine compartment. The frame and aluminum body was only slightly wrinkled. The problem was that the ELT was not functioning. It was in the "on" position, but investigators later discovered that the battery was dead (even though the expiration date was May 1991).[13] Hughes also was not on radar "flight following" from McGhee Tyson, so no one knew he had crashed.

Hughes was not as seriously injured as he could have been. Imagine hitting a telephone pole at one hundred miles per hour in a car! He had suffered a broken leg, a few cuts, bruises, and cracked ribs. The initial impact knocked him unconscious. For a few moments he was unaware of his surroundings and what had occurred. Then his rescuers arrived on the scene. When he regained consciousness, he realized that he had fallen "into the middle of some Boy Scouts."[14]

It just so happened that a Boy Scout troop was hiking in the area and actually heard the plane bore into the mountainside. Scout Troop 1519 of Alexandria, Virginia, was on a seventy-six-mile hike in the Smokies and was in the vicinity when they heard the crash. The previous night they had stayed at Spence Field and were continuing their hike. The party included two adult leaders and five scouts. Cooper Wright and Frank LaPierre were leading Carroll Connelley, Bobby Toomer, Shanon Mettlen, Erik Laaken, and Scott Miller (an Eagle Scout) on the trek.

The scouts were on the second day of the trip and had just passed Derrick Knob.

In July 1989 Patrick Hughes crashed his Cessna 172 on a heavily wooded hillside deep in the park's backcountry. The plane nosed straight down, flipped, and finally came to rest upside down. A Boy Scout troop hiking in the area came upon the plane soon after it crashed and rescued Hughes, who was not seriously injured. Courtesy of National Park Service.

They were backpacking west in two small groups toward Cades Cove at 1:00 P.M. After hearing the noise they all stopped. "It sounded like a tractor trailer when we first heard it" said one of the scouts. When they realized there were no roads in the area, they assumed an airplane had crashed. They dropped their packs and fought their way down the steep forty-degree slope in search of an airplane. The vegetation was thick, and because none of the scouts saw or smelled smoke, they were considering calling off their search. But someone saw freshly broken branches and something white that did not seem to fit into the surroundings. "We were very fortunate to have found it. It was very hard to find," stated Wright.[15] Not knowing what they were about to see, the adults took control of the situation, and together the troop came upon the wreckage.

At first, the scene did not look promising. The odor of aircraft fuel was apparent and the sight was silent and solemn. The two leaders held the boys back and slowly approached the aircraft. Crawling on the underside of a wing, the men heard fuel spilling. The two opened the door of the plane and found Hughes still alive but injured and disoriented. He was trying to get out of the fuselage when they opened the door. The men immediately discovered that the cockpit was filled with fumes.

Reaching to the pilot and speaking to him, the men assessed Hughes and decided that moving the pilot from the plane and away from the wreckage would be in his and their best interest. They pulled him out and slid him down the aircraft's wing to the boys, who calmly moved him to a safer area. Scout Scott Miller, who had previous flight experience with his father, climbed aboard the plane and turned off the electric power to prevent a fire from occurring. It was also Scott who thought to take photos of the scene (one was printed in the *Knoxville Journal*).

Once they evaluated the patient, the scouts decided assistance would be required to evacuate Hughes to a hospital. Remembering that a maintenance crew was working at the Derrick Knob Shelter, the leaders sent two of the fastest scouts to go for help. They climbed back to the Appalachian Trail and ran to the shelter. The others remained on the scene assisting with the emergency treatment of the pilot. LaPierre was trained in emergency pre-hospital medicine (a former EMT). He and the others stabilized Hughes's injured leg, kept an eye on his breathing, and kept him warm with their sleeping bags. He was in good hands and had something in common with the rescuers: he too had been a scout.

Upon reaching the shelter, the two scouts explained the situation to Park Service employees. Ronald Huskey contacted park headquarters on his radio, reported the accident, and requested additional assistance. The information was logged in at 1:22 P.M. Word quickly spread to McGhee Tyson Airport, other rangers, the Civil Air Patrol, and the media. Excitement developed quickly because the pilot was alive.

The maintenance crew followed the scouts to the scene and assisted with his treatment. Hughes's concern was for his daughter. He asked that she be contacted and told of the predicament. LaPierre used the park radio to keep the University Medical Center updated as to the pilot's condition. On everyone's mind was getting the injured man out of the backcountry.

Within a few minutes rescue teams at park headquarters were formed to begin a hike into the scene, and an army national guard helicopter was dispatched from Knoxville with a medical crew. On board was Rick Obernesser, ranger and park medic, along with the ANG crew. They picked up Obernesser at Lufty Overlook and flew him to the cleared area near Derrick Knob Shelter, where he departed the helicopter about 3:30 P.M. He joined the scouts, who escorted him to the crash site. Hughes was assessed again by the ranger and was given pain medication.

The clouds that contributed to the crash now began to produce rain. By 4:00 P.M., thunderstorms on the mountain halted the rescue operation. Backup plans were drafted to get Hughes out of the backcountry. Additional personnel and equipment arrived from the Tremont Ranger Station. The Smokies are famous for their "hit and run" thunderstorms. In this case, the rain made the carryout a slippery mess and delayed the departure of the helicopter.

It took approximately two hours to carry Hughes up the slippery and steep mountainside to the Appalachian Trail. By 6:00 P.M. they had him on the trail, and half an hour later the guard helicopter was able to find a break in the storm and lift off. Hughes was flown to the University of Tennessee Medical Center in Knoxville, where he was admitted at 6:47 P.M. (only five and three-quarter hours after the crash). There he was examined and treated for his injuries, which were not life threatening, and was listed in "guarded" condition. Most aviators who arrive at UT Medical Center are not so lucky. "Hughes is a very lucky man to survive," said NPS spokesperson Cheryl Tinsley. "If they hadn't been nearby, there's no telling how long he would have been there."[16]

Meanwhile, on the mountain there was still a great deal of activity. The scouts stayed at Derrick Knob on Tuesday night along with the park employees. A second guard helicopter was able to get into the clearing before sunset and pick up equipment and some personnel, but the scouts stayed behind. Hughes praised the scouts from his hospital room, saying,

"They were life savers. . . . I wish I could get their names so I could personally thank them."[17]

The next morning rangers and investigators hiked to the scene. Walter Stiner from the NTSB, Jim Leeder from the FAA, and Dale Carter from Continental Motors Aircraft Products Division were among the team. The men recreated the incident scenario and discovered that there was no mechanical malfunction before the crash. The investigators spoke with the pilot and examined the physician's reports. The Park Service performed another investigation before the plane was finally turned over to an insurance company.[18] Plans were then made to remove the plane from the park.

The Scouts received accolades from across the region. The persons most proud of the boys, though, were their leaders. "I was real proud of them," said LaPierre. "They were calm. They knew Cooper and I were in charge of the situation, and they did everything that needed to be done. Personally, it was real satisfying to see them react that well in that situation."[19]

The plane remained in the backcountry for eight weeks before it was removed. During that time an undetermined number of hikers located the site by following the path created by the rescuers. Radios, instruments, and engine parts were taken by curious hikers and thieves. If the plane had remained at the site, it would have probably been dismantled and carted out by other souvenir hunters, but a salvage company was hired to lift it out of the park.

On Tuesday, September 5, the "legal dismantling" began. Avemco Insurance Company contracted Dick Plowman from Swainsville, Georgia, to recover the wreckage. His plans were to airlift the Cessna to Dry Valley near Townsend and truck it to Georgia. Prior to the airlift, a crew went to the site and disassembled the plane's major parts. Trees were removed and a harness was put around three units: the wings, the fuselage, and the engine (the heaviest part). Vertiflite, from Maryville, was contracted to do the actual recovery flight. Ironically, a Hughes 500 helicopter was used to pull Patrick Hughes's plane from the scene.

Today all that marks the crash site is an area of broken and crushed trees. The wreckage is gone, but memories remain. In the mind of Patrick Hughes, it is the Boy Scouts who deserve all the credit.

SEVEN

The 1990s

Welch Ridge Skymaster

The first of eight aircraft incidents of the 1990s occurred on Sunday, January 27, 1990. Flying over the Smokies in adverse weather conditions generally puts pilots in grave danger. Fog, clouds, and up-and-down drafts are literal killers for pilots "scud-running" between the tops of the ridges and the bottom of a cloud layer. Barron Ivan Vernon, fifty, of Sylva, North Carolina, was killed when his twin-engine Cessna hit Welch Ridge on a cold, snowy Sunday evening.

Vernon departed Cleveland, Tennessee, on a short VFR flight that was to end at North Carolina's Jackson County Airport near Sylva. He departed around 5:00 p.m. on Sunday afternoon and was to arrive at his destination within an hour and a half. When he did not arrive on time, his family reported him overdue and the FAA began a preliminary investigation.

With such an overdue aircraft situation, the search process usually begins with the FAA. The Flight Service Station (FSS) tries to contact major airports along the route to determine if the pilot made an unscheduled stop. An INREQ, or "information request," is sent to all FSS and FAA towers along the route. After half an hour with no results, the FAA sends out an ALNOT, or an "alert notice." If no one has seen or heard the particular aircraft, the FAA then contacts the Air Force Rescue Coordination Center (AFRCC).

Staffed twenty-four-hours a day every day of the year, the AFRCC conducts almost all inland search-and-rescue missions for missing aircraft. The center is also the main coordinating agency for missing persons and natural disasters on the federal level. The AFRCC is located at the Langley Air Force Base in Virginia and is at the Air Combat Command Headquarters. The staff consists of two personnel during the night and five during the day. At any one time the staff may be coordinating one dozen incidents across the United States.

The normal procedure for opening a missing aircraft incident is simple. A request is made by the AFRCC by the FAA for a missing aircraft search to begin. The AFRCC evaluates the request then determines if there is in fact a need for a search and, if so, contacts the Civil Air Patrol. In this case the North Carolina, Tennessee, South Carolina, and Georgia CAP wings were alerted. Since Vernon had not filed a flight plan, no one knew his route, altitude, or alternate plans. It was a search for a needle in a haystack.

Vernon's flights, according to friends and family, were in no particular pattern. If the weather was good and he had time, he might go sightseeing. Perhaps he had flown south of the Smokies and into the Cherokee National Forest. According to the National Transportation Safety Board's (NTSB) report, the co-owner of the twin Cessna advised Vernon not to attempt the flight over the Smokies.[1] His reasoning was the poor visibility and high terrain. To make matters worse, Vernon was not an instrument-rated pilot, which means he did not have proper training for flying into a low-visibility area.

N2589S was a white and red Cessna 337C Skymaster. It is better known as a "push-pull" aircraft, having one engine in the front of the plane to pull and another engine behind the fuselage to push. The engines are manufactured by Continental and are the IO-360-C versions. This Cessna model has a large fuselage section and a "split-tail" configuration.

Because Vernon was flying without a flight plan and was not communicating with an FAA tower, he was not being followed on radar. In other words, he did not request flight following, nor did he request to be put on an instrument flight plan. As he was not being controlled via radar, his altitude was not being monitored, and it was his altitude which got him in trouble. In all probability he became lost in the mountains with the clouds above him and the ridge tops obscured by clouds. At approximately fifty-four hundred feet, flying in a southwesterly direction, the Cessna 337C began to encounter treetops at the crest of Welch Ridge.

For the next two to three hundred yards the aircraft broke into many pieces. Vernon's plane lost altitude quickly as it was torn by tall trees. It finally nosed into the ground and rolled into a large ball of metal. The plane caught fire as the fuel bladders spilled aviation fuel onto the plowed ground. Barron Vernon most likely died upon impact. The approximate time of impact was determined by the NTSB to have been 6:45 P.M.[2]

According to hikers in the area near the time of the crash, the weather was poor with visibility restricted to about two miles. The cloud layer was solid overcast in Knoxville at five hundred feet above the ground, and the next cloud layer began at five thousand feet above sea level (the plane crashed near the fifty-two-hundred-foot mark). Snow was scattered in the shaded valleys, and the overnight temperatures were in the low to mid-teens.

When Vernon did not land on time at the Jackson County Airport, phone calls were placed and the FAA put the suspected missing plane through its usual protocol. Late in the evening it was determined that the plane was indeed missing and not just overdue from a VFR flight. The AFRCC was notified, and a USAF mission authorization number was issued to the CAP and the state Emergency Management Agency. During the night additional phone calls were made to local sheriff departments along the route and nearby airports and airstrips. CAP ground crews began to patrol roads and high spots, listening for the airplane's ELT. Plans were established to decide who would fly which area, and staff assignments were made.

As the sun began to rise on Monday the twenty-eighth and searchers realized the weather would not immediately cooperate, it became obvious that this would be "one of those" searches. The good news was that the media put the word out quickly and phones began ringing in the CAP headquarters to report leads. One lead came in from a state trooper in South Carolina who reported a low-flying aircraft near Highway 107 on the North Carolina border that matched the time frame. Other calls came from persons near Copperhill, Tennessee.[3] All the leads were checked out from the air and the ground as weather permitted, but none produced positive results.

Three possible routes were considered. One was the "direct" route, which was a 90-mile flight in an almost due east direction. This route would have taken Vernon over very desolate terrain in the Cherokee and Nantahala National Forests. The second route was from Cleveland–Hardwick Field south to the Harris VOR and back up to Sylva. The third route was from Hardwick Field to the Knoxville VOR and south to Sylva. This flight would have been 130 miles over very desolate terrain.

Involved in the search operation by Monday night were the North Carolina, Tennessee, Georgia, and South Carolina CAPs, the Forest Service in North Carolina, local agencies, and private citizens. As weather permitted, CAP aircraft flew the routes, surveying the high terrain and other "hot spots." Other CAP teams flew over the area to monitor for the ELT (which was later found destroyed in the crash).

The search continued from the ground and the sky on Monday. With the relatively short flight distance, many searchers thought the plane would have been found quickly. Areas at either end of the runways at surrounding airports were searched thinking that he may have crashed shy of a runway. Tops of mountains were scoured and lakes were observed for signs of oil slicks. Finally, just before the sunset, a search plane reported a possible find.

Col. Dennis Sparks of the Tennessee CAP was flying a Cessna 182 along with aerial observers Bronce Fitzgerald and Sally Fitzgerald. They were following a possible path of flight when Bronce spotted something that did not match the surrounding terrain. The object looked like a burnt pile of metal near the top of a ridge. Snow had fallen in the drainage, but one small section had no snow. The sun disappeared in the horizon just as the search plane tried to fly closer to the sighting. The aircraft returned to its base in Knoxville and more investigative work was initiated. "What drew our attention was there appeared to be a burnt area in the snow and we were able to see the wreckage," stated Sparks.[4] His team's sighting was worth checking out. It became the actual target.

The North Carolina CAP was contacted, as was the Park Service. Colonel Sparks called Lt. Jeff Wadley and asked him to check his map collection to determine if the coordinate was near old wreckage, a building, or a Park Service supply cache. Wadley was unable to find anything on his maps relating to the request and called Dwight McCarter and Kim Delozier of the Park Service. Both men could not think of anything that matched the description Sparks and Fitzgerald gave and could not think of any Park Service project that would have resources on Welch Ridge. Sparks and Wadley agreed that with the information given to them from the two park employees, the sighting of metal must be the missing aircraft.

Sparks put plans into place during the night. At first light a NPS ground team would hike from Clingmans Dome to Silers Bald and wait to be led into the site by a CAP plane. If the weather cooperated, a CAP/ NPS crew would be taken to Silers Bald via a national guard helicopter. Within the next few hours, the CAP and NPS selected their crews and established a time to depart for the mountain.

Before daybreak the ground and aircrews met with the mission coordinators to receive additional instructions. After a briefing, and as soon as the clouds lifted, the CAP launched an aircraft from Knoxville's Downtown Island Airport. Colonel Sparks and a crew departed for the area near Silers Bald. Maj. Max Fox with the Sevier County CAP, whose job it was to dispatch the rescue teams from park headquarters, stood by at the emergency operations center to receive additional information from Sparks.

When the aircrew arrived at Silers Bald at 8:30 A.M., the burnt area was spotted again. Sparks flew the plane into the ravine for a "low and slow" look, and everyone agreed that what they saw was a crashed aircraft. In fact, a few digits of the aircraft's identification number could be seen. Sparks radioed mission base to dispatch the NPS ground team and a helicopter. The CAP plane returned to Knoxville, and another CAP plane piloted by Lt. Paul White entered the area to orbit the crash site. Also on board was Capt. Bronce Fitzgerald and Lt. Jeff Wadley.

By 9:00 A.M. the Park Service had a ground team en route up the Newfound Gap Road. Another team was ready to board a UH-1 from the McGhee Tyson Airport. At 10:00 A.M. the first team departed from Clingmans Dome. Two and a half hours later the NPS team arrived at Silers Bald. From there, the team was led into the debris field by listening to directions given to them by the CAP plane circling above. They hiked south on the Welch Ridge Trail, passed by a small clearing, and began to notice small pieces of paint flakes and metal on the trail and in the trees.

Another team consisting of NPS rangers and CAP volunteers arrived near Silers Bald on board the Huey. All trips aboard helicopters in the park bring back memories of the past. In particular, everyone recalled the tragic death of army and CAP members in the crash of a rescue helicopter years earlier. On this day, safety and precision was on everyone's mind. The UH-1 was able to land in a small clearing near the Welch Ridge trail less than a mile from Silers Bald. From there, the second team joined the first, and they all followed the CAP plane's directions and the scattered debris into the main crash site.

On everyone's mind was the question of the survivability of the missing pilot. Impatiently, the CAP plane overhead awaited to hear the

An aerial photograph of Barron Vernon's Skymaster, which crashed in January 1990. Vernon, who was not an instrument-rated pilot, probably became lost in the low-visibility conditions. His plane hit treetops near Welch Ridge, nosed to the ground, and instantly killed the pilot. Photo by Jeff Wadley.

results from the ground team. Finally, Capt. Jerry Whaley of the Sevier County CAP radioed to Wadley that the body of a man had been found in the tangled wreckage at 2:15 P.M. "Blue Chip 152 to Blue Chip 154; he didn't make it, Jeff," was Whaley's disappointed radio transmission. The information was relayed to the Park Service dispatcher and plans for an emergency rescue were put aside.

The scene was investigated by the two organizations and secured for the night. Non-essential personnel departed for the helicopter and a few rangers remained on the scene. Due to the extreme cold and the setting sun, the NTSB requested that the body of Vernon remain in the aircraft and that nothing be touched until they arrived on the scene. Rangers John Garrison, Pat Patton, and Chuck Remus were airlifted to secure the site for the NTSB.

The NTSB arrived, and once the investigation team was outfitted with warm winter clothing, they were led into the scene. Vernon's body was removed after completion of the NTSB's investigation. The plane was later removed from the mountain with a helicopter. The NTSB's March 1993 final report attributed the crash to the poor weather and the pilot inadvertently flying into it.[5]

The Eagles Collided

A midair collision is a worst-case scenario for military fighter pilots participating in combat maneuvers. The only collision incident, military or civilian, in the park's aviation history occurred on Wednesday, January 15, 1992, between two F-15 Eagles. The Smokies claimed one entire Eagle and took parts of another, but spared the lives of the crew. Although the general public is usually not aware of it, the military has used the airspace over the Smokies for years for night helicopter training, low-level terrain training, and high-altitude dogfighting for years.

Lt. Col. Barry Bierig, forty-one, was engaged in dogfighting with three other F-15 Eagles far above the Smokies on a cold and clear winter morning. The aircraft were from the 116th Tactical Fighter Wing at Dobbins Air Force Base of the Georgia Air National Guard. Along with Bierig was Maj. Bradley L. Thompson, thirty-seven, Maj. Scott Hammond, and Lt. James Murphy. Bierig was an active-duty officer assigned to the Ninth Air Force at Shaw Air Force Base in the office of the inspector general.

On this particular day, something went wrong between Clingmans Dome and Cosby and a midair collision occurred. Bierig's aircraft and the one flown by Maj. Thompson got in each other's way. Bradley's plane had one of its vertical stabilizers sheared but did not suffer severe damage. Bierig's aircraft, however, was severely damaged. It was all the experienced officer could do to keep it under control, but it became obvious to him that it was impossible to totally regain control of the aircraft.

Bierig made a decision that saved his life by "punching out" of the $30 million aircraft. He deployed his parachute seconds later, and floating above the mountains, he watched his crippled airplane spin out of control, hit the ground, and explode.

At the same time, Thompson realized that his plane was crippled. He declared an emergency and requested vectors to McGhee Tyson Airport. With fire trucks and emergency responders prepared for the worst, the aircraft landed with no problem at 10:17 A.M. According to Maj. Art Powell, spokesperson for the air base, "We scrambled our whole disaster team and had them standing by on the runway, but Thompson just brought his plane in very smoothly."[6] The other two aircraft returned to

Part of a Georgia Air National Guard F-15 Eagle, which crashed near Pecks Corner. Courtesy of National Park Service.

their home base when they saw their two team members were safe. Bierig was able to communicate to the other aircraft using his 243.0 MHz hand-held emergency beacon (similar to an ELT).

Bierig's F-15 created a small crater in comparison to what one would imagine. The impact zone was a quarter-mile in radius. Bierig ended up a good distance from his fighter jet, near Enloe Creek in the valley between Hughes Ridge and Katalsta Ridge. The only injury he reported was a cut lip, which occurred as he was falling through the tree limbs. The airplane, of course, was destroyed.

As soon as the tower at McGhee Tyson received word of the crash, a search was initiated. The Tennessee Army National Guard dispatched two helicopters to the area between Clingmans Dome and Cosby to listen for Bierig's ELT. Meanwhile, Park Service crews were trying to plot general coordinates given to them by the other fighter aircraft. The Civil Air Patrol was on standby to launch a fixed-wing Cessna 182, and park medics were preparing their gear for a rescue. All the while media were gathering information for their noon report and a frenzy of scanner listeners were calling in their reports to the authorities of where they thought the plane was.

Bierig, meanwhile, was trying to free himself from his parachute and the trees. He managed to untangle himself from the parachute, climb to another tree, and from there make it to the ground.

While park staff were driving to high spots on roads to watch for aerial flares or smoke, the national guard helicopters were closing in on the ELT signal. Bierig was able to talk with the searchers on his hand-held radio and guided them to his location. The search was narrowed to the Cosby-Cataloochee area, and the army guard made a find. Coordinates were given to the mission base, and the Park Service quickly plotted them. It was established that there was not space large enough to land the helicopter near the missing pilot, so another plan was formed. The best way to get aid to the pilot, it was decided, was to lower two rangers to Bierig.

Steve Kloster, a Cosby District ranger, and Jack Piepenbring, a Cades Cove District ranger, were taken to the scene, and both men leaned out the side of the green helicopter and rappelled 150 feet into the trees near the pilot. Just after 1:00 P.M., the pilot was assessed and found to be in good health. Although cold and hungry, he was able to walk five and a half miles out of the mountains.

The trio walked down Enloe Creek for four miles, and in some places they had no choice but to cross the knee-deep freezing water. They intersected the Enloe Creek Trail and walked to an old road. Park Service vehicles met them and transported the pilot to a landing zone at the Oconaluftee Visitor's Center, where Bierig was airlifted to the University of Tennessee Hospital. He arrived on the heli-pad at approximately 6:30 P.M. and was able to walk into the emergency room without difficulty. He was later admitted overnight for observation in satisfactory condition.

During the flurry of activity, Thompson was examined at the base hospital and was found to be in good shape. After he was released and knew that his companion was all right, he boarded a military plane and returned to Dobbins. His damaged F-15 remained on the ramp on the air national guard side of the airport.

Today the F-15 wreckage fragments are slowly being hidden by nature. Nine years of fallen leaves, precipitation, erosion, and souvenir hunters have removed just about all of the twenty-six-thousand-pound aircraft. The mountains are recovering well from the crashed Eagle. In December 1999, a cross-country hiker located part of the engine in a creek almost two miles from the crash site.

Mount Love Cessna 310

On the afternoon of Sunday, April 26, 1992, a cold and snowy day, Derrick Romines, a member of the Sevier County Civil Air Patrol, was sightseeing at Newfound Gap on his day off. Unknown to him, a Cessna 310R had just crashed nearby onto the side of Mount Love. As was his general practice, Romines was monitoring his scanner, but at the time he was not close enough to detect the aircraft's automated distress transmission.

On board the Cessna 310-R was the pilot, Mark Williams, who was making a personal flight over the Smokies from the Cartersville–Bartow County Airport in Georgia. He was flying to Greenville Airport in Tennessee. A thirty-three-year-old instrument-rated, commercial pilot who had flown 768 hours, Williams worked as an aircraft mechanic in Cartersville, where the plane, registered to CSF Air, was based.[7] He did not file a flight plan for this cross-country flight, nor did he have radio contact with the Knoxville tower before his accident.

According to the FAA's radar tracking analysis program, Williams was flying north over the Smokies and somewhere east of Pigeon Forge he made a 180-degree turn and began to fly south.[8] The aircraft was high enough heading north to make it over the Smokies, but after turning south he was approximately 750 feet too low.

At 1:53 P.M. he was in a climb as the airplane began to hit the tops of trees. For a few seconds the airplane's propellers and the underside of the fuselage cut into the trees, and then the Cessna struck the earth. The wings separated from the fuselage, and the nose of the plane dug into the ground. The cockpit split open and ejected the pilot from the plane, catapulting him approximately seventy-five feet. The plane did not burn but lay silent in the forest as the temperature dropped and a heavy snow began to fall.

According to the National Transportation Safety Board's accident report, there were no mechanical or structural malfunctions associated with the cause of the incident. The final suggestion as to the cause of the crash was the pilot's "continued VFR flight into [IFR conditions] and his failure to attain a proper altitude over high, mountainous terrain."[9] Recordings from a local automated weather observation station revealed that the lowest cloud ceiling was broken at twenty-three hundred feet and visibility under the layer was seven miles. There was a six-knot northwest wind blowing cool air into the Tennessee Valley. Near the time of the crash the temperature was forty-seven degrees.

The ELT began transmitting upon impact, just as designed. Ninety-seven percent of all ELT searches are nondistress missions. Most ELTs begin transmitting when they are inadvertently turned on during installation, battery replacement or when their power switches are accidentally turned on. The remaining 3 percent of ELT searches are for crashed aircraft whose ELTs are transmitting an actual distress signal. Nevertheless, all ELT missions are treated as emergency searches until the teams learn otherwise. On this particular mission, several aircraft flying over the area heard the ELT signal and reported it to the Knoxville and Asheville towers. A powerful C-130 army transport aircraft, for example, tracked the signal and provided a fairly accurate location to the CAP. This particular ELT unit (Donse Margolin) transmitted on two frequencies simultaneously (121.5 MHz and 243.0 MHz).

At the time of the crash and for several hours later no one knew Williams had crashed. The first key to the need of a search was the search-and-rescue satellites (SARSATs) that orbit the Earth monitoring for ELT distress beacons. The satellites were able to almost pinpoint the location of the signal transmitting from the Cessna. The U.S. Air Force Rescue Coordination Center in Virginia plotted the satellite data and activated the Tennessee CAP for an ELT search.

Once Williams's family reported him overdue, the Rescue Coordination Center saw the correlation and converted the ELT mission to a missing aircraft search. Search urgency increased. Since Derrick Romines was on the mountain earlier in the day, he was contacted and met Ranger Kenny Slay. They drove to the top of the Smokies to monitor for the ELT, and the signal was heard. Additional personnel were quickly summoned, and a ground search was initiated since the weather would not allow for a safe and effective aerial search.

The Park Service and CAP both knew that due to the poor weather conditions a difficult search was ahead. During the evening, highly trained persons from the CAP and NPS were called upon to prepare for a cold and wet off-trail search. The ground was covered in eighteen to twenty-four inches of snow, that was hip deep in some areas. The search area was narrowed to the north slope of Clingmans Dome, approximately one mile east of the observation tower.

Ground teams in the next two days encountered severe weather and exhaustion. At the end of the first and second day, three teams had tried to track the ELT signal. The terrain was extremely steep and covered with icy rocks and boulders. Very high cliffs were a constant obstacle. Clouds kept the mountain

The cold search for a Cessna on the Appalachian Trail near Mount Love. Rangers George Minnigh and Pat Patton, along with CAP searcher Jeff Wadley, prepare to hike off trail. Photo by Jeff Wadley.

shrouded, prohibiting good visibility. To make matters worse the batteries in the ELT tracker would get so cold that the "juice" in them would quickly die out, making reception difficult. The searchers came out of the woods on both days, tired, cold, and disgusted. "Ghost" signals (the ELT signal reflecting off rocks, trees, cliffs, and so on) made tracking the signal a nightmare. Many searchers described the search as their most difficult. Frustration and stress levels were high.

At the end of the search's second day a helicopter from North Carolina was flown into the area at the request of the CAP. Despite the incredible snow cover, the helicopter crew was able to make out a tiny piece of metal that was inconsistent to the terrain. They had located the aircraft.

Once the site had been located, the helicopter landed on the Clingmans Dome Road to explain to rangers and the CAP how to get to the scene. The pilot described all the lines of cliffs and the multiple ravines and drainages. Rangers drew a line on a map from where the helicopter landed down the mountain to the site. It was decided that the helicopter would drop a roll of orange surveyor's ribbon at the place the searchers should leave the Appalachian Trail and in several places down the mountain leading them to the crash site. However, before the searchers could reach the ribbon, darkness and clouds again stopped the search for the night.

On the third day two NPS and CAP teams left the Little River Ranger Station just after daybreak. One team led by Ranger Steve Kloster with two rangers and one CAP member began on Mount Love at the Appalachian Trail and went downhill. A second team led by Ranger George Minnigh included Ranger Pat Patton and CAP member Jeff Wadley. They hiked to the west of Mount Love. Wadley's portable direction finding unit was receiving a weaker signal than the past two days. That was good. Strong signals sometimes cause so much reflection that it is impossible to accurately track an ELT.

The morning was bright and clear. For the first time in three days the ground searchers could see just how much snow had blanketed the mountains. The blue sky was an incredible sight against the white hoarfrost on the frozen trees. Snow and rain had frozen on the balsams and firs for almost a week, and the scenery was breathtaking. At least two inches of rime ice covered the tree limbs. By midmorning the temperature had risen just enough to burn the top layer of the frozen precipitation off branches. This presented a "good news–bad news" situation. The bad news was that the melting snow was drenching the searchers. The good news was that the snow was melting, and if the ELT were to stop working, it would be easier to visually spot the crash site.

Col. Dennis Sparks and Maj. Phil Robbins of the CAP were performing an air search while the two ground teams were closing in on the weak ELT signal. The ELT would probably have stopped transmitting that afternoon due to the power drainage over the past four days. Within the first few moments in the search area Sparks had spotted the downed aircraft as a "smudged spot on a page of white paper." He radioed the find to the ground teams and they proceeded to the area.

The ELT tracking radio pointed the team in an easterly direction and they proceeded until the signal strength meter was pegged at "maximum." They were right on top of the aircraft. They began to wonder what they were going to find at the crash site. Would the pilot be found alive? If he had not died on impact, how would they deal with the fact that he had survived but they did not find him in time? The trio walked faster through the snow and were preparing each other for the entry into the site.

The private helicopter arrived on the scene again and began to hover over the site. A crew member radioed to the team that there "appeared to be no life around the crash area." Still, the hopes of the ground team were high as they struggled through the deep, wet snow. Minnigh, Patton, and Wadley arrived on the scene and quickly surveyed the wreckage. No

The wreckage of a Cessna 310 on Mount Love, April 1992. According to the National Transportation Safety Board's accident report, the plane probably crashed due to cloud cover and the pilot's failure to maintain sufficient altitude in the mountainous terrain. Photo by Jeff Wadley.

pilot was found. At first they thought he had survived and walked away from the crash, but where was he now?

The three radioed their report to the incident command center and were instructed to expand the search to include five areas: below, above, beside, beneath, and beyond the aircraft. Patton positioned himself along the aircraft while Minnigh began looking below the wreckage. Wadley began a walk uphill from the plane. Wadley waved off the hovering helicopter so that the three-member team could listen for signs of life. All that was heard was melting, dripping snow and an occasional sight-seeing helicopter flying over head. Each man used a long hiking staff to poke through the snow like avalanche searchers. CAP put in a request for a search dog if the team could not locate the pilot.

Half an hour after the initial find, Wadley found four red cloths hung in tree at eye level. He thought the cloths might be a signaling device put there on purpose to attract the attention of searchers. His first reaction was excitement, then disappointment. "What if the pilot lived and we did not get here fast enough?" While probing the snow, he hit a hard object. He dug through the snow and found a yellow flashlight. As he dug farther, he found clothing and, finally, Williams's body under two feet of snow. It was obvious he had not survived the initial impact of the crash.

Once the team dealt with the facts of the crash, the report of a "DOA" was radioed to the CAP aircraft flying above and to the park incident base. Word was then sent to the AFRCC, the FAA, the NTSB, and, of course, Williams's family. The search was now over.

Minnigh and Patton made plans for the recovery of Williams's body. The incident base through the NTSB arranged for his body to be removed from the scene that afternoon. A contract helicopter (Vertiflite) was called to the scene, and airspace in the Clingmans Dome area was restricted. Additional supplies were dropped to the ground team from the helicopter. Soon, the other NPS and CAP teams arrived on the scene. A preliminary investigation was accomplished, a safe area was created for a sling "short haul" operation, and the plane's ELT was turned off.

Williams's body was lifted from the forest by the helicopter and taken to the Collins Gap pull-off near Newfound Gap. Additional officials were on hand to transport the body off the mountain. The crash site was guarded overnight by a ranger, and the other team members began their walk out of the backcountry to the Clingmans Dome Parking Area. They arrived in late afternoon, wet, cold, hungry, and tired but filled with a sense of accomplishment. They were glad the pilot's body had been found; it would give the family some sense of closure.

The team and the other support personnel departed just before dark from the Dome Parking Area and were debriefed at park headquarters before heading home. The NTSB went into the site the next day and investigated the incident before turning the plane over to the owner's insurance company. A few weeks later, the plane was completely removed from Mount Love.

Today, nothing remains at the crash site because the recovery company did a remarkable job of cleaning the scene. In the past few years nature has reclaimed the spot and the wounds have healed. For the family and friends of Mark Williams, the pain of loosing a friend, husband, and parent to an aircraft crash will not be healed so easily.

Three Persons Die on Tricorner Knob

Ronnie Baldwin, Tammy Dial, and Savannah Dial had just finished a Memorial Day weekend get-a-way in Gatlinburg and were on their way home when tragedy struck. The airplane in which they were flying fell out of the air over the Smokies at 2:52 P.M. on Sunday afternoon, May 24, 1992.

Thunderstorm clouds were boiling high into the atmosphere above the Smokies, and precipitation, moderate winds, and lightning were reported in the Tennessee Valley. It was not a great day to fly.

Baldwin, age twenty-seven, was a Georgia Bureau of Investigation agent in Atlanta. Tammy Dial had been employed by the Floyd County, Georgia, sheriff's department for three years and was twenty-three years old. Her daughter, Savannah, was five months old and she is the youngest person to have died in an aircraft crash in the Smokies. All three made their home in Rome. "They were both important members of the law enforcement community," Sheriff Mike Thornton said. "We're going to miss them both."[10]

The trio was flying in perhaps the most popular civilian aircraft flown today, the Cessna 172. White with red stripes, the aircraft departed the Gatlinburg–Pigeon Forge Airport around 2:45 P.M. en route to Rome. The flight would not be very long (140 miles, or about two and a half hours). It would take them over the Smokies as they flew southwest from Sevierville. Instead of gradually climbing toward the final destination, pilots who fly over the mountains sometimes climb in large circles, gaining altitude first before leveling off. Baldwin apparently did just this.

According to news reports, Baldwin got into trouble quickly.[11] He apparently flew into the clouds and experienced "spatial disorientation." It is like diving into a swimming pool and loosing your sense of "up," or like driving a car with your eyes closed: you feel yourself moving but you cannot determine which way you are moving. Spatial disorientation is horrifying for both low- and high-hour pilots. The only thing a pilot has to aid the flight are the instruments on the front panel of the aircraft.

An aircraft instrument panel to the non-aviation-minded person seems confusing and overwhelming. To a trained pilot, each light, switch, button, and gauge tells a story of what is going on with the aircraft. When "flying by instruments," the pilot relies on an artificial horizon, compass, and rate of climb indicator to show the orientation of the plane in relationship to the horizon. An airplane can be flown entirely by observing the instruments if the need arises. The skill is honed by time, practice, and, unfortunately, trial and error. The problem of "error" often leads to injury or death.

In Baldwin's case, he became an apparent victim of spatial disorientation. Whatever the case, he contacted Knoxville approach and requested help, stating that he was lost and requesting "radar vectors to the nearest airport." Knoxville gave him a transponder (radar) code and a direction to fly, but it was too late.[12]

The controller watched N8102X very carefully. The "blip" that represented the aircraft told a horror story, and all the controller could do was give directions, watch, and hope for the best. Prior to dropping off radar, the Cessna made "several climbs, descents and erratic turns" that indicated that Baldwin was having a very difficult time keeping his airplane level with the horizon. What a horrifying few minutes it had to have been for both the tower personnel and the three persons on the aircraft.

At 2:52 P.M. the tower lost radar and radio contact with the Cessna. It was obvious what had occurred. There was the hope that Baldwin's plane had electrical problems, that his radio and transponder were not operating and he had actually made it to an airport. The facts, however, did not stack up in the favor of the trio on board the aircraft. The tower made a phone call to the Gatlinburg–Pigeon Forge Airport. No plane. Other aircraft in the sky tried to radio the missing aircraft. No response.

The flight turned into tragedy as the aircraft nose-dived deep into the ground one hundred yards off the Appalachian Trail near Tricorner Knob. A hiker in the area reported that a "thud" was heard; however, he could not tell from which direction it came. On impact, Ronnie, Tammy,

and Savannah were all killed. Buried under the wreckage and the soil were the three bodies. Once the violent crash occurred it continued to rain, and clouds shrouded the silent mountain.

Pilot Ronnie Baldwin most likely experienced spatial disorientation after flying into heavy cloud cover in May 1992. His Cessna 172 crashed near Tricorner Knob. On board was Savannah Dial, five months old, the youngest person to die in an aircraft crash in the park. Courtesy of Duane Devotie.

The Park Service was called within minutes, as was the Atlanta Center. The Air Force Rescue Coordination Center confirmed the report and issued a search mission number for the Tennessee Civil Air Patrol to respond as quickly as possible. Heavy rain and clouds disrupted the planned air search until the late afternoon. All the CAP plane was able to do was fly above the clouds and monitor for a distress signal. While flying over the general search area, the CAP plane reported to the Park Service that no ELT was being heard. The next step was to insert a small team on the mountain between thunder showers and before night fall. Additional ground teams readied themselves to hike in during the night.

The army national guard dispatched a helicopter to a landing area near Tricorner Knob. On board were two rangers who would stay the night at the shelter and be on hand at first light to begin a visual search. In the meantime the CAP prepared a large contingent of ground searchers who were briefed at the Cosby Ranger Station and were sent into the back-country late in the evening. Trampling through heavy rain most of the night, the team, led by CAP members Duane Devotie and Earl Mysinger, finally made it to Tricorner Knob in the early morning hours.

Luckily, Monday morning brought fair weather. The overnight low at Newfound Gap was twenty-two degrees, which was accompanied by stable air and clear skies. A CAP plane was sent to the search area to once again listen for an ELT signal or watch for signs of life. Once the plane was able to get "low and slow" at the area of the last radar plot, the spotters saw only thick evergreens and heavy underbrush. After a few passes a crew member spotted what appeared to be a pile of trash. The "trash pile" was the missing aircraft. Exact coordinates were plotted, and the CAP plane radioed the sighting to the NPS incident command center.

At this point the search had ended and the second phase, rescue, was launched. The CAP and Park Service units climbed the steep mountain while a guard helicopter was summoned by the CAP to hover over the site and lead the ground crews through the maze of trees to the airplane. Additional rangers were airlifted to the scene along with food and sup-plies. The task of determining if there was life inside the cockpit began.

Once on the scene the team had to literally cut through the belly of the plane to gain access. There was not a lot room to move around at the crash site, let alone to do an extrication, due to the extremely thick vege-tation. "It took four hours," said park spokesperson Bob Miller. "The thing was flipped over on its top so they had to cut through the rear underside of the aircraft. That got you into the body of the plane where they had to cut through a bulkhead behind the passenger compartment."[13]

Taking turns using various improvised tools, the team finally found the three bodies buried under ground. The impact penetrated the forest floor with such force that all three occupants had no chance of survival. Rangers and CAP personnel were devastated at the tragic scene of a child and two adults who had to endure such trauma. By 3:00 P.M., twenty-four hours after the crash, the find was complete; the plane's three occupants had been found.

Although the search and extrication had ended, the carryout was about to begin. Again, bad weather set in and detained the recovery. The carryout and airlift were canceled and the bodies were instead taken to the Tricorner Knob Shelter and guarded throughout the night.

On Tuesday morning an alternative plan was put into motion. Due to safety concerns regarding low clouds, a contract helicopter was unable to be used. Instead, mules were guided to Tricorner Knob and the animals were used to transport the three bodies off the remote mountain. After nightfall Tuesday, the victims' bodies finally reached the Smokemont Campground, where they were transferred to a hospital in Bryson City, North Carolina.

A Federal Aviation Administration agent, a National Transportation Safety Board agent, a representative from Cessna, and an engine manufacturer representative all went to the site the next day (Wednesday) to perform a routine investigation to try and determine why the plane had crashed. The NTSB findings, filed as report number ATL92FA108, stated that "spatial disorientation[,] . . . lack of total flight time," and the rain were contributing factors to the crash.[14]

The plane was released over to a salvage company for complete removal from the park. Today, the forest has fully recovered and there are no signs of the tragedy. But for the men and women on the search and recovery, the memory of the scene will stay with them for some time.

Right on the Yellow Line

Ranger Bobby Holland was the first to arrive on the scene of a helicopter incident that occurred on Little River Road on Friday, April 16, 1993. Marc A. Corder landed his Bell 204 Huey UH-1F on the double yellow line just west of the Laurel Falls Parking Area. When Holland arrived, he found Corder somewhat injured but walking up the road with his suitcase. "He said his neck was hurting," Holland was quoted as saying.[15]

At 3:36 P.M. Corder experienced engine trouble and was forced to auto-rotate the aircraft into the terrain. Luckily, he saw the two-lane highway below him and aimed the disabled aircraft at the road. Aircraft N4040P suffered substantial damage as the main rotor blades cut into the trees and the fuselage struck the pavement. About ten gallons of aviation fuel leaked from the fuel tanks and onto the road but did not flow into the nearby stream (the team put sandbags around the helicopter to dam the leaking fuel and used absorbent clay and pillows to clean up the spill). The helicopter did not burn. The aircraft was equipped with auxiliary agricultural spraying tanks and nozzles but there were no chemicals stored in them.

Corder's last departure point was from Greenville, Tennessee, on a flight to Dalton, Georgia. The nearest weather observation facility recorded the temperature at the time of the crash as fifty-one degrees; winds were from the southwest at fifteen knots, with a forty-five-hundred-foot overcast cloud layer. The visibility that day was good at ten miles, which accounted for his Corder's VFR flight. Corder was a fifty-year-old commercial helicopter pilot with 3,824 total hours recorded in his log book. He had flown 2,104 hours in this particular aircraft model.[16] He was from Midlothian, Virginia, and the helicopter was registered to Ranger Helicopter Services in Roanoke.

Corder's trouble began as he was flying over Gatlinburg en route to Dalton. As he entered over the park, for no apparent reason, the engine began to loose power and he was forced to land the aircraft. Making his way to the nearest airport was out of the question because the Gatlinburg–Pigeon Forge and McGhee Tyson Airports were too far away. As the power decreased even more, he began to auto-rotate (allowing the rotors to rotate the aircraft through the air relatively slow) until he crashed.

The emergency descent came to an abrupt halt when the helicopter landed "right on the yellow line" on the Little River Road facing traffic.[17] Pieces of trees, leaves, and ground debris swirled through the air as if in a tornado. Corder suffered abrasions, and injuries to his chest and neck. Motorists were on the scene almost immediately, and many persons stood from a distance taking photographs and talking. Luckily cars were not in the way of the helicopter as is dropped from the sky and no one on the ground was injured.

As Holland was responding to the call, he topped the hill at Fighting Creek Gap looking for smoke coming from the mountain side but was surprised to see a line of cars and the helicopter sitting in the middle of the road. Once on the scene Holland confirmed the report of the crash and requested an ambulance. Also dispatched was the Gatlinburg Fire Department, an aircraft wrecker from McGhee Tyson Airport, and the Sevier County Volunteer Fire Department's Hazardous Materials Team. UT Hospital's Lifestar medical helicopter arrived on the scene and landed at the Sugarlands Visitor's Center. The pilot was transferred to Lifestar by an ambulance and he was at UT Hospital at 4:25 P.M. He was evaluated and admitted in stable condition.

In the meantime, Little River Road was blocked from Elkmont to the visitor's center for several hours. Traffic traveling to Sugarlands was diverted through Metcalf Bottoms, Wears Valley, and Pigeon Forge, while traffic west bound from Sugarlands was diverted back through Pigeon Forge and Wears Valley. The aircraft wrecker lifted the helicopter onto a truck and was transported to the park maintenance area to be secured through the weekend. On Monday the nineteenth, the NTSB arrived and performed their investigation before the craft was hauled away.

Why did the helicopter loose power? During the investigation and after a close observation of major components, there was no evident reason why the helicopter's General Electric T58GE-3 engine had failed. The cause was listed as "loss of power for unknown reasons."[18]

As the incident concluded, Holland praised the agencies involved. "We couldn't do it without them," he said.[19]

"N6749S, Do You Copy, Knoxville?"

A flight into the mountains turned tragic for a Knoxville man on Saturday, February 11, 1995, when his Beechcraft BE-60 Duke crashed and burned in the Smokies. Physician Ed Malone probably never knew what happened as his twin-engine aircraft struck trees then nosed into the ground near Laurel Falls. Although snow was falling heavily, the flames were fanned by high winds and kept the wreckage burning all night.

The excited voice of a pilot calling Knoxville approach got the attention of this book's coauthor, Jeff Wadley, who was listening to a scanner at his residence. The pilot reported that he was in the clouds near Gatlinburg and needed help in getting out. Approach asked the pilot to switch his transponder to a particular code, and the pilot responded. Seconds later approach gave the pilot a direction in which to fly to escape the cloud-covered mountains.

Malone's plane was dangerously deep in the heart of the mountains near Laurel Falls. He was making a turn when the plane's underside began to make contact with a few tall trees. At a direction of 210 degrees the Beechcraft created a 491-foot path through the forest from the first tree he struck to the edge of the debris field. Paint and pieces of metal flaked off the plane and slowly drifted to the ground. The twin engines then began to chew up oak trees and pines, hitting a very large oak almost at its base. The oak's base was forced forward and up as its top fell backward and down. The plane dug into the frozen ground, cartwheeled, and came to rest near the crest of a steep hill. Immediately the plane caught fire. According to investigators, Malone died from injuries resulting from the crash, not the fire. The time was 1:27 P.M.[20]

Malone had begun his flight fifteen minutes earlier from McGhee Tyson. His flight became a nightmare when the Smokies' notorious weather reached out and grabbed the large aircraft. He called McGhee Tyson approach on his radio and requested an ILS approach. Two minutes later he requested a vector, or direction, out of the mountains. The radar "painted" only one "blip" of him. By the time the radar was supposed to receive his signal again, the "blip" had already disappeared.

Some hikers were in the Mount Harrison area when the plane crashed. The group heard an aircraft in the clouds, heard what sounded like a gunshot, then heard only silence. Apparently, they heard Malone's plane hit the earth and burst into flames.

At the time Malone had gone down, another aircraft was flying near Pigeon Forge. Knoxville tower asked the pilot of that aircraft to call Malone's aircraft on the radio and listen for him. He was also asked to listen on his aircraft radio to the 121.5 MHz frequency (the ELT and distress frequency). The pilot flew closer to the area and reported that an ELT signal was not being received.

Wadley interpreted the situation correctly. Malone had gone down. With plenty of daylight left, Wadley quickly called the Sevier County CAP commander, Maj. Kevin Tarwater, and requested he put together a ground team to rush to park headquarters. A ground team from Knoxville was also alerted, led by Maj. Gary Milton. In a matter of minutes CAP was en route to the area. The obvious issue was to narrow the search area. All the Knoxville tower had to go on was one radar hit near Gatlinburg, but there was no way to determine the direction of flight. Where was Malone?

Within minutes of the plane's disappearance, Wadley's phone rang. It was the Knoxville tower. Controller Jerry Haynes informed Wadley of the incident and gave him all the known details. Although the missing aircraft was not being seen on radar, the fact remained that Malone could have gotten out of the terrain and weather and lost electric power to his radio and transponder which would account for the loss of contact. He could have flown back to Knoxville or to another airport without radio communications. The situation appeared dreary.

Haynes left work and drove to Wadley's home, where he showed him the exact "point of last contact" on a map: Cove Mountain near Laurel Falls. Wadley immediately asked his two CAP teams to split. One would go to the top of Mount Harrison above the Ski Lodge, the other to the Laurel Falls Parking Area. Another team stood by at park headquarters.

In the meantime McGhee Tyson tower informed Atlanta Center of the situation. One of the first things to do was to listen to the voice tapes and interpret the raw data of the radar images. While that was going on,

an INREQ went out to all area airports and Flight Service Stations in the area to find out if anyone had seen or heard from the missing aircraft. No one had.

Ed Malone's Beech BE-60 Duke, which crashed near Laurel Falls in February 1995. As with so many other pilots, Malone probably lost his way in the Smokies' notoriously bad weather and failed to maintain altitude. The underside of his plane clipped a few tall trees then cut a 491-foot path through the forest before striking the ground. Photo by Jeff Wadley.

The Tennessee Emergency Management Agency was contacted, as was the Air Force Rescue Coordination Center. They became involved to do a primary investigation and to call local law enforcement agencies to determine if anyone had something to report. The Sevier County Sheriff's Department, the three local police departments, the Blount County Sheriff's Department, and Alcoa and Maryville Police Departments were called. The Park Service was also contacted to see if any reports had come into their dispatch desk. No news.

Maj. Joe Meighan of the CAP designated Wadley as mission coordinator, and the search was assigned mission number 95M266A. With things happening so swiftly, Wadley did not have time to drive to the mission base; instead, he set up the command center in the basement of his home. The Tennessee Emergency Management Agency called Wadley and assigned state incident number 039 to the investigation. A staff member and additional resources were available if needed.

In the meantime, the teams were in place and ready to hike into the mountains. Gary Milton and Brent Thatcher were hiking up the Laurel Falls Trail toward the Cove Mountain Fire Tower while Jerry Whaley's team had arrived at the top of Mount Harrison. Whaley reported to Wadley that snow was falling heavily and the roads were covered. The cloud layer was around twenty-five hundred feet. A search aircraft was out of the question due to weather. This would be a ground team search. Their task was to hike into the search area and use their senses (hearing, smelling, and looking) for signs of the missing aircraft. Both teams also planned to monitor for the aircraft distress frequency on their specialized tracking equipment. Minutes seemed like hours. The teams checked in every few minutes, and both reported heavy snow and wind.

Meanwhile, the National Park Service dispatcher contacted three experienced searchers, George Minnigh, Ron Parrish, and Kenny Slay, to prepare for the search. Slay asked the two other rangers to drive to Cove Mountain Fire Tower by the way of Wears Valley and hike along the mountain top to Phils View. From there they were to decide if going cross-country would be advantageous and if not they were to return to the mission base. Slay soon arrived at headquarters and set up an incident command center for the entire operation.

Slay called the army national guard at McGhee Tyson and requested a helicopter to come immediately to the search area and do an aerial survey. The operations officer ruled that the impending snow showers would not allow the unit to respond in their Hueys and smaller "scouts." Slay then requested that the army at Fort Campbell dispatch a Blackhawk helicopter, which could probably navigate through the storm more safely. The army agreed. Later, however, Operations called Slay and said that even their larger helicopters could not be released to fly due to the extreme weather. Once again, air cover was out of the question.

The weather on Mount Harrison was getting worse. The CAP's two ground teams searched until dark with no leads. As the mountains grew darker, the teams turned to walk out of the backcountry and were going to regroup at park headquarters. Whaley found that his team's vehicle was covered in snow, and the wind made the cold temperatures seem even colder. The team departed Mount Harrison and slid down the mountain toward Gatlinburg.

At about the same time, Wadley sent a CAP team to McGhee Tyson Airport. Their task was to walk the flight line and look for the missing pilot's car. After locating the car and not finding the airplane on the ramp it was obvious that he had not arrived in Knoxville. That bit of information confirmed even more that Malone was in the Smokies. Another team walked the flight line at the Sevierville Airport and another at the Downtown Island Airport hoping that Malone had actually made it back. There was no sign of the plane at the other two airports either. He had to be down.

Although tainted by some as a nuisance in the backcountry, the tourist sightseeing helicopters have come in handy. Some have reported forest fires and have helped in searches for lost hikers, but for the most part, the relationship among the Department of Interior, the hiking public, and the tourist helicopter business is at odds. Dale Williams, who now flies for a news station in Florida, was a tourist helicopter pilot who worked for Rainbow Helicopters. He was also a lieutenant in the Sevier County CAP squadron and a former army flight instructor. On this particular evening, Williams and CAP's Ray Sager heard about the search and met at the heli-pad in Wears Valley before sunset to make a flight over the area. The owner of Rainbow, Rob Thompson, gave Williams permission to make the flight on donated company time. The two CAP members departed the heli-pad in fairly good weather and went to the top of the mountain just above the heli-pad.

Almost immediately the two got into a snowstorm. As long as there was daylight Williams said he could fly over the mountains. They searched from the air as the CAP and NPS crews were hiking below. The ground teams could only hear and occasionally see the Jet Ranger.

Just as one CAP team turned back, Wadley's phone rang at his residence. On the other end was Kenny Slay. He wanted to know what the CAP plans were for the next day. As they were discussing the plans and were about to recall the teams, Wadley received another phone call. Dale Williams was on the other line.

"Jeff, this is Dale Williams," said the pilot.

"You better not be where I think you are," Wadley replied.

"I do not see an airplane, but I do want to report a forest fire," indicated Williams.

"A forest fire? There is no way on earth that the mountains could be—" Wadley stopped. "Dale, you've found my airplane haven't you?"

The helicopter pilot was hovering over a fire that he described as being approximately forty feet long and ten to fifteen feet wide along a downed tree. Williams told Wadley that there was absolutely no sign of metal below, nor was he receiving an ELT signal. Wadley asked Williams to hover above the fire and get high enough for Knoxville's radar to track him. Williams complied. Wadley now knew via Knoxville's radar plot not only where Williams was but also the location of the crash site. Wadley got off the phone with Williams and discussed the matter with Slay. Neither of the men could believe the news.

Slay had his two-person team prepare for an off-trail search while Wadley asked his two teams to return to the area. Whaley's team was already slipping down the mountain and could not make it back. Sleet and snow had made the road impassable. Milton and Thatcher stopped at an overlook below Fighting Creek Gap and could not see the fire on the mountain nor the helicopter flying overhead due to the snowstorm. Whaley's team dropped him off at the Ober Gatlinburg Ski Resort. He was so determined to meet with the rangers and go in with them that he asked the resort personnel to turn on the chair lift to give him a ride to the top of Mount Harrison. In fact they kept the lift running until he returned later that evening. (Thank you Ober Gatlinburg!)

Parish and Minnigh waited near Phils View for the helicopter to fly over them and point the direction to hike off trail. Whaley opted to turn back due to being improperly prepared for the extreme weather, and Milton and Thatcher returned to park headquarters.

Williams began a flight up and down the mountain, one he would make dozens of times that night. Wadley relayed to the rangers on their radio the information from Williams who was on a cell phone. The three-way conversation enabled communications between the rangers and the aircraft that would have been impossible years earlier. Williams flew over the fire, hovered, and looked for the flashlights of the rangers. Once he spotted them, he would fly up to them, turn, and fly in the direction of the fire. Back and forth he did this for more than an hour until Minnigh and Parrish arrived on the scene at 8:25 P.M.

The two rangers arrived after descending from Phils View through rhododendron, laurel, and briers. The men quickly surveyed the scene and found Malone's body beneath the tangled wreckage. At 8:29 P.M. the two radioed to Wadley and the NPS command post that the pilot was dead. Wadley also informed Williams. For a few moments the radio was quiet. The rangers could hear the helicopter directly over head until Williams broke the silence and asked to return to his helipad. Remaining at the scene during the night, the two rangers posted guard until fresh personnel arrived in the morning.

Malone's wife was notified. A spokesperson for the family called Wadley and asked that he convey to the searchers how much he and the family appreciated their efforts to locate the missing aircraft so quickly, especially considering the weather conditions. The word was passed to the searchers.

In the next few hours, the CAP teams returned home, the news media called for a briefing, and the NTSB and FAA were notified. Plans were made by District Ranger Slay for a carryout at first light Sunday morning.

At 8:00 A.M. on Sunday morning the twelfth, the carryout crews organized at park headquarters. Along with the Park Service were members of the CAP and the Smoky Mountain Nordic Ski Patrol. Once they arrived at the scene with the proper equipment, the crew rotated its members for the long carryout down the mountain. Through snow and very cold temperatures, the carryout crew brought Malone's body to a waiting ambulance at the Laurel Falls Parking Area at 1:00 P.M., almost twenty-four hours to the minute of the crash.

Edward M. (Ted) Malone Jr. was fifty-six years old and lived in Knox County. He was a 1965 graduate of the Medical School at the University of Miami and served in the U.S. Army. As an ophthalmologist, Malone was known by friends, colleges, and clients as a man who was a servant to humanity. Malone was known for his work with the Knoxville based "Remote Area Medical," a project organized by Stan Brock to provide medical care to the rural poor. He is survived by his wife of thirty-three years, Joyce, and three daughters. On the Wednesday following his crash, a memorial service was held in Malone's honor at Rose Mortuary Highland Chapel in Knoxville.

On Sunday afternoon, the NTSB, FAA, and representatives from the aircraft's manufacturer began the task of piecing together the story to determine the cause of the crash. On Monday they hiked to the scene and collected information from the crash site. Included in the investigation was a background check on the plane's maintenance records and the pilot's flying credentials. Malone was a "very experienced and skillful" pilot according to his friends and had accumulated over fifteen hundred flight hours. Their investigation "failed to disclose a mechanical problem," according the NTSB report.[21]

The joint effort between CAP and NPS was at its prime during this search. The quick response by the McGhee Tyson controllers by informing the CAP was in direct correlation to the rapid find. "The only thing that could have been better was to have heard the two rangers radio me and say 'we have a survivor,'" said Wadley.

A few days later, Roger Stallcamp of Hartzell Propellers and Eddie Webber of Beechcraft contacted the Park Service's Slay and CAP's Wadley to inform them that during the investigation and recovery it was found that a propeller was missing from the crash site. Questions were centered on it coming off in flight, being carried off by a souvenir hunter, or being buried in the earth. Wadley volunteered to return to the area and search for the missing three-bladed propeller. After three trips up the mountain with no results, he reported that the propeller was not on the ground in a quarter mile radius of the crash site. Retired ranger Dwight McCarter (coauthor of this book) was also contacted, and the two made another trek to the scene.

Wadley and McCarter studied the drawings the investigators provided and concluded that if the propeller was still on the plane and was turning at full speed when it hit the ground, it must have buried itself very deep underground. Measuring (but mostly guessing), Wadley began to dig in the trench that the plane had made. McCarter used a metal detector (its use approved by the NPS for the day) and discovered a large "hit." The two spent two hours digging and finally found the three-blade propeller under three feet of soil. Once it was brought to the surface, the propeller was "hog-tied," carried out, and shipped to the insurance company. The two solved the question of the propeller coming off in flight. It had not.

Today, six years after the crash, nature has fully healed the site. Small trees are growing where the shearing of the large trees opened the forest canopy. Undergrowth has covered the bare earth. The forest has a way of doing that. All the metal, glass, and fabric was removed by the recovery company, and the spot is marked by only photographs and memories. Malone has been missed since his untimely death, but his impact upon hundreds of people is a sign of his love for humanity. He gave them sight.

A Textbook Search

In the next two sections the authors wish to overload the reader with facts, figures, times, and statistics. The information presented is what a typical mission coordinator and investigator works with in putting together the story of how an aviation incident occurred.

Jeffrey W. Mann of New Berlin, Wisconsin, perished in an airplane crash near Russell Field in the late afternoon of December 1, 1997. Mann's flight was from Capital Field in Brookfield, Wisconsin, to Gainesville, Florida. In preparation for his trip, he checked the weather on Sunday, November 30, at 7:23 P.M. with the Green Bay automated FSS. As a result of the conversation with the briefer, he postponed his flight due to unsuitable flying weather. Monday morning at 7:45 A.M. Central Time, he called again. He indicated that his plan was to attempt the flight and he would stay under the forecasted and observed overcast cloud layer.[22] He was not trained or certified to fly in IFR conditions.

Between 11:00 and 11:30 A.M. Eastern Time on Monday the first, Mann departed Capital Field. He did not file a formal flight plan with the Federal Aviation Administration, nor did he request flight following.[23] He flew toward Gainesville with a checkpoint at Anderson, Indiana, and after flying for two hours and forty five minutes, he planned on stopping for fuel at Bowman Field in Louisville, Kentucky.

After arriving without incident between 2:00 and 2:30 Eastern Time, Mann took on 37.8 gallons of fuel at the Triangle Flying Service in Louisville. He departed around 3:00 from Bowman Field, with knowledge that the clouds en route were overcast. At the time Mann would have been over Knoxville the ceiling or overcast cloud layer was at 3,200 feet above the ground (or 4,200 feet above sea level). A hiker who was on the Appalachian Trail near the time of the crash indicated that the "temperature was cold enough that some ice had formed on the trees and there was no wind."[24] Visibility on the trail was between 100 and 150 feet with dense fog on the 4900-foot mountaintop.

Mann was flying a white, red, and black Cessna 182-E. It was registered to Mann with the "tail number" N9033Y. The pilot did not have radio contact with an air traffic control facility after he left Bowman Field's airspace. He was also not being tracked on radar, nor was it a requirement for an aircraft on a VFR flight. Although this is a legal, safe, and an accepted method of flight, many pilots will not fly in marginal weather without at least asking to be "followed" on radar or communicating with a tower. Even if Jeff had communications with the tower in Knoxville all that is required of them is to control him through their airspace. As a courtesy, the tower controllers will ask pilots if they are familiar with the rising terrain in their flight path. As a safety consideration, Mann would have been warned of the mountainous terrain.

Jeffrey Mann had logged 460 hours of flight time as a private pilot. His logbook, recovered in the crash, indicated that he had logged no instrument flying time.[25] He had gone through his biennial review in January and had flown eight hours since the end of August. The aircraft was in good condition and had been thoroughly inspected the morning of the crash. The pilot and aircraft were "signed off" as airworthy. December the first was just not a good day for both.

Investigators know that after leaving Bowman Field in Louisville, Jeffrey did in fact fly over Knoxville and was heading toward Gainesville at 171 degrees.[26] The plane's positioning equipment (LORAN) was downloaded at an inspection facility after the recovery. The information downloaded confirmed that his checkpoint behind him was Knoxville and the "to" waypoint was Gainesville. However, if you draw a line from the McGhee Tyson Airport to the Gainesville Regional Airport, his flight path would have been just to the west of Parsons Bald. The crash site was several miles to the east near Russell Field. In hindsight one would say that either Jeffrey did not fly directly over Knoxville before turning toward Gainesville or as he approached the mountains he moved off track looking for a low gap to fly between the cloud layer and the mountain tops. The wreckage path pointed the plane at 170 degrees, which points to Gainesville. Apparently he saw the 4,328-foot McCampbell Gap and was trying to shoot through. The bottom of the overcast layer was 4,200 feet, a difference of 128 feet.

At approximately 4:15 P.M. Eastern Time, Mann flew over the Knoxville area and turned toward Gainesville, Florida. If he was following the proposed plan he had discussed with the Green Bay FSS, he was flying at or below 4,200 feet due to the overcast. On a cloudy, winter day such as this, the mountains looked dark and looming. At this time of day it would look lighter and less ominous to turn west toward the sunset rather than into the dark mountains. Perhaps Jeffrey thought he could make it across the main ridge and stay below the clouds; however, this thinking was a trap. In conditions like these, the mountains become a spider web for airplanes. Fifteen minutes later Mann hoped for the best. But hope does not buy altitude.

By the look of the accident scene, the Cessna 182 flew straight and level into the side of the mountain. It was not in a climb or a turn. This told the investigators that he probably was in the clouds and was trying to ride it out. More than likely he did not see the terrain. Perhaps (and this is pure speculation) he was in a momentary white out and was simply keeping the plane straight and level hoping to pop out of the cloud after the crossing through the gap.

McCampbell Gap (4,328 feet) is just east of the Russell Field Shelter. From a distance this feature sticks out as the lowest dip in that area of the main ridge system. It is the low spot between Thunderhead Mountain at 5,527 feet and Mollies Ridge at 4,775 feet.

The impact took place at 4,280 feet and was spread over a 150-foot area. The first point of contact with the Smokies was two tall trees. These trees tore off the aircraft's entire right wing and the outer portion of the

left wing. The collision turned the aircraft slightly to the right and dropped it quickly to the ground. The speed was around one hundred miles per hour as the fuselage abruptly stopped. The propeller hit a dead, rotting tree-trunk and splintered it into sawdust. The wood chips were scattered all over the wreckage and the crash site.

The wreckage of a Cessna 182 piloted by Jeffrey Mann in December 1997. It was later determined that Mann most likely did not see the surrounding terrain and flew straight and level into the side of the mountain. He was probably trying to cross over McCampbell Gap, the lowest point of the main ridge system in the area. Photo by Jeff Wadley.

A large box of photographs was jettisoned from the plane and flew into the air. Hundreds of photos spread throughout the area. The authors of this book have a photograph of the crash scene that shows two of Mann's pictures embedded in a tree trunk at least a half-inch. From above in the search aircraft, the plane looked shredded because of the white backs of the hundreds of pictures.

Most likely the pilot from Wisconsin died on impact still strapped to his seat. In the blink of an eye he lost his life because the clouds shrouded his sight and robbed him of keeping his aircraft out of danger. He needed only 148 feet (plus the height of the trees) to have made it over the Smokies. This was a tragedy.

At impact the plane was demolished, the pilot died, and the orange Narco ELT self-activated. Although the pilot could not summon searchers himself, the ELT was doing it on his behalf. That is the beauty of an ELT. At the same time the ELT turned on, several satellites were in Earth's orbit monitoring the frequency for the electronic pulsing signal. The time of the crash (by estimating the time of departure from Bowman Field and factoring a cruise speed for the Cessna 182) was approximately 4:34 P.M. As soon as a SARSAT was over the area, it locked onto the transmission. The time was 5:06 P.M.

The first set of coordinates relayed to the Air Force Rescue Coordination Center was 35 35.1′ by 83°41.3′. This is considered a "first alert" and is logged as a hit. Another satellite was over the area at 6:21 P.M. and locked the location as 35 36.0′ by 83°35.9′. The third hit was at 6:47 P.M. with the coordinate of 35°35.8′ by 83°38.4′. The three sites are considered a "merge," which means as the satellites pass over the area they will continue to "home in" on the exact location. Overall the SARSAT system is correct only within a few miles of the exact location. At times it can pinpoint a signal. In this incident these hits were within two to five miles of the actual crash site.

Airman Cordaro was on duty at the Air Force Rescue Coordination Center at Langley Air Force Base that night. He reviewed the transcripts of the satellite information and, after plotting the coordinates on a map, determined that an ELT mission should be opened in East Tennessee. At 6:47 P.M. Cordaro notified Capt. Todd Rodgers of the Tennessee Civil Air Patrol. USAF mission number 97M2507 was activated to search for an unknown ELT signal. The Tennessee Emergency Management Agency in Nashville was also notified because CAP is an agency of TEMA. At this point the aircraft that activated the ELT was not known to have been overdue. All the investigators knew was that an ELT had been transmitting for one hour and forty-one minutes. No one knew a plane had crashed.

Captain Rodgers notified Maj. Rick Grindstaff of the East Tennessee Group 1 Headquarters that his unit was to begin to track the source of the ELT. Grindstaff put together a plan and put Group 1 members on mission status. Grindstaff dispatched two ground teams and had an aircrew on standby if the ground teams could not promptly locate the ELT.

Ground teams were activated. One call was placed to the Sevier County Squadron and another to coauthor Wadley. The Sevier County team assembled and met at the airport in Sevierville. Much to their surprise they could hear the ELT from the airfield! They thought that the ELT was probably at the Gatlinburg–Pigeon Forge Airport and the SARSAT was in error reporting the coordinates. When Wadley heard their report, he thought that they had it under control and he called Grindstaff to tell him that the Sevierville team was tracking it in Sevierville. The CAP radio became busy with traffic from all over east Tennessee. One unit in Oak Ridge heard the ELT as well as units in Knoxville, Oliver Springs and Kodak. Either there were multiple ELT signals or this one was very strong and high in elevation. Grindstaff assumed the later option. With so many people hearing the signal from so many places the ELT had to have been transmitting from high in the Smokies.

Wadley called a unit in North Carolina and had them listen for the ELT. All CAP members in North Carolina who reported back indicated that they were not hearing the signal. This confirmed even more that the signal was being transmitted on the Tennessee side of the Smokies. Still, no word on an overdue aircraft; no one knew yet that Mann had crashed.

Turning on his tracking equipment, CAP member Dennis Sparks, who lives in east Maryville, heard the ELT right away. He relayed to Wadley that the signal was coming from southeastern Blount County. Wadley also turned on his equipment from his home in the Montvale area and immediately heard the signal loud and clear. With Sparks's information in the back of his head he drove to the Lookrock Observation Tower on the Foothills Parkway to gain altitude. Wadley's tracking radio gave a reading toward Russell Field.

The Sevier County crew led by Maj. Jerry Whaley met Wadley at the Cades Cove Ranger Station. Ranger Ken Davis joined them and the CAP and Park Service gathered additional data. The tower at McGhee Tyson Airport and the Airway Traffic Control Center were interviewed. The supervisors reported that there were no missing or overdue aircraft. McGhee Tyson listened to their voice tapes from the past few hours and reported that they had not "worked" any aircraft through the area that was VFR or any that had gone off their radarscopes.

With this information the CAP and park investigators were at a loss to explain the activated ELT. Other scenarios were considered, such as a drug drop or a personal ELT. In the past some drug dealers had actually dropped drugs from an airplane in duffel bags with an ELT attached. The receiving dealer then tracked the bag, and after it was found, the ELT was turned off. This practice is not wise on the dealer's part because the ELTs are tracked by satellite, air, and ground by the U.S. government (CAP, coast guard, AFRCC, and so on).

The other scenario was that this was a personal ELT. Although it is not legal in most of the continental United States, some hikers and outdoors enthusiasts have purchased ELTs to carry with them on their hikes and activities. The user would simply switch on the unit and wait for help to arrive. Lastly the investigators considered that an airplane had crashed that had not been worked by the tower.

With the scenarios in mind, Davis, Whaley, Wadley, and the other members decided to continue the search through the night with the insistence of their respective supervisors. Whaley requested that a CAP aircraft be dispatched to the area. By that time the clouds had lifted and the night sky was clear so flying was permissible. Ground teams decided to drive through Cades Cove to "triangulate" the signal during the night.

Upon entering the cove, the CAP/NPS team used spotlights to scan the fields in case there was a plane in an open field. While driving around the desolate loop road the team stopped at specific points to listen for the signal. From the extreme northwestern overlook referred to as the "wildlife overlook" the team was able to hear the ELT signal well. Davis took a compass bearing along the line that the tracking unit was pointing. They plotted their location on a topographical map and drew a line from their location along that line. The direction on the map was toward Russell Field and Spence Field.

They moved to the back of the Cove and plotted again. This bearing was still in the direction of Russell Field. In fact it was very close to the direction of the backcountry shelter near the field. Again they moved around the loop to the extreme eastern end of the cove and took another reading on the tracking unit. This time the signal was very strong and pointed almost due south toward Ledbetter Ridge and the Smoky's crest.

The last reading was from the end of the gated access road above the Anthony Creek Horse Camp. Again, the plot was to the south up the Ledbetter Ridge. After taking all their readings the team saw that the lines crossed just three-quarters of a mile north of the Appalachian Trail and just east of Russell Field.

While the ground team was plotting on maps the source of the signal from the ground, a CAP aircraft had made its way in the darkness above Cades Cove. It began to track the signal upon liftoff from the Downtown Island Airport in Knoxville. Lt. Gerald McLinn and Maj. Ted Bumbalough were flying a Cessna 182 (N9307X) in the direction of the Smokies crest. They departed the airport at 10:25 P.M., and as soon as they were in the air the ghostly warbling tone of an ELT blared over their headsets. Flying toward the source of the ELT signal, the two pilots could barely distinguish the very dark horizon from the mountains. With plenty of mountain flying and night-flying time under their belts, they maintained an altitude of seventy-five hundred feet during the operation.

Wadley radioed the aircrew and had them fly directly over the spot that had the greatest signal. As they flew over the source of the ELT, Bumbalough read his coordinates to Wadley at the Ranger Station: 35°33.7′ by 83°43.9′. The ground crew plotted the coordinates and determined that their plot and the aircrew plot were very close. McLinn and Bumbalough peered into the darkness seeking a light, fire, strobe, or flare. They saw only the color black. With still no indication that an aircraft was missing or overdue, and for the safety of the team, the aircrew was eventually called back to its base.

The ground team continued searching until 2:30 A.M. and decided that they would rest until sunrise and hike the five miles to Russell Field. Wadley requested additional personnel to relieve his team. The group would leave Cades Cove at 6:30 A.M. and track the ELT with rangers. Another team was summoned and met Wadley at the ranger station an hour later for a briefing. The Sevierville team, Wadley and Ranger Davis called it a night.

Before sunrise two CAP members from Knoxville (Tres Monceret and Marcus Bersaglia) were packing their gear to join Ranger Al Voner. Their task would be to hike to Ledbetter Ridge and track the ELT. They had hopes that the weather would be good enough to have a helicopter or aircraft spot the wreckage and lead them in to the scene. First, there was a two and one-half hour hike ahead of them.

Cades Cove District ranger Jack Piepenbring met with the three men, briefed them on their instructions, and sent them into the woods. Ranger Voner was the team leader and a very experienced searcher in the Smokies. As they departed, there was still no report of a missing aircraft. The ground team did not know for sure what they would encounter.

Meeting at the Knoxville Downtown Island Airport were CAP members Col. Dennis Sparks, Maj. Ted Bumbalough, and Lt. Gerald McLinn. Their Cessna 182 started in the cold morning air, and the crew was airborne at 8:08 A.M. Just as they had done a few hours earlier but in total darkness, the crew began to track the ELT. Ten minutes later they were over Cades Cove with the sun rising over the mountains revealing a cloudless day. Keeping their eyes peeled, the threesome scanned the terrain in search for an indication of what was transmitting the ELT signal. Two minutes later, the aircraft tracked the ELT to an exact spot just east of Russell Field. The highly trained search pilot maneuvered the plane right over the highest transmission signal of the ELT and immediately the three spotted a debris field of white, red, and black metal. Making a quick turn the pilot reduced speed and altitude so that the two other searchers could see into the wreckage. To their amazement they could see the pilot sitting in his seat. There was, however, no sign of life.

The CAP aircraft radioed their mission base and gave an exact coordinate of the crash site: 35°33.94′ by 83°46.14′. In the area was a Knox County Sheriff's Department helicopter. The CAP aircraft radioed the pilot and asked that he hover over the wreckage to try and read the large registration number on the side of the plane and see if there were signs of life. The sheriff's pilot quickly moved into the area and read the tail number: N9033Y. Using heat-sensing equipment, the crew did not discover signs of life in the tangled wreckage. It was now 8:30 and the ground crew were still hiking toward the crash site.

Using the registration number on the side of the plane and a general description, the Park Service notified the FAA of the source of the ELT signal. Through the proper channels, the FAA notified the family of the situation and began an investigation. Paul Jones of the FAA was on call and given the case. He left his office and flew to Knoxville within the hour.

Hiking up the trail to Russell Field, Ranger Voner was notified via his radio that the source of the ELT was a crashed airplane. Since a CAP airplane and a sheriff's department helicopter were circling the wreckage, he left the trail before arriving at the summit. Beating the bushes and hurrying to the site, the ranger was lead into the scene by the helicopter at 10:45 A.M. Twenty minutes later, Monceret and Bersaglia arrived by way of McCampbell Gap and Russell Field.

Approaching the aircraft from below the scene, Voner cautiously walked around to the front of the fuselage and determined that there was one person on board. As he was checking for vital signs, he realized that the pilot probably had died upon impact. This is always a bittersweet revelation. Searchers would rather locate a pilot alive, but at the same time it eases the minds of family, friends, and searchers to know that the person did not suffer while anxiously waiting for help that did not arrive in time.

Just prior to Voner's discovery, Piepenbring had asked another team consisting of CAP and NPS Rangers and Maintenance employees to hike to Russell Field to aid the first team. At 10:30 a crew led by Assistant District Ranger Jeff Carlisle departed the ranger station for the hike to the Appalachian Trail. In this team was a *Knoxville News Sentinel* reporter

(Marti Davis), CAP member Wadley, and ten Park Service personnel. By 12:47 the twelve rescuers were on the scene.

FAA investigator Paul Jones flew on board the Knoxville sheriff's helicopter to the landing zone and met with Wadley and Ranger Steve Kloster. The three hiked the short distance to McCampbell Gap, where they met the carryout crew extricating the body of Jeff Mann. At 12:58 Mann's body was at the Russell Field landing zone ready for transport off the meadow.

At the wreckage scene Jones examined the airframe with the NPS and CAP representatives. The orange ELT was located and turned off. It was attached to the inside of the tail of the aircraft and was in great condition. Jones and Marti Davis took a photographic inventory of the airplane while Carlisle made a video recording. Personal affects were also inventoried and guarded overnight by two rangers.

Once the preliminary investigation was complete, the body was loaded in the helicopter for transport. The contingent of searchers also began their hike back down the mountain. Mann's body was flown to the Cades Cove landing zone just off Sparks Lane at 2:20 P.M., and the team was off the mountain by 4:30. After a short debriefing, the Park Service and CAP closed the mission at 5:58 P.M.

Jeffrey Mann's body was taken to the University of Tennessee Medical Center, where an

The carryout of Jeffrey Mann to a waiting Knox County Sheriff's helicopter in December 1997. Photo by Jeff Wadley.

Silhouette of a Knox
County Sheriff's helicopter
at the end of the recovery
of Jeffrey Mann the day
after his crash. Photo
by Jeff Wadley.

autopsy was performed the next day. Dr. Sandra Elkins determined that the pilot had died from "blunt force injuries."[27] Blood work was sent to a national investigation lab as required by the FAA. His body was then released to the family for a funeral service.

On December 18 the aircraft was released to the owners insurance company. Bob Jones assumed the responsibility for removing the aircraft from the de facto wilderness area. Atlanta Air Salvage in Griffin, Georgia, removed the aircraft from the Smokies. The recovery was hampered because the mountains were enveloped in clouds. In fact, the contract helicopter pilot tried several times to depart from Russell Field and hover over the site but the clouds made it unsafe. The helicopter was grounded and guarded until finally after a week of waiting the crash was hoisted off the mountain to a waiting flatbed truck.

The NTSB investigation into the fatal crash lasted several weeks. A time line was developed, witnesses were interviewed, and the aircraft itself was thoroughly inspected. In the end the investigators found that the "flight controls and airframe components showed no signs of pre-crash failure or malfunction."[28] The NTSB studied the power plant, controls, instruments, and airframe. It was determined that the probable cause of the crash was "the pilot's failure to maintain VFR conditions in a mountainous area resulting in in-flight collision with rising terrain."[29] In others words, Jeffrey Mann flew into the Smoky Mountains' spider web and perished.

The Last Crash of the Century

When Frank "Bo" Thomas's airplane crashed in the Great Smoky Mountains National Park on May 5, 1999, many lives were touched. Without warning, Rhonda, his wife of twenty-three years, lost her husband. His sons, Josh, twenty, and Nate, fifteen, lost their father. Kelly, seventeen, his daughter, lost her dad. Co-workers, friends and other relatives would never forget hearing that "Bo" died an untimely, accidental death. Rose Mortuary in Knoxville along with a pastor ministered to the grieving survivors within the week.

This story will be told in a different fashion. A time-line format is used to enable searchers and the public a glimpse into the procedures and unfolding drama of a search-and-rescue mission. The information is a combination of radar data, CAP, and NPS mission notes and radio logs.

May 5, 1999. 4:36 P.M. The forty-nine-year-old pilot departs Jacksonville, Florida, for a return trip home to Knoxville, Tennessee. The aircraft Bo Thomas was flying was a 1956 Cessna 172. It was light blue in color with dark blue stripes. The registration number was N30DS. Thomas, a stockbroker, was the assistant vice president and resident manager of Merrill Lynch at the First Tennessee Plaza in Knoxville. Formerly of Columbia, South Carolina, he was a 1971 graduate of the Citadel. He was a lieutenant colonel in the South Carolina Air National Guard, flew the A-7 Corsair in Vietnam, was an F-16 pilot and had worked for Eastern Airlines as an airline transport pilot. He had accumulated more than twenty-three thousand flying hours.

4:57 P.M. Thomas contacts the departure controller and begins flying a heading of 20° at 3,000 feet. He asks for "flight following" at 4,500 feet and is issued a discreet transponder code of 2662. At this point he is 23 miles west of Brunswick, Georgia.

5:10 P.M. The air traffic controller tells Thomas about some bad weather along his route, so Thomas turns and flies just west of his intended heading. This is a typical pattern in cross-country flying. He is "handed off" to Macon approach, then to the Atlanta Air Route Traffic Center.

7:32 P.M. Atlanta center hands him off to Knoxville approach and tells him to switch frequencies. He is over Clay County, North Carolina.

7:34:02 P.M. Thomas checks in with Knoxville East approach at 8,500 feet. He indicates that his intention is to fly to the Downtown Island Airport. He is over the vicinity of Nantahala Lake.

7:34:15 P.M. Knoxville approach has radar contact with him and informs him of how far away from Knoxville he is and what the weather is in the area. The cloud bases are 3,400 feet above the ground in the Knoxville area, and the top of the cloud layer is at 7,000 feet east of Knoxville.

7:34:27 P.M. Thomas reports seeing the cloud tops below him and says that he has visual contact with the ground. He mentions that he "ought to be able to come down" through it.

7:34:39 P.M. The radar controller asks him if he is familiar with the rising, mountainous terrain.

7:34:42 P.M. Thomas acknowledges that he is familiar with the terrain.

7:35:47 P.M. Flying near the Nantahala power house (35°19.06′ by 83°42.27′) Thomas declares that he is ready to descend and is leaving 8,500 feet. This is his last radio contact, in which he does not indicate a problem. What happened between this conversation and the crash is unknown, but after the postcrash investigation, the following details were discovered.

7:40:42 P.M. At 5,000 feet over Pickens Gap, radar plots him at 2,500 feet above the terrain. By all indications (Knoxville tower's weather observation system) he is flying through a cloud layer and has been for approximately 1,500 feet of altitude. As an experienced instrument-rated pilot, this is not a problem; it is what he has been trained to do. The problem is he is not all the way over the main range of the mountains.

7:40:54 P.M. At 5,400 feet the radar plots him again. He is approaching Woodward Knob at a normal angle of descent. He is now 2,000 feet above the ground and still likely in the clouds.

7:41:06 P.M. Radar plots Thomas at 5,000 feet over the Jenkins Ridge Trail, apparently still in the clouds and not over the main ridge line. He is 1,400 feet above the ground.

7:41:18 P.M. Now only 829 feet above the ground, he has descended to 4,800 feet and is above the Jenkins Ridge Trail according to the radar plot.

7:41:30 P.M. The last radar hit puts Thomas at 4,700 feet over Haw Gap Branch.

7:41:41 P.M. The Knoxville radar site was plotting him every twelve seconds. Because this is the last radar reflection, in theory, the plane would be located within an eleven second circle. He struck Forrester Ridge at a heading of 360° at 4,440 feet above sea level. The Cessna's underside struck small-diameter treetops first, and in a split second, at around 138 miles per hour, the plane hit the ground and turned upside down, traveling approximately 200 feet on a 30-degree slope. More than likely the pilot died instantly. Measuring the weather reports in comparison to the elevation of the terrain, Thomas was probably riding the plane through the cloud layer as he had done with F-16s, commercial aircraft, and A-7s. This time he likely miscalculated the position of the aircraft in conjunction with the main ridge, thinking that he would "pop out" of the cloud layer at about 3,400 feet. With the leaves just budding in the open, second-growth forest, scattered with new ferns and rocks, Thomas's life was halted. Once the plane came to a stop in the steep ravine, the forest became quiet again. The clouds covered the trees, the plane, and pilot for the night.

7:41:42 P.M. Knoxville's radar "coasted his tag" (the blip on the screen stayed stationery and blinked).

7:41:54 P.M. Knoxville's radar coasted his tag.

7:42:06 P.M. Knoxville's radar coasted his tag.

7:42:18 P.M. The Knoxville radar's tag, which had repeatedly blinked "N30DS," disappeared from the screen. This alerted the controller to a problem, and he attempted to contact the aircraft by radio several times in the next few minutes. No response.

7:49:52 P.M. After several minutes of calling on the radio, hoping the blip would come back or that another aircraft would hear N30DS, the controller realized that the plane had probably crashed.

7:53 P.M. Knoxville weather (METAR): winds 130° at 7 knots; 10-mile visibility; altimeter, 29.84 Hg; temperature, 70 degrees; dew point, 64 degrees; a scattered cloud layer at 2,000 feet; a broken cloud layer at 3,600 feet; an overcast layer of clouds beginning at 5,500 feet.

7:54:37 P.M. Still no radio contact or radar returns. The tower discovers the airplane owner's name and calls the contact number. Thomas's wife answers the phone and reveals that Bo was expected home but had not yet returned. The family is informed of the situation.

8:00 P.M. The Knoxville approach supervisor contacts the Air Route Traffic Control Center (ARTCC) in Atlanta, which was previously working with the Thomas aircraft. They review their tapes and radar data. A statement is gathered from the controllers in Knoxville about what had occurred. A determination is made to begin a search. This is the earliest time that Thomas could have been at Knoxville. The time came and went with no contact.

8:02:40 P.M. N575CC is flying in the general area and monitors for an ELT signal on 121.5 MHz and 243.0 MHz. Nothing is heard.

8:45 P.M. The Atlanta ARTCC contacts the Air Force Rescue Coordination Center (AFRCC) and briefs the supervisor regarding the missing aircraft. Mission authorization number 99M0892 is issued. For the next three hours the AFRCC analyzes the radar data, voice transcripts, and tapes and makes contact with the Knoxville 911 center. Surrounding airports are contacted. Police departments and airport operators visually check the airport runways, parking areas, and hangars to see if the missing airplane had landed. Although this standard procedure takes time, it has in many cases turned up an airplane that has had electrical trouble and has been unable to contact the tower. In this case, all reports came back negative. With this data in hand, the AFRCC agrees that the plane is in fact down in the mountains. They notify their call-out list.

May 6. **12:07 A.M.** Capt. Todd Rodgers of the Tennessee CAP is on call and receives the alert from the AFRCC. Rodgers is given all the vital information, and after plotting the coordinates on a map, he appoints Maj. Gary Milton incident commander. The AFRCC contacts the North Carolina CAP. Their membership is alerted, and many members respond to their emergency operations centers to plot the incident and make plans for the ground search in the backcountry and by airplane.

2:00 A.M. Tennessee CAP ground searchers and aircrews are briefed and prepare for a first-light deployment. The SARSAT system is still not receiving an ELT signal.

6:00 A.M. CAP incident commander Walter Zohrn is appointed to take over the search operation. Still, no ELT is heard.

6:50 A.M. Zohrn calls the Great Smoky Mountains National Park dispatcher and briefs them.

7:00 A.M. Zohrn interviews Rhonda Thomas, Bo's wife. He asks questions pertaining to Bo's flying habits and other personal issues. Sometime during the day a fax will arrive describing Bo's profile. This is from a friend, Paul Bissell, of the U.S. Coast Guard Auxiliary:

> flies the west end of the Smokies
> he would have called if he had landed somewhere else
> flies to the letter
> calm pilot
> not likely to lose it in an emergency
> has sharp survival skills

7:10 A.M. The Knox County Sheriff's Department calls. Chief Lyon offers the use of their helicopters and crew. They will be able to fly as soon as the weather cooperates. They indicate that they would like to fly to the last known position and work towards Downtown Island Airport.

7:52 A.M. Atlanta center offers more specific radar data.

8:44 A.M. CAP relays all their information to the Park Service in an update. Weather is too bad to fly. Clouds hide the mountains and fog still shrouds the Downtown Island Airport.

8:55 A.M. Sergeant Noble with the AFRCC gives another archived radar hit: 7:41 P.M., 4,800 feet, 35° 31.31′ by 83°43.02′, heading of 360°.

9:30 A.M. Ranger Jack Piepenbring from Cades Cove is notified about the search by his dispatcher. Ranger Mike Farley prepares a landing zone for the Knoxville sheriff's helicopters near Sparks Lane in the Cove.

11:07 A.M. The sheriff's department is finally able to depart safely from Knoxville and begin their search between Downtown Island Airport and the Smokies.

11:52 A.M. A CAP ground team (Steve Cantrell, Caleb Joiner, and James Massengill) is dispatched to Cades Cove. They are to stage with the Park Service team. The helicopters arrive in the cove and decide to land due to the very high wind and thick cloud cover.

12:00 noon. Piepenbring meets with Lieutenant Burnette and Tim Lickliter at the landing zone to discuss the search plan. The pilots report the wind to be in excess of 45 miles per hour near the summit of the Smokies. The Bell 206 Jet Rangers are unable to fly safely.

12:25 P.M. CAP aircraft N9307X departs toward the search area with pilots Bill Dritt and Mike Wood on board. They plan to conduct a contour search of the south slope of Thunderhead Mountain, staying 1,000 feet above the terrain.

1:00 P.M. The CAP ground crew arrives in Cades Cove.

1:05 P.M. CAP and NPS request the aid of the Tennessee Army National Guard. Weather forces them to not commit. By this time everyone is wondering if any aircraft will get in any search time on the mountain. It is very disheartening and frustrating for all involved.

1:42 P.M. The crew of CAP's N9307X decide that because of the low cloud cover and turbulent winds, conditions are unsafe to fly. They return reluctantly to their mission base. North Carolina CAP pilots have the same problem and return to their base. We were told that it was so turbulent that "you would drop several feet then be forced back up in a matter of seconds over and over again." Alternate plans are made to prepare a ground team to hike toward the last known position. It would take until after dark to get there if they left now.

2:50–2:57 P.M. The Knoxville sheriff's helicopter pilots try again to enter the search area around the last known position. Their target was Cherry Knob, DeArmond Bald, and Blockhouse Mountain. Again they were turned away by the erratic winds. They return to the landing zone.

3:51 P.M. The sheriff's helicopters decide to return to the Knoxville Airport before the weather closes in on them and keeps them in the park overnight.

3:52 P.M. CAP aircraft N97018 piloted by Gerald McLinn tries to search the 161-degree radial of the volunteer VOR to the last known position and back at 4,500 feet. His plan is to fly a route search, a contour search, and a search around the last radar hit.

4:00 P.M. Jeff Miller of the Park Service at Deep Creek plans to put together a crew to fly into a high-probability area in the morning.

5:30 P.M. Maj. Jeff Wadley of the Tennessee CAP meets with Piepen-bring to debrief the day's frustrating results. They also make plans for the next day's search. They decide to send a small CAP/NPS crew to Spence Field Shelter, spend part of the night, and hike cross-country to the last known position in the morning. Another larger crew of CAP and rangers would assemble at the Cove at first light and hike to Thunderhead Mountain for a search. These two teams would hike along the flight path in hopes of discovering the crash site. It would be like finding a needle in a haystack. If the weather cooperates the CAP or Knoxville sheriff's helicopter would be used as well. During this planning session Major Wadley spoke with CAP pilot Lt. Mike Wood and asked him to stay airborne over the suspected area until dark in case the clouds lifted.

6:20 P.M. CAP aircraft N97018 returns to Knoxville, unable to see the mountaintops.

7:00 P.M. At the North Carolina CAP's incident command center, pilots and coordinators discuss their displeasure with the way the search had progressed. Everyone agrees that if the clouds had cleared an aircraft would have been able to see Thomas's plane. At the Asheville Regional Airport sat a solution to the problem. A CAP member knew that a unit of large and heavy U.S. Air Force helicopters was temporarily stationed just down the runway from the CAP base. These gray MH-53 Pavelow helicopters were attached to Hubert Air Base in Florida. They were using the mountains in western North Carolina as a classroom in night-flight operations. Lt. Col. Steve Siske of the CAP asked the crew if they would be able to fly a mission. They quickly agreed. After securing proper authorization, the crew was briefed and given a search area. They departed Asheville with plans of returning three and a half-hours later. With four and half hours of fuel on board and eight crew members they flew to the last known position of N30DS.

7:07 P.M. CAP search plane N9307X departs Downtown Island Airport and prepares to stay in the area until sunset. A CAP ground search team leaves Knoxville en route to meet Wadley for their night trek into the backcountry.

7:25 P.M. Lieutenant Wood and Lt. Randy Patterson have the break-through everyone had been waiting on. Flying at 7,500 feet, the men notice that the clouds are clearing just enough so they can see the trees. They make a beeline for the "hot" area south of Thunderhead Mountain.

8:00 P.M. Wadley meets with Farragut High School Junior ROTC coordinator Bill Trisler and Nate Thomas (son of the missing pilot) at the Cades Cove Ranger Station. The assistance of the JROTC is presented. Wadley asks that they meet with Ranger Piepenbring at 7:30 A.M. the following day. Wadley sends the message to the family through Tresler that everyone is frustrated, there will be a search plane flying until sunset, and a ground team is being inserted quickly. The group agrees that the best things to do is wait until morning and offer their assistance rather than walking through the woods at night.

8:07 P.M. Wood and Patterson catch a glimpse of scattered metal in a steep ravine around 4,500 feet near Haw Gap and Blockhouse Mountain. The geographical coordinates are 35°32.56´ by 83°42.65´. "Tally Ho!" indicated the air crew to mission base. The two-person crew flies as low as practical and safe trying to make a positive ID on the plane's tail number. Orbiting the site at almost sunset and watching the rolling clouds, the men decide to leave the area in case they too end up on the side of the mountain. Twenty-four hours had passed since the crash occurred.

8:20 P.M. Just as the CAP aircraft is turning to fly home, the air force helicopter contacts them by radio. "Knife 51" said that they were able to go low and slow over the last known position and Wood informed them of the find. Knife 51 received the coordinates from Wood and flew over the area until they also located the plane. The pilot hovered over the plane and did not notice any signs of life but was able to read a partial tail number. As quickly as the clouds lifted they again covered the mountain, and both search aircraft immediately left the area.

8:30 P.M. Lieutenants Wood and Patterson notify Major Wadley of the situation and announce the find.

The wreckage of Bo Thomas's Cessna 172, which crashed into a steep ravine near Haw Gap in May 1999. After several days of searching, the family was able to have closure. Photo by Jeff Wadley.

8:55 P.M. N9307X arrives at its mission base in Tennessee, as does the MH-53 in North Carolina. Wadley and Ranger Randy Scoggins plot the coordinates and prepare to leave Cades Cove.

9:15 P.M. The CAP mission base informs the Park Service command center of the specific details of the location and about plans for the night.

9:30 P.M. Maj. Duane Devotie, Lt. Greg Summers, and Lt. Meyers arrive at Cades Cove and join with Wadley and Scoggins for a briefing.

10:30 P.M. The five-person search team departs for a five-mile night hike. On the North Carolina side of the park, Rangers Jenkins and Murphy and one other ranger boat across Fontana Lake and hike toward the south end of the Jenkins Ridge Trail head. Both teams will camp in the backcountry.

May 7. **Midnight.** At the end of the day, forty-six persons from four different agencies had been involved in the search, and the result was a definite location of the missing aircraft. The search was half over. By 2:00 A.M. the teams had arrived at their predetermined campsites. They took time to eat and rest.

6:00 A.M. The two teams rise after a short night of rest and prepare for the search. At Spence Field the weather was cool, the winds were 15 to 20 miles per hour from the southwest, and visibility was less than 100 feet.

6:30 A.M. The teams begin their hike on the Jenkins Ridge Trail.

6:39 A.M. Pipenbring contacts the three Lake District team members and asks them to meet the Cades Cove team near Haw Gap. If the Knox County Sheriff's Department helicopter can fly, it will attempt once again to fly over the site. If the crew is able, they will guide the ground search teams into the crash site.

7:30 A.M. Additional park rangers, maintenance workers, and CAP members gather at the command center at the cove. They gather a wheeled liter, extrication gear, and personal equipment and prepare to leave.

7:45 P.M. The sheriff's department calls to say that they will be airborne around 9:00 A.M.

9:15 A.M. The two search teams meet below the Haw Gap meadow and plot the last known position and the coordinate of the crash site in reference to where they are. They divide into three smaller teams and leave the Jenkins Ridge Trail. One team walked up the facing ridge, one walked down the ridge, and the third went directly east off the trail. They knew that even though they had good coordinates it would still be difficult to locate the crash because it was described as being in a steep ravine about a mile off the trail and in a forested area. Visibility was hampering the effort because clouds were still covering the mountain. The team knew that the helicopter or the CAP plane would not be able to guide them.

9:24 A.M. Airspace above the western Smokies is restricted by the FAA to search-and-rescue aircraft only.

9:43 A.M. CAP flight N9307X with McLinn and Patterson depart from the Knoxville Downtown Island Airport to assist with radio communications over the search area. A few minutes later the sheriff's helicopter also departs.

9:51 A.M. Ranger Jenkins and CAP Wadley locate the crash site. The find is radioed to the command center. They find Bo Thomas in the aircraft and realize that he did not survive the crash. They call for the other two teams to meet them at the scene.

9:59 A.M. The additional CAP and NPS members are 1.2 miles from Spence Field and report light rain and low visibility. The CAP and sheriff's aircraft also report that the overcast cloud layer is above 7,000 feet. They decide to stay in the area above the clouds until the weather clears.

The helicopter declares an intention to land at Spence Field when the clouds dissipate.

10:09 A.M. Once the other teams gather at the scene they carefully, and with great respect, remove Bo Thomas from the crumbled wreckage. An inventory was made and photographs of the scene were taken.

10:15 A.M. The family is notified of the situation.

11:05 A.M. A rescue sleeve is dropped to the team by the helicopter during a short break in the weather.

11:15 A.M. The helicopter tries multiple times to land at Spence Field but cannot due to the "soup."

11:41 A.M. A severe thunderstorm warning is issued by the National Weather Service in Morristown for most of East Tennessee and the Smokies. The Park Service opts to transport the body to Fontana Lake rather than up to Spence Field and down to Cades Cove. Transportation is arranged.

11:50 A.M. 07X returns to Knoxville, trying to beat the approaching storm.

1:00 P.M. The additional carryout crew arrives and meets the exhausted search team members who had begun the carryout up the steep slope. After securing Thomas's body in the litter, the crew continued the evacuation. Thunder is heard rumbling in the distance. The twenty rescuers know what is coming.

1:31 P.M. It begins to rain while the crew is at the bottom of a ravine, with half a mile to go before reaching the Jenkins Ridge Trail.

2:29 P.M. As the team arrives with the body at the Jenkins Ridge Trail, wind blows against the mountain and lightning is heard cracking to the northwest. Rain comes down in sheets, then, as quickly as it came, it stopped. The twenty-person team divides into two teams. One will do the carry out to Fontana and the other will return to Cades Cove by climbing back up Jenkins Ridge Trail to the Appalachian Trail.

3:45 P.M. Ranger Al Voner and his team arrive back at Spence Field at the Appalachian Trail. They encounter pea-sized hail, horizontal-blowing rain, lightning, and extremely high winds. The carryout crew slip and slide down the Jenkins Ridge Trail toward Fontana Lake.

5:30 P.M. Voner's crew arrives at Cades Cove, are debriefed, and head home.

7:00 P.M. The carryout crew arrives at the Fontana Boat Dock with the body.

7:45 P.M. All personnel return to the cove.

10:00 P.M. The crew meets a Rural Metro ambulance, which transports the body to the hospital.

10:50 P.M. Everyone returns home, except Ranger Jenkins, who remains at the crash site to guard it through the night. Forty-one persons are involved in the operation on the seventh. Plans begin for Thomas's funeral service at Rose Mortuary in Knoxville (it was held on Tuesday, May 11).

May 8. In the morning, Ranger Scoggins of the Park Service leads a team of investigators to the site. Along with him are Al Yurman of the National Transportation Safety Board (NTSB), Ron Robson of the Federal Aviation Administration (FAA), Seth Buttner of the Cessna Corporation, and Dale Carter. The NTSB investigation was filed as report number MIA99FA150.

The men inspected the engine, fuel tanks, instruments, and fuselage and documented their findings. A ranger recorded Thomas's personal property, and the scene was released to the owner's insurance company. The plane was removed from the park a few weeks later by Atlanta Air Salvage. Except for a few broken tree limbs, no sign of the aircraft remains today.

On July 15, Phil Powell of the NTSB examined the plane's airframe, engine, and propeller. He found no discrepancies or mechanical malfunctions. The final NTSB report indicated the opinion to the cause of the crash: visual flight into a reduced-visibility area.

A few weeks after the operation a critique was held at park headquarters to discuss the aspects of the search. Both the CAP and Park Service learned once again that their job usually begins as a search to find a pilot alive but often turns into a quest to bring closure to a family. The Thomas family continues to miss Bo and grieves at his untimely death. On May 5, 1999, the Smokies claimed their last aircraft and life of the century.

EIGHT

A Few Minor Incidents

Although minor aviation incidents do not receive much press, nor do they make for exciting search stories, five incidents are included here.

April 12, 1941

Pilot L. D. Warren was flying over the Cherokee Orchard on April 12, 1941, when he was "forced down" into the terrain. Warren, of Nashville, found himself sitting in his airplane, not on a landing strip or on a field, but on top of an apple tree. Records indicate that Warren did not receive any injuries in the crash; in fact, he was able to crawl out of the plane and down the limbs of the tree.[1] Apparently, his airplane survived the crash as well, with minimal damage.

It is not known why Warren was in the area or if he was on a cross-country or local flight. There was a small airstrip near Airport Road in Gatlinburg, and he may have been taking off or landing there when the incident occurred. It is also not clear how many passengers he had with him that spring day.

The area of the crash is an interesting destination for hikers. Within the loop road of the orchard, the curious hiker can still find evidence of the once-cultivated and well-maintained orchard with its perfectly aligned rows of shrubs and flowers and unmaintained apple trees. Do not go into the loop looking for airplane parts, however; the plane was completely disassembled soon after the event and reassembled for flight.

August 8, 1946

The Oconaluftee fields are located at the park boundary near Cherokee, North Carolina. The area, famous for its Cherokee history and its old lumber camps, is also home to many trout streams. The large, beautiful meadows welcome visitors as they enter the park from Cherokee. The Park Service has landed search-and-rescue aircraft at Oconaluftee, and two aviation incidents have occurred here.

Park records indicate that a single-engine, light aircraft from Grapevine, Texas, became lost while flying over the Smokies on August 8, 1946.[2] While trying to find his way, the pilot decided to stop and ask for directions. Although Oconaluftee did not have an airport, a field below the ranger station did the job. The pilot landed the plane successfully and inquired about his location and how to get where he wanted to go. After reorienting himself, he continued his cross-country flight.

March 12, 1952

In another incident a Gatlinburg resident, Clyde Cooper, was flying over the Smokies en route to a Knoxville airport when he experienced engine trouble. Being a smart pilot, he decided not to try his luck by flying over the mountains but instead landed safely in the Oconaluftee meadows. The pilot was able to correct the aircraft's problem, and he continued his flight the following day.[3]

May 5, 1949, and November 24, 1961

One of the most beautiful autumn scenes in the nation is within a day's drive of half the population of the United States. This particular area of the park has a generous history of limestone erosion, affording visitors a view of the results of the Great Smoky Overthrust Fault. Locals call it Cades Cove. Durwood Dunn's *Cades Cove; the Life and Death of a Southern Appalachian Community* and *The Cades Cove Story* by Randolph Shields explain the story of the Cherokee inhabitants and the new settlers inhabiting the cove.

Although there is no airstrip within park boundaries, several airplanes have made their way into the cleared fields of this cove. Tall mountain peaks and steep slopes characterize the mountains, and suddenly a "hole" appears. The cove has been a landing zone for search-and-rescue aircraft on occasion, and it has been the scene of two minor incidents.

On May 5, 1949, a pilot from Maryville landed a small airplane in the fields of Cades Cove. Park Service records indicate that he did not think he would get into trouble, but was ordered to remove the aircraft and never land his plane in the park again.[4] Apparently, he obliged, as his name is not mentioned again in park files.

The Tri-Pacer was manufactured by the Piper Corporation primarily for use by private pilots. This small plane was fabric-covered but strengthened by a metal frame and powered by a strong engine. The four-place single-engine aircraft was popular among aviators in the 1960s, and many are still flying today. It was this type of light aircraft that made an emergency landing in the dry, brown grass of Cades Cove. The date was November 24, 1961.[5]

Flying out of New Orleans, William Fowler was low on fuel and time was running out. He was in serious trouble over the Smokies as his fuel gauges told him that he did not have enough fuel to reach an airport. Seeing the cove below, he picked a landing spot in the open fields. He descended and without incident landed the plane safely.

Park Service records indicate that Fowler found help and was able to fly out of the park that day. A woman gave the pilot ten gallons of fuel, enough to get him to McGhee Tyson Airport. Once he checked out the improvised airstrip, Fowler started his plane and departed. He flew to the airport in Alcoa for fuel as he continued his journey.

NINE

Supplying Mount LeConte

LeConte Lodge atop Mount LeConte is a commercial bed and breakfast inn operated to give park visitors a rustic but comfortable feel for the backcountry. Pauline Huff began to feed tourists passing through the area in the early 1900s as her husband, Jack, literally carved the lodge, the beds, and other furnishings out of the mountain. Since the inception of LeConte Lodge, its operators and staff have made it a home away from home for both locals and tourists.

The lodge has been supplied in different ways through the years. Human muscle has brought much of the needed supplies to the summit, as have horses and llamas. Hikers and staff members make hundreds of trips a year to the mountaintop, bringing everything from fresh fruit to cellular phone batteries. Although supplying the lodge seems adventuresome and romantically glamorous, unexpected events have spelled tragedy for many.

Death on Deep Creek

Helicopter sightseeing is the only way some visitors can see the backcountry of the vast Great Smoky Mountains National Park. The majority of the park visitors never leave parking areas or paved roads, so an aerial view is ideal except for hikers who desire quietness. The loud helicopters tend to spoil their day, thus a problem.

Gene Henry operated a helicopter sightseeing business in Pigeon Forge and flew tourists over places that only a handful of hikers had ever seen. Henry's last flight over the Smokies was on Tuesday morning, August 12, 1969.

Installing a sewer and water system one vertical mile above Gatlinburg was no easy task. The Egli and Spradlen Construction Company of Gatlinburg was contracted to install the new system at LeConte Lodge. Simply off loading pipe and pumps from Ralph and Lynn's truck was impossible because there were no paved roads to the lodge. That is where Gene Henry came in.

Indian Gap and the Luftee Overlook are pullouts primarily used for viewing the mountains from a car or recreational vehicle. On occasion they are used for helicopter landing areas for search-and-rescue operations, wildlife management, and to supply LeConte Lodge. Another landing zone used frequently on supply trips is a large gravel parking lot at the old Hunter Hills/Chucky Jack outdoor theater off Highway 321 near Gatlinburg-Pittman High School. Gene Henry was using the Indian Gap for a landing zone.

Henry, age thirty, worked for the Knoxville Helicopter Services and also flew out of the old Apple Tree Inn heli-spot in Pigeon Forge. In the early 1970s this was at the upper end of Pigeon Forge; now it is in the middle. Just a week prior to this incident, it was reported that he had crashed on takeoff in Pigeon Forge but was uninjured. On this fatal occasion he was transporting building materials, not people, into the mountains. Having never flown this route with materials, Henry made a practice run from Indian Gap to LeConte and back without incident. At around 10:00 A.M. his aircraft was loaded with materials and he took off, circling to gain altitude.

In an instant Henry's life was taken. Turning his helicopter, he crashed into the trees just below Clingmans Dome Road into the Deep Creek drainage. Witnesses watched in terror as the helicopter dropped out of sight and failed to come back up. Several persons began to make their way down the slope to search for the helicopter while others darted down the highway looking for a ranger. The hasty search found nothing.

At 10:40 A.M. maintenance worker Herb Chambers was found at the Alum Cave Parking Area by a visitor and was told that the helicopter had gone down. Chambers immediately notified park dispatch and requested additional resources to aid in the search. Shortly after noon another helicopter, this one piloted by Ron Smith, who operated a similar sightseeing tour operation, arrived on the scene at Indian Gap. Smith flew his tours from Hillbilly Village in Pigeon Forge. District ranger Bob Morris and Smith searched in the immediate area but saw nothing from the air.

Weather began to hamper the search as additional crews arrived. Lynn Spradlen, one of the construction company owners who witnessed the crash, flew with Smith on another search of the mountain and made a possible sighting at 1:20. The clouds covered the mountaintop, and the air search was temporarily halted.

At 1:30 a team consisting of five rangers began a ground search, and forty five minutes later another aerial search attempt was made from another helicopter. This chopper was from yet another sightseeing service in Gatlinburg. Frenchie Devall operated from the old American Legion Football Field heli-spot (the current Gatlinburg Wastewater Treatment Plant) on the "Spur." Devall and John Haynes, a friend of Henry, flew three sorties over the area. On the third trip, at 4:09, the crashed helicopter was located.

At 4:58, guided by the Devall helicopter, the ground crew arrived on the scene. They found that Gene Henry had died in the crash, and a carryout was arranged. The National Park Service called the Cherokee Rescue Squad and others for assistance. By 5:30 a team was assembled, and at 6:00 the team departed down the mountainside with food, lights, and a litter. Almost one hour later the team met with the ground crew and the body was prepared for transport. At 7:23 the carryout began. Although the actual crash site was found approximately half a mile off Clingmans Dome Road, the carryout was best accomplished by going downhill toward Highway 441 near the Luftee Overlook. After carrying Henry for almost three miles through very thick summer vegetation, the team arrived at the hearse at 9:50 P.M., almost twelve hours after the incident occurred.

Henry's body was transported to the University of Tennessee Medical Center in Knoxville and examined by Robert Lash, the FAA medical examiner. Two seasonal rangers guarded the crash site until the FAA and the Civil Aeronautics Board arrived in Gatlinburg. Their investigation of the crash took place on Thursday the fourteenth.

Close by, in North Carolina, the Nantahala Power and Light Company had hired Carson Helicopter Services out of Parkasis, Pennsylvania, to set power poles for power lines near Bryson City.[1] The powerful, converted military H-34 had a 1,525-horsepower engine that was cable-hoist equipped. It was this helicopter that several days later lifted Henry's crashed helicopter from Deep Creek drainage back to Indian Gap.

Captain Crunch's Crash

Three years and two weeks after Gene Henry died, the park's first aviation accident of the 1970s occurred. Interestingly, the incidents in 1969 and 1972 had something in common: both aviators were trying to supply LeConte Lodge.

The Sevier–Gatlinburg Airport, as it was called until the city of Sevierville sold its ownership to the cities of Gatlinburg and Pigeon Forge, was the home of Great Smoky Mountains Aviation. Allen Moore, of Maynardville, worked there as an aviation mechanic and flew with Jack Neiman Jr. of Gatlinburg on occasion.

Neiman, forty-eight, was a lieutenant commander in the U.S. Navy and was that service's first astronaut. At the time of the crash, or "crash landing" as the *Knoxville News Sentinel* correctly called it, Neiman had logged nine thousand hours of flight time.[2] His experience probably led not only to the soft landing but also to the reduction of injuries sustained in the crash. In his twenty-one years of flying up until the LeConte accident, he had never been involved in a crash.

He had experienced several close calls, however, such as losing power in a jet over the Gulf of Mexico and his plane being blown up by the enemy during the Vietnam War as he walked away from the fuel pumps. In 1958 he tested a lightweight, full-pressure suit for simulating space travel for the navy. Although he did not actually exit Earth's atmosphere, Neiman spent forty-four continuous hours in a pressure chamber at simulated altitudes between 80,000 and 105,000 feet, paving the way for Alan Shepard's Earth orbit. At the time of the crash, Neiman was also an aerial fire controller for the Chattahoochee National Forest in Georgia. This was the caliber of pilot who, rather than landing on the moon, landed instead on Mount LeConte.

Neiman and Moore had planned to drop four fifty-pound bags of horse feed onto a landing area near the lodge from a Cessna 172. That's when their trouble began. This was Neiman's first experimental drop of supplies onto the mountain, but not his first such drop as a pilot. Herrick Brown, the operator of LeConte Lodge, needed horse feed for his horses, and Neiman was trying to deliver the order.

Neiman said that they were making their approach to the top of the mountain when lift was lost. He said that he was flying at about sixty miles per hour when the incident occurred. He had to make a quick decision to either attempt a landing on the helicopter pad or turn and dive off LeConte and hope to regain lift on the way down the slope. He set the plane's nose high and allowed the tail to begin to slowly touch the small trees and eventually slide into the forest. The plane rested in fir saplings approximately two hundred yards southeast of the lodge near the present-day backcountry shelter. The entire emergency took "from 30 to 45 seconds," according to the pilot.[3] Except for a small scratch on Neiman's forehead, neither of the two men was injured and both were able to step out onto the ground and walk away from the aircraft.

Campers and other hikers near the top of the mountain witnessed the incident. Tommy Stover of Gatlinburg was at the lodge at the time and heard and saw the whole thing. "He did a marvelous job of landing that aircraft," he told a *Gatlinburg Press* reporter. "He cut his engine, so he wouldn't by-pass the drop zone, had engine trouble and couldn't regain speed. He landed in small shrub pine trees, which acted as a cushion."[4]

N9285C was worth $19,500. The FAA made an investigation and the craft was removed from the scene a short time later.

Bell 206 at Indian Gap

Eleven years had passed since the last aircraft incident involving Mount LeConte Lodge. Then, in 1983, in the space of eleven days, two aircraft transporting supplies to the lodge went down within a few yards of each other. On Tuesday, July 26, the Smokies claimed another aircraft, and on August 6, another. The first was a Bell 206-B, the second, a Sikorsky S-58. The last time a helicopter had crashed in the park was in 1978, when a UH-1 went down during a rescue operation near Parsons Bald killing four persons. The crews of these aircraft fared better.

In July 1983 a Jet Ranger piloted by Robert Bailey crashed near Indian Gap after ferrying supplies to Mount LeConte Lodge. Courtesy of National Park Service.

It was a typical hazy, warm July afternoon in the Smokies with thousands of visitors making their way along quiet "nature trails" and motor homes creeping up the steep mountain grades. On Mount LeConte, staff were busy emptying loads of supplies being airlifted to the lodge by Robert Bailey, age forty-two. Vertiflite Air Service, a Blount County–based helicopter contracting service operated by Bailey, was using Indian Gap as a landing and loading zone.

Indian Gap is rich in pre-park history. Along Road Prong is a foot trail used previously by the Cherokees as a major thoroughfare. Settlers used it as a major route between North Carolina and Tennessee until the Newfound Gap Road was completed. This "gap" is used as a popular trail head, pull-off, and landing zone. It is located on the Clingmans Dome Road a couple of miles from the Newfound Gap Road. It was here that Bailey almost lost his life.

The Bell 206, or Jet Ranger, is a popular helicopter. The aircraft is used for cargo hauling, search, rescue, and transporting people, among other things. In this case the Bell 206-B, N5733M, was transporting supplies to LeConte Lodge.

Bailey had already made several trips to the lodge from Indian Gap and had dropped off a load when he was returning to land shortly before 5:00 P.M. At the end of a long steel cable connected to the underneath of the helicopter was a thirty-gallon bucket filled with straps. Either at the lodge, in flight, or just as he was about to land, one of the straps began to dangle out of the bucket. This fabric strap apparently wrapped around the tail rotor, causing it to malfunction.

Six persons were either near or at Indian Gap when the incident occurred. In fact, it was reported that one person took photos of the helicopter as the crash occurred. Bailey was approaching the gap to land at about forty knots when he felt a "bump" in the tail rotor pedals (the pedal control turns to the left and right). The National Transportation Safety Board investigation revealed that the bump was the tail rotor being "entangled" in the dangling fabric strap.[5] Without the tail rotor rotating, the main rotor blade's torque causes helicopters to turn in a circle. Imagine being able to grab the main rotor with your hand causing it to stop; the body of the aircraft would receive the engine's power and would begin turning. The tail rotor counters the main rotor torque, and in this instance the helicopter began spinning out of control.

The helicopter began to spin to the right. Bailey auto-rotated into the treetops at approximately 125 feet above the terrain. He dropped

through the balsams and became inverted in the last few feet before striking the ground. The helicopter hit nose first, breaking off the main rotor
blades and destroying the small helicopter. From the road, onlookers ran
quickly but cautiously two hundred yards into the forest, hoping to find
the pilot alive. They found the crash site in just moments as a small fire
was beginning to ignite.

Amazed at the total destruction of the aircraft, witnesses were elated
to see that Bailey had survived the fall. They pulled him from the burning
helicopter and carried him to the road away from the danger of fire and
explosion. He was found to have suffered numerous head injuries, a broken finger, a bruised lung, and various cuts and bruises. Carrying him off
the hillside were William Gilbert of Kentucky, William Miller of Lebanon,
Tennessee, Jim Ayre of Midland, Michigan, and an unidentified person.

Ranger Charlie Garren was the first official to arrive on the scene.
"I've never seen anyone come away from anything like that," he said. "It
blows my mind that he came out of it."[6] Onlookers had already extin-
guished the fire and had taken Bailey to the road before Garren arrived.

At the scene, a passerby nurse, Sherry McCulley of Lake Junaluska,
North Carolina, stabilized Bailey. She was his primary care giver until medical crews from Gatlinburg arrived. The Gatlinburg Fire Department sent
an ambulance and a fire truck to the scene. Capt. Dave Brown attended to
him at the scene, on the ambulance trip to the Sevier County Medical
Center and on the army national guard helicopter flight to UT Hospital.

The aircraft was airlifted out of the forest on Thursday the twenty-
eighth and placed on a truck that took it back to Blount County for an
investigation. The site is now clear of all wreckage. The NTSB investigated
the incident and assigned it the number ATL83LA294.[7] A probable cause of
the accident, according to the investigators, was the trailing strap becoming entangled in the tail rotor, restricting its movement and subsequently
causing the aircraft to loose altitude and auto-rotate through the trees.

Sikorsky S-58 at Indian Gap

When Jack and Pauline Huff began to operate LeConte Lodge in the
1930s most of the supplies were carried on the backs of either employees (sometimes volunteers) or pack animals. Today, llamas are the choice
method. In a 1997 supply operation to Mount LeConte Lodge, a highly
skilled helicopter pilot was able to set a dangling load of supplies on the
front porch of one of the buildings. In August 1983 the facility was

undergoing a massive renovation and a great deal of construction supplies were needed where trucks could not deliver. A week and a half earlier Vertiflite had been contracted to do the moving, but unfortunately, the company's Bell 206 was destroyed and its president hospitalized.

St. Louis Helicopter Airways was hired to do the job. The company was no stranger to the Smokies. One of its missions involved pulling a slightly damaged Cherokee Six out of the forest near Clingmans Dome. The helicopter of choice for such operations is the Sikorsky S-58, which has taken supplies to LeConte for years without an accident (unless you count a load of suitcases, books, food, and other personal belongings of the staff being dropped into the Dudley Creek area in the early 1990s; luckily the "accident" was witnessed and all of the belongings were recovered).

The wreckage of a Sikorsky helicopter near Indian Gap, July 1983. Luckily no one was seriously injured. It crashed a few feet off Clingmans Dome Road. Photo by Jeff Wadley.

Greg Honer was the pilot of the large and powerful S-58-D; N6488 was the aircraft's registration number. He, along with Terrance Lahey and Steve Koemig, were attempting to lift off when the accident occurred. At 4:20 P.M. he powered up the aircraft, hovered a few feet above the ground, and, when he determined that he had enough power to depart, pushed

the yoke forward. He traveled twenty feet and the helicopter fell to the ground. The pilot stated that all at once the aircraft lost power and, subsequently, its lift, requiring him to abort the takeoff. But it was too late. The helicopter was too far from the road to land, so it cleared its way through small trees to the steep incline just below the road.

This accident occurred on the opposite side of the road from the Bell 206 but only twenty-five feet or so off the roadway. In fact, a person could stand on the road and see the large aircraft sitting crippled in the trees just off the asphalt.

The three persons exited the aircraft and crawled on their hands and knees back to the road, where they were met by concerned bystanders and ground crew members. The Park Service was contacted, and rangers arrived on the scene. Later the National Transportation Safety Board arrived to investigate.

According to the NTSB report (ATL83FA312), the crash was due to a long list of factors. Among the "probable causes" were low compression on four cylinders of the engine (through exhaust valves), a partially clogged carburetor screen (with fiber lint), a fuel filter partially obstructed with contaminants from the fuel barrels at the landing zone, and pilot fatigue.[8] Today, all that remains of the crash are a few pieces of metal and broken glass.

Supplying Mount LeConte has proven to be fatal. The employees, guests, contractors, and others mourn the loss and injury of the aircrews. Everyone prays that incidents such as these will not happen again.

CONCLUSION

The threefold purpose of this book is to have a definitive collection of documented Great Smoky Mountain National Park history, provide a resource tool for persons involved in search and rescue, and to warn pilots of the dangers of mountain flying.

Since 1920 there have been fifty-four known aircraft incidents in the Great Smoky Mountains National Park involving 127 persons. We say "known" because surely there have been other, unknown incidents. In fact, the Civil Air Patrol and Federal Aviation Administration have a listing of many aircraft still classified as missing. The cases mentioned in this work illustrate a variety of scenarios, such as aircraft running out of fuel, encountering icing, working aircraft, military maneuvers, aircraft flying into clouds, pilots becoming lost, dare-deviling, loss of power, midair accidents, and aircraft simply flying too low.

Categories

Of the fifty-four incidents, sixteen involved military aircraft and thirty-eight involved civilian craft. Three-quarters (thirty-nine) of the accidents occurred when aircraft were flying across the Smokies en route somewhere.

One interesting category of incidents involve the working aircraft. These seven aircraft were working under hazardous conditions (low and slow). They are considered "working" because they were not en route across the Smokies, sightseeing, or involved in other general aviation. Two were involved in photography (the L5 on Mount Sequoyah and the Cessna 150 on Noisy Creek), one in a rescue operation (the UH-1 near Parsons Bald), and four were transporting supplies to LeConte Lodge. Four of the seven working accidents involved helicopters. In fact, of the five helicopters that have crashed in the park, four were working helicopters.

Search

Twenty-four (slightly less than half) aircraft required a search. Four aircraft were located by persons simply walking up to them (Staggerwing, B-29, Commanche, and Balsam Mountain Cessna 180). Six crashes were witnessed (of those, three were of working aircraft), and one aircraft has not been located.

In nineteen aircraft incidents, part or all of the crew walked out of the backcountry either while a search was being organized or conducted or before anyone reported the plane overdue. Only one incident required a search and walkout (the McCarras' Cherokee Six). The pilot of this plane walked out to report the accident and get help for his passengers then a search proceeded.

Survivability

Of the 127 persons involved in airplane crashes in the Smokies, 56, or 44.1 percent, survived. *An interesting statistic is that once rescuers arrived, there was a 100 percent survivability rate.* No one died from the time rescuers arrived on the scene until the injured were discharged from medical care at the scene or in a hospital. Forty-five persons who lived were either not injured at all or had very minor abrasions and cuts. Only 11 survivors were injured severely.

Rescue

It was not until the Mollies Ridge crash (thirty-two incidents) that a person required an actual search *and* a rescue. Up to that point the crew either died or walked out on their own. Of the 127 persons involved in aircraft incidents, 44 needed no rescue and 12 needed help to get out.

Causes

We recognize that most incidents in the park are based upon a *sequence of events* leading up to the incident rather than an isolated decision or event. Since we are not aircraft incident investigators, we relied upon the summaries of NTSB reports and other sources of aviation incident "causes."

Nationwide in 1998 for instance, 83.1 percent of all *fatal* aircraft accidents were weather related.[1] In the Smokies, we have discovered, about 50 percent (twenty-six out of fifty-four) of the incidents were weather related, but not all included a fatality. *Almost all of the weather-related incidents in the Smokies were the result of a pilot flying the aircraft at cruise into instrument meteorological conditions.*

Probable Causes or Major Events Leading to an Incident	
CAUSE/EVENT	NUMBER OF INCIDENTS
Too low over the mountains	18[a]
Unverified	8[b]
Engine problems	7
Fuel exhaustion/starvation	5
Too low while maneuvering	3
Carburetor ice	3
Interference with flight	2
Airframe problem	2
Wing/airframe ice	2
Controlled landing	2
Spatial disorientation	1[c]
Extreme turbulence	1

[a]Plus 7 unverified, for a possible total of 25. [b]Of these, 7 possibly due to poor visibility, and 1 possibly due to spatial disorientation. [c]Plus 1 unverified, for a possible total of 2.

A Word to Pilots

"Visual flight into instrument meteorological conditions (IMC) and low maneuvering flight continue to be the two areas of flight producing the largest number of fatal accidents," according to the Aircraft Owners and Pilots Association (AOPA). Nationwide, landings and takeoffs produce the most number of accidents but have fewer fatalities due to low speed and low altitude. In 1998, with an estimated 26.8 million flying hours, there were 1,679 general aviation accidents. Of these accidents, there were 619 deaths. *In fact, in consideration of national statistics, a pilot's visual flight into IMC conditions increases his chance of fatality by 83 percent.*[2]

Considering all the stories, the AOPA findings, and the NTSB reports, it would be wise to at least do the following before a flight:

1. Get a weather briefing, consider your experience and your aircraft's limitations, and decide if the flight is worth it.
2. File a flight plan and activate it.
3. If you are on VFR and do not intend to file a flight plan, at least request "flight following."
4. Before you take off, make sure your ELT is in the "armed" position (not "on" or "off") and that the battery is up-to-date.

It is certainly OK to turn around or cancel the flight.

Search Planning

CAP search managers have used these standards when searching for missing aircraft nationwide (from the Air Force Rescue Coordination Center's incident commanders' course):

55 percent of missing aircraft are found on course
64 percent are located within 5 miles either side of course
79 percent are located within 10 miles either side of course
87 percent are located within 15 miles either side of course

In our study of the Great Smoky Mountains National Park, the average find is 8.5 miles to the left of course and 11.8 miles to the right of course. With an operating ELT, the average time to locate an aircraft is 14.2 hours. Without an operating ELT, the average time increases to 65.88 hours. The average time to locate an aircraft on a flight plan was 18.13 hours. Without a flight plan, the time escalated to 62.5 hours.

What does all this mean to those involved in search and rescue in the Smokies? First, expect an incident on the average of one every seventeen months (eighty years divided by fifty-four cases). The incidents in this book occurred in all twelve months of the calendar year, with August and January having eight each and September having only one. The temperature may be extremely hot and the rescuer may have to battle yellow jackets and heat stress, or it may be very cold and the rescuers may have

How Did They Survive?	
PERSON	WHAT THEY HAD AND DID
Follin	Two cigarettes, one match, no food; started a fire with pine needles and cigarette package; walked out
Sullenbarger	Can of sardines, bag of peanuts; walked out
Toomey and Tallent	Used plane's fabric for fire starter and bedding; walked out
Pasquet and Giardina	Two matches, small survival kit; walked out
Miller	Lighter fluid and lighter, almonds, pack of mints; used rolled up papers from his briefcase for a fire, ate leaves, piled up clothes for bedding, stayed awake for fifty-six hours, used a necktie for a tourniquet, used Scouting knowledge, and said he was going to make it
Hunter	Had nothing; walked out
Pettit and Aptt	Had nothing; walked out
Postelnek	Stayed with aircraft until help arrived
Acree, Wyman, Thurlow, and Harbin	Used park radio to summon help
Rutland	Had nothing; walked out
Hughes	Luck—and the Boy Scouts of America
McCarras	Clothes for vacation; one walked out, the rest stayed at the scene, remembered their Christian faith, flagged down motorist, and used plane as shelter
Shrewsbury	Had each other and chocolate candy
Bruning	Wrapped himself in plastic bags, used interior of plane and maps for insulation, turned on ELT, contacted tower on radio, stayed in plane, maintained a positive attitude
Wheeler	Walked out, summoned fishermen
Oliphant and Hayes	Walked out, summoned fishermen
Suteu	Broke into NPS cabin, called on NPS radio, found sugar, blankets, matches, and a map
Bierig	Stayed put, used ELT to call for help

to contend with hypothermia. The incidents' range of elevation was from the balsam zone at 6,643 feet at Clingmans Dome down to the cove hardwoods at Oconaluftee and Cades Cove.

The incidents ranged from aircraft being totally obliterated by an explosion to aircraft left almost untouched and able to take off again after refueling. Most of the crashes were very near a ridge top (most were less than half a mile from the top of a ridge line, and the average was 698 feet from the top). The majority were within a mile of a road or trail. Be prepared for searches in all types of weather and on all types of terrain all year long.

When an aircraft crashes in the Smokies, more than half the occupants will die. Most of the other half will find their way out or be rescued by a witness to the crash. Only a handful will require medical evacuation. Not every time the report of a crash comes in will it be a Mollies Ridge, Cherokee Six, or Shrewsbury incident. Most likely it will be a Parsons Bald Cessna 421 or a Gunter Fork Cessna 150 crash. Searchers do what they do to save lives and to help families bring closure to a tragedy. They do it *"that others might live."*

Pilots, be careful! Searchers, be prepared. Historians, be informed. In Memory of pilots and passengers.

NOTES

1. The 1920s

1. "Aeroplane Falls in the Great Smokies," *Newport Plain Talk*, Nov. 8, 1922, p.1.
2. Ibid.
3. Ibid.
4. Ibid.
5. Much of the "Rooster" Williams story belongs to Vic Weals, who wrote of him in newspaper articles and in his book *Last Train to Elkmont* (Knoxville, Tenn.: Olden Press, 1993). Vic was more than happy to do an interview and provide details.
6. Vic Weals, "Spirit of Rooster Takes Wing," *Knoxville Journal*, May 2, 1977.
7. Ibid.
8. Vic Weals, "Rooster Was Bold but a Big Rock Was Boulder," *Knoxville Journal*, May 9, 1977.
9. Vic Weals, "Homesickness Fatal to Mountain Logger," *Knoxville Journal*, May 16, 1977.

2. The 1940s

1. "Whereabouts of U.S. Plane Missing since Monday Is Mystery," *Asheville Times*, Feb. 3, 1944.
2. Ibid.
3. "Logger Picks-up Fabric of Lost Plane," *Waynesville Mountaineer*, Sept. 10, 1946, p. 1.
4. "Helicopters to Be Used When Army Men Return," *Waynesville Mountaineer*, Jan. 28, 1947, p. 1.
5. "Staggerwing Is Popular," *Maryville-Alcoa Daily Times*, May 9, 1974, p. 8.
6. "Antique Plane Owners Gather for Dedication," *Maryville-Alcoa Daily Times*, June 17, 1974.
7. Hank Leonard was a major contributor to this story. He lent us letters, photographs, interviews, a short story, and his journal as references.
8. Information from Hank Leonard's journal.

9. Ibid.

10. "Lost Plane Hit Green Mountain, Searchers View," *Maryville-Alcoa Daily Times,* Aug. 21, 1944, p. 1.

11. Smoky Mountain Hiking Club newsletter of January 1947.

12. Office of Flying Safety of the U.S. Army–Air Force, "Report of Major Accident." Much of the data used in this chapter pertains to this report. The times, passenger list, navigation, and so on were determined from this public but semicensored report.

13. Willard Yarbrough, "Big Army Transport Reported Crashed Near Foot of Mt. Guyot," *Knoxville News Sentinel,* Oct. 15, 1945, p. 9.

14. "Mules to Bring Crash Dead Out," *Knoxville News Sentinel,* Oct. 17, 1945, p. 10.

15. "Searchers Reach Crashed Plane near Guyot, Craft Carried 6 Men," *Knoxville News Sentinel,* Oct. 16, 1945, pp. 1, 8.

16. Ibid., p. 1.

17. "Memorandum for the Director," Oct. 1945 monthly report of activities, Nov. 8, 1945.

18. Jack Pettit has contributed interviews, photographs, and letters to this chapter.

19. "Light Army Plane, Circling Site of Wrecked C-45, Crashes," *Knoxville News Sentinel,* Oct. 18, 1945.

20. Ibid.

21. Pettit to authors, Feb. 9, 1990.

22. "Four Navy Fliers Leap from Bomber," *Knoxville News Sentinel,* Dec. 10, 1945, p. 1.

23. Ibid.

24. The Civil Air Patrol and National Park Service had this aircraft listed as a PBY, or flying boat, until the late 1980s.

25. "Bodies Nine Fliers Burned, Mutilated, W. R. Miller Reports," *Maryville-Alcoa Daily Times,* June 13, 1946, p. 1.

26. Carson Brewer, "Army Board Probing B-29 Crash in Smokies," *Knoxville News Sentinel,* June 13, 1946, p. 2.

27. "B-29 Hits Smokies, 12 Killed," *Knoxville News Sentinel,* June 12, 1946, p. 1.

28. A "ferry flight" refers to the transporting of an aircraft from one airfield to another.

29. The propeller and engine were buried at least three feet into the mountain. Looters, and eventually "Bootstrap," hauled away 100 percent of the aircraft.

30. Bob Scott, "Pilot Bailed Out before Fighter Crashed into Smokies 44 Years Ago," *Asheville Citizen Times,* Nov. 13, 1992.

31. Ibid.

32. Doug Elfman, "Firm Rescues Crashed Plane from the Ashes," *Maryville-Alcoa Daily Times,* Nov. 12, 1992, p. 2-A.

3. The 1950s

1. "Aeroplane Incidents in Great Smoky Mountains National Park." Mary Ruth Childs was perhaps the first person who put together a listing of all the crashes on January 9, 1978. In her report she wanted to give a short synopsis for media reference.

2. "Plane Is Found between Happy Valley, Cades Cove," *Maryville-Alcoa Daily Times,* Apr. 6, 1951, p. 10.

3. Ibid.

4. *Maryville-Alcoa Daily Times,* Nov. 3, 4, 7, 1955, and *Knoxville News Sentinel,* Nov. 5, 1955, p. 1.

5. "Plane Crash Victim Walks Out of Smokies," *Maryville-Alcoa Daily Times,* Nov. 7, 1955, p. 1.

6. David Dickey, "Missing Doctor Safe after Crash," *Knoxville News Sentinel,* Nov. 5, 1955, p. 1.

7. Ibid.

8. "Aeroplane Incidents."

9. "Richard M. Cox, Founder of Sky Ranch, Dead at 80," *Daily Times,* Aug. 31, 2000, p. 4A.

10. "Alcoans Crash Land in Smokies, Escape Injury," *Maryville-Alcoa Daily Times,* Aug. 27, 1956, p. 1.

11. Ibid.

12. "Two Youths Uninjured as Plane Crashes," *Maryville-Alcoa Daily Times,* Aug. 29, 1956, p. 1.

13. "Aeroplane Incidents."

14. Bob Gilbert, "1933 Map Which Didn't Show Fontana Lake, Ranger Station, Radio Help Suteu to Safety," *Maryville-Alcoa Daily Times,* Dec. 11, 1956, p. 1.

15. "Two National Guard Pilots Rescued in Smokies," *Maryville-Alcoa Daily Times,* June 23, 1958, p. 1.

16. Ibid.

17. *Maryville-Alcoa Daily Times,* Jan. 21, 1959.

18. This scene was similar to that of the F-15 in 1992, a crater and scattered debris.

4. The 1960s

1. This quotation is from a newspaper report titled "Radio Plea May Lead to Lost Plane." We cannot determine from which paper; it is one of many old clippings we were given.

2. "CAP Commander Feels Certain Plane in Area," *Maryville-Alcoa Daily Times,* Nov. 13, 1962.

3. "Search Continues for Airman Sucked from Plane; Jacket Is Found," *Maryville-Alcoa Daily Times,* Mar. 4, 1964, p. 1.

4. Ibid.

5. "Smokies Plane Crash Kills Six," *Maryville-Alcoa Daily Times,* Mar. 23, 1964, p. 1.

6. Ibid.

7. Ibid.

8. "2 Killed as Plane Crashes Near Mt. Sterling," *Waynesville Mountaineer,* June 8, 1964.

9. Ibid.

10. "Two Survive Crash in Great Smokies," *Maryville-Alcoa Daily Times,* Sept. 7, 1966, p. 1.

11. "Aeroplane Incidents."

12. *Park News and Views* 16, no. 11, June 9, 1970.

5. The 1970s

1. "Smokies Crash Plane Was OK, Investigators Say," *Knoxville News Sentinel,* Feb. 1, 1973.

2. At the time of the initial search on the fourth, the dog was not found in the wreckage, and it was assumed that the animal had perished in the fire.

3. This is not always the case. Some of the aircraft that went down in winter were not found for months. This happens usually when no large branches are broken and the aircraft falls straight down rather than taking out a large swath of trees. Broken branches are fairly easy to see from a search aircraft.

4. "Five Plane Crash Victims Rescued," *Knoxville News Sentinel,* Feb. 19, 1974, p. 2-A.

5. "Last 2 Crash Victims Rescued," *Knoxville News Sentinel,* Feb. 20, 1974, p. 7.

6. Ann M. Black, "God Was with Me on That Mountain," *Sunday Digest* 90, no. 3 (June, July, Aug. 1976): 2.

7. Mission notes from the Civil Air Patrol HQ at Sevier County, Tennessee.

8. Keith Bennett, "Three Survive Plane Crash," *Knoxville Journal,* Aug. 15, 1975.

9. Quote from an unknown newspaper source.

10. *Knoxville Journal,* n.d., n.p.

11. "Physician Calls Plane Crash Survivors 'Very Hardy Kids,'" *Knoxville News Sentinel,* Dec. 6, 1977.

12. Carson Brewer, "Jeff and Jennie, Survivors of Smokies Plane Crash, Fly Home to Michigan," *Knoxville News Sentinel,* Dec. 18, 1977.

13. Tom King, "2 Smokies Plane Crash Victims to Visit Here," *Knoxville News Sentinel,* Nov. 26, 1978.

14. "McGivney to Get Another Honor for Rescue in Smokies," *Knoxville News Sentinel,* Jan. 7, 1979.

15. King, "2 Smokies Plane Crash Victims."

16. "Nine Bodies Removed from Park," *Maryville-Alcoa Daily Times,* Jan. 5, 1978, p. 1.

17. Carol Byrd, "Jesus we've got an engine out . . . ," *Knoxville Journal,* Jan. 5, 1978, p. 1.

18. Ibid.

19. Ibid.

20. Ibid.

21. "Tennessee Wing Makes First Find in Mountains," *Civil Air Patrol News,* n.d., unknown issue.

22. The times mentioned in the rest of the story were recorded at Tennessee Wing HQ by Lt. Col. George Hudson the night of the crash in his radio log.

23. "Tennessee Wing Makes First Find."

24. Ibid.

25. Sharon Fitzgerald, "Pilot Survives Crash," *Gatlinburg Press,* Feb. 15, 1979.

26. "Tennessee Wing Makes First Find."

27. Fitzgerald, "Pilot Survives Crash."

6. The 1980s

1. "Search Underway for Balloonist Feared Lost in Smoky Mountains," *Knoxville News Sentinel,* July 3, 1980.

2. Rebecca Ferrar, "Crash Searchers Held Little Hope," *Mountain Press,* n.d., n.p.

3. Ibid.

4. "Air Force Aircraft Crash Site Located by Tennessee Volunteers," *Civil Air Patrol News,* n.d., unknown issue.

5. Gilbert Soesbee, "Residents See Orange-Red Burst, Feel Ground Shudder," *Newport Plain Talk,* Jan. 6, 1984.

6. Ferrar, "Crash Searchers Held Little Hope."

7. "Air Force Aircraft Crash Site Located."

8. From an overheard radio transmission from the search helicopter.

9. Ferrar, "Crash Searchers Held Little Hope."

10. The investigation took months. The reports were made public through the local television, radio, and newspaper.

11. Ray Snader, "No Mechanical Problem Found in Smokies Crash," *Knoxville News Sentinel,* n.d., unknown issue.

12. "Pilot Praises Scouts Who Found Him after Crash." *Knoxville News Sentinel,* July 13, 1989, n.p.

13. From a National Park Service (NPS) report (Form 10-344B) on Feb. 15, 1989.

14. "Pilot Praises Scouts Who Found Him."

15. Susan Robertson, "Scouts Thought Crash Was Big Truck," *Mountain Press,* July 13, 1989, n.p.

16. Ralph Dosser, "'Lucky Man' Survives Plane Crash in Smokies," *Knoxville Journal,* July 12, 1989, p. 10A.

17. "Pilot Praises Scouts Who Found Him."

18. NPS Form 10-344B.

19. Robertson, "Scouts Thought Crash Was Big Truck," 2A.

7. The 1990s

1. National Transportation Safety Board (NTSB) report number ATL91FA043.

2. Ibid.

3. Other "hot" spots were along the North and South Carolina line, in the Cherokee National Forest, and a call in Copperhill from a resident. Almost all the leads plotted at or about the alleged time the aircraft would have been in the area but none developed into a solid clue.

4. Randy Kenner and John Stiles, "Body Found in Wreckage of Small Plane," *Knoxville News Sentinel,* n.d., n.p.

5. NTSB report number ATL91FA043.

6. Jim Balloch and John Stiles, "Fighter Planes Collide over Smoky Mountains," *Knoxville News Sentinel,* Jan. 16, 1992. p. A1.

7. NTSB report number ATL92FA091.

8. The NTAP data was not available until after the search was completed. It is not confirmed that the data available was in fact the missing aircraft.

9. NTSB report number ATL92FA091.

10. John Stiles, "3 Victims Found in Smokies Crash," *Knoxville News Sentinel,* n.p., unknown issue.

11. Susan Robertson, "Search on for Missing Plane," *Mountain Press,* May 25, 1992, p. 1, and Skip Lackey, "Scanners Loose Light Airplane over Smokies," *Knoxville News Sentinel,* May 25, 1992, p. A5 (no quotations used but good information regarding the details of the weather and the problems the pilot encountered).

12. In other words, before the tower could help Baldwin with directions and an altitude, the aircraft was already out of control and began falling to the ground.

13. Robertson, "Search on for Missing Plane."

14. NTSB report number ATL92FA108.

15. John Stiles, "Chopper Drops 'Right on the Yellow Line'; Pilot Walks Away," *Knoxville News Sentinel,* n.d., n.p.
16. NTSB report number ATL93LA075.
17. He literally landed the aircraft on the yellow line parallel with traffic.
18. NTSB report number ATL93LA075.
19. "Copter Crashes in Smokies," *Mountain Press,* Apr. 17, 1993, p. 1.
20. NTSB report number ATL95FA050.
21. Ibid.
22. NTSB report number MIA97FA038.
23. "Flight following" is a procedure in which a pilot asks the control tower to record their movement on the radar record for search purposes if they go down. It also enables the tower to notify the aircraft in case another aircraft is flying near them.
24. NTSB report number MIA97FA030.
25. Ibid.
26. Ibid.
27. Ibid.
28. Ibid.
29. Ibid.

8. A Few Minor Incidents

1. "Aeroplane Incidents."
2. Ibid.
3. Ibid.
4. Ibid.
5. Ibid.

9. Supplying Mount LeConte

1. *Park News and Views* 15, no. 19 (Sept. 18, 1969).
2. Willard Yarbrough, "'Capt. Crunch' Has 1st Crash in 31 Years," *Knoxville News Sentinel,* Aug. 27, 1972, p. 12-A.
3. Ibid.
4. "After 31 years of Flying Neiman 'Bends' an Airplane," *Gatlinburg Press,* Aug. 31, 1972, p. 6
5. NTSB report number ATL83LA294.
6. Rebecca Ferrar, "Pilot Lives; Witnesses 'Amazed,'" unknown paper, n.d., n.p.
7. NTSB report number ATL83LA294.
8. According to NTSB report number ATL83FA312, he had made sixty-four previous trips to LeConte that day.

Conclusion

1. John Steuernagle and Kathleen Roy, eds., *Nall Report—1999* (Frederick, Md.: Bruce Landsburg, Aircraft Owners and Pilots Association/Air Safety Foundation, 2000), 19.

2. Ibid., 3.

SELECTED BIBLIOGRAPHY

Childs, Mary Ruth. "Aeroplane Incidents in Great Smoky Mountains National Park." Library of Great Smoky Mountains National Park, 1978.

Farabee, Charles R. "Butch," Jr. *Death, Daring and Disaster.* Niwot, Colo.: Roberts Rinehart, 1998. Roberts Rinehart web site:
www.robertsrinehart.com.

LaValla, Rick, and Skip Stoffel. *Search Is an Emergency.* Olympia, Wash.: Emergency Response Institute, 1987.

McCarter, Dwight, and Ronald Schmidt. *Lost!* Yellow Springs, Ohio: Graphicom Press, 1998.

National Transportation Safety Board. Aircraft accident monthly synopsis on the web at www.ntsb.gov/aviation.

Steuernagle, John, and Kathleen Roy, eds. *Nall Report—1999.* Frederick, Md.: Bruce Landsberg, Aircraft Owners and Pilots Association/Air Safety Foundation, 2000. Aircraft Owners and Pilots Association web site:
www.aopa.org/asf.

Weals, Vic. *Last Train to Elkmont.* Knoxville, Tenn.: Olden Press, 1993.

INDEX

MayDay! MayDay! was designed and typeset on a Macintosh computer system using QuarkXpress Passport software. The text is set in 11/14 Garamond Book and condensed to 95%. Chapter opener text is set in Helvetica condensed black and Helvetica Neue light extended. This book was designed and typeset by Cheryl Carrington and manufactured by Thomson-Shore, Inc. The paper used in this book is designed for an effective life of at least three hundred years.